Blogging
and RSS
A Librarian's
GUIDE

Blogging
and RSS
A Librarian's
GUIDE

Michael P. Sauers

 Information Today, Inc.
Medford, New Jersey

First Printing, 2006

Blogging and RSS: A Librarian's Guide

Copyright © 2006 by Michael P. Sauers

Library of Congress Cataloging-in-Publication Data

Sauers, Michael P.
   Blogging and RSS : a librarian's guide / Michael P. Sauers
        p. cm.
  Includes bibliographical references and index.
     ISBN: 1-57387-268-7
1. Communication in library science--Technological innovations. 2. Library science--Blogs. 3. Librarians--Blogs. 4. Library Web sites--Design.   I. Title
   Z680.3S38 2006
   025.04--dc22

                          2006026421

Printed and bound in the United States of America.

ISBN-13: 978-1-57387-268-3
ISBN-10: 1-57387-268-7

President and CEO: Thomas H. Hogan, Sr.
Editor-in-Chief and Publisher: John B. Bryans
Managing Editor: Amy M. Reeve
VP Graphics and Production: M. Heide Dengler
Book Designer: Kara Mia Jalkowski
Cover Designer: Shelley Szajner
Copyeditor: Wendy Catalano
Proofreader: Barbara Brynko
Indexer: Beth Palmer

To Gwynneth

I missed out on your first 10 years,
I promise not to miss any more.

Contents

Acknowledgments

I'd like to thank the following individuals and institutions for their contributions to the writing of this book: Louise Alcorn, Aurora Public Library, Barnes & Noble Café (Clive, IA), Bibliographical Center for Research, John Bryans, Frank Cervone, Steven M. Cohen, Karen Coombs, Miles Davis, DEN, DSM, Jane Dysart, Darlene Fichter, Rosario Garza, Rachel Singer Gordon, Kathy Groth, Sylvia Hall-Ellis, Amy Helfman, Sarah Houghton, John Hiatt, Jenny Levine, Laura Martinez, Andrea Mercado, Mary Norman, PHX, Aaron Schmidt, Greg Schwartz, Michael Stephens, Steve Walker, Jessamyn West, Irene Wood, and the reference staff at the Smoky Hill branch of the Arapahoe Library District.

Introduction

If you're reading this book, chances are you're a librarian who wants to know more about blogging and RSS. Even if you're not ready to dive in head first, I'm assuming you are interested enough to take a closer look. Blogs and RSS have received a lot of press in recent years: 2004 was widely hailed in the press as "The Year of the Blog" and blogging has proliferated at a remarkable pace since then. I realized blogs had gone mainstream while watching an episode of *The Daily Show with Jon Stewart*. Stewart was listening to a report from one of his "correspondents" about what was going to happen in Iraq the next day, as though it had already occurred. When Stewart questioned the fact that the correspondent had written his report in advance and asked what he'd do if something different and significant happened, the correspondent responded, "Jon, that's what the bloggers are for."

Blogs and RSS have also received a significant amount of attention in the library world. Today, librarians use blogs to share their experiences with their peers, while libraries as institutions use blogs to get information out to patrons. In some cases, blogs are the core of library Web sites. Go to any major library conference, especially Computers in Libraries or Internet Librarian, and you'll find entire tracks devoted to these topics. The movers and shakers among next generation librarians are blogging, and if you're not reading what they're saying, you're falling behind.

This book is designed to give you a baseline from which to start taking advantage of blogging and RSS technologies. As readers of my previous books will know, my style is practical and straightforward. Yes, the book will discuss history and theory, but its central purpose is to give you practical advice on how to get started at little to no cost. There may be more advanced ways to accomplish some of the tasks I'll be discussing, but typically such options involve significant financial investment or technological know-how. There are plenty of other places you can go for that information. This book is for those of you who want to be able to read blogs and their feeds tomorrow and have your own blog up and running the next day. With these two goals accomplished, you can move on (if you like) to mastering some of the more advanced and complex options that are available.

So, what exactly will I be covering in this book?

In Chapter 1, we'll be taking a look at just what blogs are, where they came from, and the significance of the blogging phenomenon. In Chapter 2, you'll learn about some of the most significant blogs in the library world today and about dozens of other blogs of potential interest to you as a library professional. In Chapter 3, I'll introduce you to the people behind some of these blogs.

Chapter 4 focuses on creating your first blog. I'll briefly discuss the various blog-creating services and software packages, but in the interest of cost and ease of use, the focus will be on Blogger.com. This free Web service will allow you to have your own blog up and running in less than five minutes. Once your blog is live, I'll walk you through the options available for customizing it.

In Chapter 5, we'll move on to RSS. Here, I'll take you through an introduction to RSS, explaining what it is, where it came from, and its value. This chapter will also demonstrate XML code, but don't let that scare you. I'm a firm believer in showing the "back-end" once—in this case, if you feel like forgetting it after that, that's okay. In Chapter 6, we'll take our knowledge of what RSS is and apply it to your life as a librarian. I'll introduce you to RSS aggregators, which are Web sites or software solutions that let you take advantage of RSS feeds to get all your information in one location.

Chapter 7 is a directory of RSS feeds you might consider subscribing to, though not all of them are directly LIS-related. Some might be useful in reference situations, while others simply illustrate the possibilities of the technology. Lastly, Chapter 8 will show you how to create your own RSS feeds. There are several options and, depending on the source of your original material, setting up your first RSS feed can take as little as two minutes and typically no more than 20.

Although I wrote *Blogging and RSS* to be read from cover to cover, you may prefer to only browse the topics that are of greatest interest to you. If you are just looking for a basic background in these technologies, you can read Chapters 1 and 5 for now. If you already have some background and are interested in resources and pointers to starting places as an information consumer, check out Chapters 2, 3, 6, and 7. If you're already using blogs and RSS and are planning to become an information supplier, Chapters 4 and 8 are for you.

Regardless of how you approach the book initially, I recommend that you eventually read it in its entirety. As a trainer for the past 10 years, I've discovered that there's always something you can learn about a topic, even if you already know "everything." You never know where and when a gem might turn up.

Welcome to the blogosphere!

An Introduction to Blogs

Welcome to the wonderful world of blogs, bloggers, and blogging! In this chapter, I'll essentially be answering the following questions:

- What are blogs?
- Why are blogs important in today's online world?
- What can blogs do for you and your library?

By the end of this chapter, you'll be ready to start using blogs not only as an information consumer but also as an information provider.

What Is a Blog?

According to Wikipedia (wikipedia.org), a blog is "a Web application which contains periodic posts on a common Web page. These posts are often but not necessarily in reverse chronological order. Such a Web site would typically be accessible to any Internet user." Blogging is the act of creating posts for a blog, and the person who creates those posts is known as a blogger. The collective environment of all blogs and bloggers is commonly referred to as the blogosphere.

Blog is a shorthand form of the word "Weblog," which in this context is pronounced "we blog."[1] The term Weblog (pronounced "Web log") is older than the concept of blogs and refers to the computer files generated by Web servers to log their activity. When blogging became popular, some technologists decided that, to prevent confusion between the two concepts, Weblog would be pronounced as "we blog." This, in turn, was shortened to "blog," from which other blog-based terms arose.

The first important part of the Wikipedia definition of blog is *Web application*. A Web page comprised of your thoughts and interesting links isn't necessarily a blog. One of the key components of a blog is the automatic generation of a page comprised of individually created entries, known as posts. Bloggers use either a Web-based service, such as Blogger.com (covered in detail in Chapter 4), or a client program, such as Radio's Userland software. Posts are created using one of these methods, after which the software takes over and generates the code needed to display your posts to users.

The next important part of the definition of blog is *reverse chronological order*. This means that the newest posts are presented at the top of the page, followed by older posts. When a new post is added to a blog, it appears as the first item to be read and shifts other posts down. As the definition states, posts are "not necessarily" presented in reverse chronological order, but this is the prevailing practice by far.

Lastly, the definition states that a blog is *accessible to any user*. Technically, a blogger can use blogging software to create a blog, then password-protect it or place it within a corporate Intranet, but there is some debate as to whether this would be considered a true blog. It is generally understood that a blog should be available to one and all without restriction.

Common practice indicates some additional features of blogging not mentioned in the Wikipedia definition of a blog:

- Blog posts are marked with the date and time of publication. This is important both for timeliness and for the working of aggregators. (Aggregators are covered in Chapter 6.)

- Blogs are more than just lists of sites someone thinks are cool. The original intent of blogging was to create online journals. In many cases, bloggers may link to other sites of interest but will usually add commentary as to *why* these sites are of interest.

- Unlike items on a standard Web page, which may be modified regularly, a blog entry typically remains unchanged once posted. Updates to a topic discussed in one post may be revisited in a new post or appended to an existing post. Revising and deleting old posts often warrants, at a minimum, a harsh and public verbal flogging.

- Most blogs by individuals allow readers to post comments. These comments are automatically attached to the end of a post for all readers to view. Blogs of large organizations tend not to have this feature, as allowing public comment may be determined as more hassle than it's worth. Additionally, an organization needing to retain control of its public image may not want to host uncensored reader commentary on its blog.

Types of Blogs

From the user's perspective, there are three types of blogs: individual, subject, and organizational.

Individual blogs are those run by individuals for their own reasons. This is the original blog style. Typically resembling an online journal, these blogs are commonly personal in nature, relating to the blogger's life experiences or professional life. Examples of individual blogs in the LIS (Library and Information Science) circle include my own blog, travelinlibrarian.info, Jenny Levine's The Shifted Librarian, and Michael Stephens's Tame the Web.

Subject blogs are produced by one or more people and are focused on a particular topic. Such topics or events may include hobbies, politics, pets, or other topics of interest to the group. War blogs have become popular due to the recent wars in Afghanistan and Iraq. One notable LIS subject blog is LISNews.com. Other subject blogs include Romensko's Obscure Store, which comments on offbeat and weird stories in the news, and Gizmodo, which reviews the latest gadgets, gizmos, and technology.

Organizational blogs represent the views, opinions, and events of an organization. For example, the Waterboro (ME) Public Library has a blog that informs its patrons about events at the library (www.waterborolibrary.org/blog). Sun Microsystems encourages all its employees to blog and has developed a system for them to do so at blogs.sun.com. (Many of these blogs reflect what employees are doing at Sun, although this is not a requirement.) The Microsoft Developer's Network has a blog called Channel 9 (named for the channel on which passengers can listen to tower communications while on an airplane) on which Microsoft developers post details about current projects.

It is important to keep in mind that these three categories are generalizations to help you learn about blogging and are not meant as hard and fast rules. Many blogs may fall into more than one category or may not easily fit into any of them.

The Blog Effect

The Merriam-Webster 2004 word of the year was "blog" (www.m-w.com/info/04words.htm). *Time* magazine's 2004 Person of the Year issue included an article titled, "Person of the Year 2004: 10 Things We Learned About Blogs" (www.time.com/time/person oftheyear/2004/poymoments.html). To say that 2004 was the year that blogs gained mainstream notoriety, if not mainstream accept-ance, would be an understatement. From those of us who have been reading and writing blogs for years, there was a collective response of "It's about time!"

Why was 2004 a watershed year for blogs? The answer is that several events that year made it clear that blogs were a force to be reckoned with. Two such events impacted "traditional" media, while the influence of other events was felt in the world of search engines, specifically Google.

The Impact of Blogs on Traditional Media

By the end of 2004, the traditional media of print, radio, and tel-evision could no longer ignore the impact bloggers were having on how people received their news. In that year alone, there were two significant cases in which blogs and bloggers either scooped major media or directly influenced if or how a story was reported:

- **John Kerry's Choice of Vice-Presidential Running Mate**—On the morning of July 6, 2004, John Kerry announced that his choice for a vice presidential running mate was Senator John Edwards. Unfortunately for the Kerry campaign, the announcement was not the big surprise it was meant to be. On the previous evening, an airport technician in the hangar where new decals were being applied to Kerry's campaign plane saw the decals and posted the news to the USaviation.com message board. The information was quickly picked up by bloggers and posted on hundreds of sites within hours. The word was out, and the bloggers spread the word ahead of the traditional media.

- **60 Minutes and "Memogate"**—In September 2004, Dan Rather anchored a report on CBS's *60 Minutes II* about a memo allegedly written by Lt. Col. Jerry Killian in 1973, which stated that President George W. Bush had not fulfilled his National Guard duties. The memo turned out to be a fake, a fact first reported by bloggers on the Free Republic blog (www.freerepublic.com). The post pointed out that the typeface used in the memo was generated by a computer rather than a typewriter—something not likely in 1973. In response to this post, many other bloggers took up the charge and continued the investigation. Traditional media picked up the story and eventually confirmed the suspicions. CBS offered an official retraction in October.

Blogs continued to gain greater attention in traditional mainstream media throughout 2005 with such blogs as the Shuttle Blog (aolsvc.news.aol.com/news/article.adp?id=20050706102209990034), documenting the first space shuttle mission since the demise of the *Columbia* and its crew three years earlier; the Fat Man Walking blog (www.thefatmanwalking.com), documenting Steve Vaught's walk across America to lose weight; the Blogging Fifth Nail blog (fifthnail.blogspot.com), written by Joseph Duncan who was later convicted of kidnapping and murder; and the MLBlogs (mlb.mlb.com/NASApp/mlb/mlb/news/blogs/index.jsp), the official blogging service of Major League Baseball. Additionally, 2005 saw the demotion of National Guardsman Private First Class Leonard Clark for posting classified information on his blog.[2]

The Effect of Blogs on Search Engines

Search engines started to feel the effects of blogging in 2003, but those effects grew in 2004 during the presidential election cycle. Google became a victim of what is known as "Google bombing." To understand how this works, here is a quick introduction to how Google ranks its search results.

Google's relevancy ranking algorithm (PageRank) is complex, but one of its main criteria is the number of other pages that link to a page. The more links found, the higher the ranking of the page in search results. Additionally, Google looks at how that linking occurs. If the linked text contains the keywords searched, that page receives an even higher ranking. To influence Google's ranking system, all someone needs to do is pick a word or phrase and then convince a lot of people to link to the exact same page using the exact same text as the link. This might take tens of thousands of pages, all creating the same link to the same page, but that isn't as difficult as it may sound.

Two cases of Google bombing involving blogs received significant press in 2004. The first involved the phrase "miserable failure." When this phrase was searched in Google, the first result was the official biography page of President George W. Bush on the White House Web site. As of March 2006, this was still the first result received when performing this search (Figure 1.1). For the most part, the effect on Google was considered minimal since most users viewed this as a humorous and essentially harmless manipulation of the system.[3]

In another case, a Google search on the word "Jew" resulted in the site for Jew Watch—which bills itself as "Keeping a Close Watch on Jewish Communities & Organizations Worldwide"—rising to first position. In this case, there was considerable public outcry, given the anti-Semitic nature of the site.[4] In retaliation, bloggers banded together, creating thousands of links to the Wikipedia article on Judaism, and bumping the Jew Watch site to the second position (Figure 1.2).

Both cases of Google bombing were the direct result of bloggers banding together to create the exact same link on their sites with the express purpose of influencing Google results.

Why Blog?

What makes blogs an important information resource and tool for you and your library? There are two perspectives from which this question can be answered: from the perspective of an information user and from the perspective of an information provider.

All libraries are information users. We constantly retrieve, access, sort, and store information for our patrons. Blogs are just one more source of information. Blogs, however, are unique in several ways:

- *Blogs are timely.* They are typically updated more frequently than Web sites—many times a day in some cases. Unlike newspapers and other traditional publications where reporting is fact-checked and edited as part of the publishing process, the information provided in blogs is likely to be raw

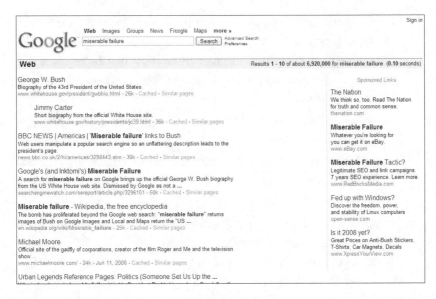

Figure 1.1   Google's results for "miserable failure"

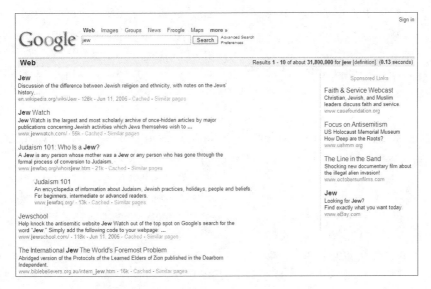

Figure 1.2   Google's results for "Jew"

and unfiltered (of course, in some cases, the lack of editorial review may be viewed as a downside). News and information can be posted with minimal delay, and if it is sufficiently interesting or important, it will be quickly picked up and spread by other bloggers.

- *Blogs are opinionated.* More often than not, a blogger has a personal point of view and expresses it in no uncertain terms in his or her postings. Of course, whether or not a particular blogger's opinions are valid is subjective.

- *Blogs are accessible.* While many Web sites are difficult to navigate or make users jump through hoops to read (or just to find) what they're looking for, blogs are designed for open access. A blog that *isn't* accessible won't be widely read or referenced and will eventually disappear.

- *Blogs are omnipresent.* In February 2002, *Wired* magazine reported that there were "more than 500,000 [blogs]."[5] In April 2006, Technorati reported that they are monitoring more than 35.3 million blogs—doubling its numbers from the previous six months.[6] Any type of information resource of this size will have an affect on the results presented in search engines (as with the "miserable failure" and "Jew" episodes).

Blogs are excellent means by which a library can fulfill its role as an information provider. Calendars of events along with news of recent acquisitions, upgrades, and staff changes can be efficiently disseminated through a library blog. As we'll see in Chapter 4, the level of technical know-how needed to begin a blog is minimal, and the cost is even less. Because blogs are so widely accessible, they can help to increase your library's Web site traffic. Once a blogger starts supplying his or her posts via RSS feeds (covered in Chapters 5–8), accessibility further increases.

Now that you have a basic understanding of how blogs have developed and what they can be used for, let's look at a number of excellent blogs that you can use both as resources and models.

Endnotes

1. Rebecca Blood, *We've Got Blog*, Perseus Publishing, 2002, p. 7.

2. KPHO News 5, "National Guardsman punished for information on blog" (www.kpho.com/Global/story.asp?S=3668667), and Leonard Clark's blog (leonardclark.com/blog).

3. More information on "miserable failure" and Google can be found in "Google's (and Inktomi's) Miserable Failure" by Danny Sullivan (searchenginewatch.com/sereport/article.php/3296101).

4. More information on "Jew" and Google can be found in a discussion from the Association of Jewish Libraries' electronic mailing list (www.mail-archive.com/hasafram@lists.acs.ohio-state.edu/msg02143.html) and "Jew Watch, Google, and Search Engine Optimization" by Seth Finkelstein (www.sethf.com/anticensorware/google/jew-watch.php).

5. Farhad Manjoo, "Blah, Blah, Blah and Blog," Wired News, February 18, 2002 (www.wired.com/news/culture/0,1284,50443,00.html).

6. "State of the Blogosphere, April 2006, Part 1: On Blog Growth," Technorati, February 6, 2006 (www.sifry.com/alerts/archives/00432.html).

Chapter 2

The Library Blogosphere, Part 1: The Blogs

This chapter will introduce you to a number of noteworthy blogs by librarians and from libraries, along with some additional blogs that may be of interest. The related chapter that follows— "The Library Blogosphere, Part 2: The Bloggers"—will take a close look at some of the most notable librarian bloggers in the field today. Much of the information presented in these two chapters was gleaned from the bloggers themselves through interviews, e-mail exchanges, and blog posts. I found it fascinating and I hope you will, too.

For each blog listed, you'll find the title, author name, URL, and brief description of the blog—in the blogger's own words when available—followed by an excerpt (or excerpts) intended to give you a feel for the tone and content of its posts. In many cases, the excerpted posts originally included links to other posts, blogs, and online resources; those links do not appear in this text.

Note that my coverage of these blogs is based on the content that was available at the time I viewed them. As with all Web resources, blogs will come and go, and metamorphose over time.

Librarian Blogs

There are hundreds of blogs written by librarians, library staff, library school students, and other bloggers in the LIS field. This chapter contains a sample of what I believe to be some of the best written, most informative, and in a few instances, the funniest blogs by librarians. In many cases, there are RSS feeds associated with these blogs that will make them easier for you to track. I'll show you how to take advantage of feeds in Chapters 5–8.

025.431: The Dewey Blog

Jonathan Furner, with contributions from other members of the Dewey editorial team

ddc.typepad.com/025431

"[A] weblog covering topics related to the Dewey Decimal Classification (DDC) and knowledge organization" (Figure 2.1).

Do stupid things faster with more energy

Short of the medical establishment's confirming the health benefits of my beloved national dish (six pints of Stella and a chicken tikka masala), there is surely no more unexpected-yet-welcome news than the recent rediscovery that coffee is in fact exceedingly good for you. Such a timely announcement gives me the fortitude I need to finally throw off the cloak of shame, peel back the facade, and proudly reveal Dewey Manor as the den of iniquity it really is. All that guff about tea at four in the drawing room? Merely a smokescreen, a pathetic attempt to deny the simple fact that, quite frankly, we're all addicted to the hard stuff, even the Vicar. And not just because it tastes good and clears the head, but because the ritual of ordering coffee is such a celebration of correct citation order. Fancy an iced decaf triple grande skinny hazelnut latte? Get one of those facets out of order, honey, and you won't be welcome at our pricey pastry-parlor of Pacific-Northwest provenance again. The interdisciplinary DDC number for coffee is **641.3373** (under 641.3 Food, not 641.2 Beverages); **633.73** is for **Coffee—agriculture**; and works about coffeehouses go in **647.95 Eating and drinking places**, under 647 Management of public households.

Beyond the Job

Sarah Johnson and Rachel Singer Gordon

librarycareers.blogspot.com

"Professional tips for librarians: Articles, job-hunting advice, professional development opportunities, and other news and ideas on how to further your library career. Compiled by the Library Job People, Sarah Johnson and Rachel Singer Gordon" (Figure 2.2).

The Library + Information Show, 26 + 27 April 2006, NEC Birmingham

Where the Library + Information Community Comes Together With an exhibition showcasing the latest products and services in the market and a free seminar programme featuring leading figures and authors from the nations library community, The Library + Information Show will help professionals from the workplace, school, academic and public sectors to face the challenges in the library community today. Register now for free entry: http://www.lishow.co.uk/promo/freepint [freepint]

Copyfight

Donna Wentworth, Ernest Miller, Elizabeth Rader, Jason Schultz, Wendy Seltzer, Aaron Swartz, and Alan Wexelblat

copyfight.corante.com

"Here we'll explore the nexus of legal rulings, Capitol Hill policy-making, technical standards development and technological innovation that creates—and will recreate—the networked world as we know it. Among the topics we'll touch on: intellectual property conflicts, technical architecture and innovation, the evolution of copyright, private vs. public interests in Net policy-making, lobbying and the law, and more" (Figure 2.3).

MPAA vs Usenet

Following its strategy of smashing torrent-linking sites, the MPAA has filed suits against three companies that provide searches for Usenet content including illegally copied movie files. All three of the current targets have the air of shadiness about them, being essentially anonymous registered shells. However, as Bray points out in his Boston Globe story, success here will likely embolden the Cartel to tackle more well-known Usenet index sites like Newzbin.com and Nfonews.com. And sitting at the far end of that road is Google, which owns a huge database of old Usenet postings and whose index likely contains more than a few files the MPAA wouldn't approve of.

Crime in the Library

Anbolyn

crimeinthelibrary.blogspot.com

"News about crimes affecting libraries" (Figure 2.4).

Textbooks Stolen from NC Library

Several students are arrested after stealing textbooks from the library at N.C. State.

Youth Gang Terrorizes UK Library

A gang of "yobs" has taken over the Ashburton Library in Croydon.

Paintings Stolen at VT Library

Two paintings are stolen from an exhibition at the Aldrich Public Library.

Free Range Librarian

Karen G. Schneider

freerangelibrarian.com

"K.G. Schneider's postcards from the edge of librarianship" (Figure 2.5).

When Analog met Digital: Michaels Golrick and Stephens Talk L2

I heard a voice from the past when I read Michael Golrick's comments to Michael Stephens in this TechSource interview: "At the same time, I do not disagree with what I see as the underlying thought behind of L2: excellent customer service."

The voice was that of Marvin Scilken, a beloved librarian pioneer who for forty years ran his own "Library 2.0" campaign. I can hear Marvin's voice rasping over the phone, "The bottom line is public service. You hear me, Karen? A library, it doesn't have a book that suddenly shows up on the best-seller list, that director should run to the nearest bookstore and buy two copies. Karen, you hear me?"

I hear you, Marvin. Like Michael Golrick, Marvin was a non-techy administrator. Marvin didn't even grok email, let alone the Web. But Marvin believed in many principles of service that I see reiterated in a new framework in the ideas proposed in Library 2.0.

I have a longer piece I'm working on about L2, probably not for this blog, but I felt such a moment of warmth, remembering Marvin, that I just had to share.

Librarian's Rant

Louise Alcorn

lblog.jalcorn.net

"Planning the Revolution ..." (Figure 2.6).

Well, there's one option off the table...

I mentioned previously a town in British Columbia, Canada that was for sale. I'd envisioned, with some fellow library types, a librarian utopia where we'd escape the insanity of the day, and our major export would be information services. Sadly, the town has been sold and will likely end up full of pretentious California ski bunnies. C'est la vie.

librarian.net: a library Weblog

Jessamyn West

www.librarian.net

"Putting the rarin' back in librarian since 1993" (Figure 2.7).

plinkit: scalable solutions to library tech rollouts

One of the problems that library consortiums have frequently solved is technology centralization. While I am not denying that consortiums have caused other problems, having one central go-to technology platform, software set, team of trainers and help desk has made many non-tech savvy librarians able to provide a higher level of service to their customers. For tech savvy librarians, this has sometimes come with a downside of lack of control of their own technology, or dumbed down interfaces to robust tools. We've been looking for a happy medium solution.

Two newish projects have been getting talked about lately in the states of Iowa and Oregon. Oregon is using Plinkit, a web authoring tool that is built on an open source CMS called Plone. This tool allows libraries to create nice looking professional websites with some standard modules (calendar, lists of links,

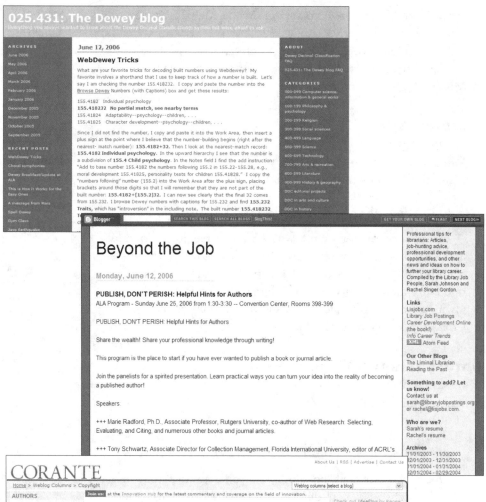

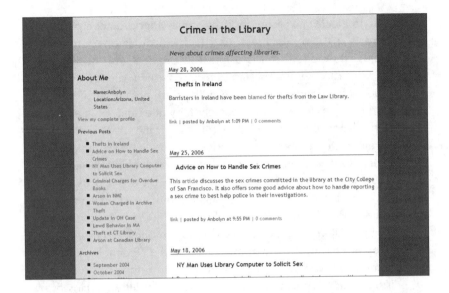

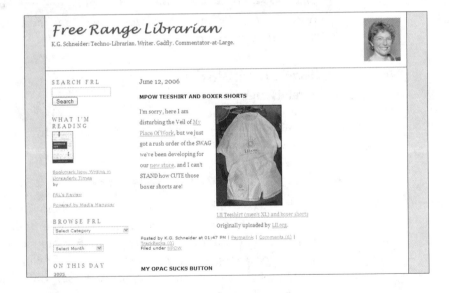

links to electronic resources) and some standards compliance. Here is a list of libraries using it. Iowa got money from the Gates Foundation and is using it to provide web hosting for libraries along with an email hosting service (please don't let it be an Exchange server) and a helpdesk person available by email and phone (and I bet chat by the end of the grant period) for all state libraries. One of the best things the Vermont Department of Libraries has done is to make sure every library in Vermont has a fixed and memorable email address that either forwards or links to an easy to use web-mail interface. They have had this for years and it's done a lot to help libraries stay connected and feel like part of the larger library system, even when they're up a mountain serving 600 people. I'm not usually one to jump on the "technology builds community" bandwagon, because I think there are certain irreplacable virtues to face to face interactions. However when done properly and effectively, technology can help support communities that are already built, and help them put their best face forward.

Librarian in Black

Sarah Houghton

librarianinblack.net

"Resources and discussions for the 'tech-librarians-by-default' among us ..." (Figure 2.8).

Google selling books?

Ah, it was only a matter of time. Ad space, wireless, now books. Books that are indexed in Google Book Search will soon be available for full-text purchase online. In a new section of Google Book Search's Help Center, Google explains how publishers can choose to sell online full-text access to their books. Eric Bangeman has a good explanation of whence this comes and how it will work over on ars technica.

How does this impact libraries? Well, how will our library holdings show up (for *eBooks* and print books) in Google Book Search? So far, they're not showing up well. So how do we let people know that they have free access to these titles, perhaps even online through the library's eBooks collections? That is the challenge and one which I think we're going to have to figure out on our own—Google most likely isn't going to help us on this.

LibraryLaw Blog

Mary Minnow

blog.librarylaw.com/librarylaw

"Issues concerning libraries and the law—with latitude to discuss any other interesting issues. Note: Not legal advice—just a dangerous mix of thoughts and information. Brought to you by Mary Minow, J.D., A.M.L.S." (Figure 2.9).

Library liability for pirating patrons?

Is the library responsible for bad patron copyright behavior? That is, when you notice (or let's face it, sometimes the patrons **proudly tell you**) that a patron is checking out DVDs purely to duplicate and then returning for more, is there a legal responsibility to do something about it? Ethical?

I wrote an article about library liability for patron copying *when they use library equipment* to download stuff off the Internet. The copyright law graciously lets libraries out of the liability loop ... as long as the equipment displays a notice that *"making a copy may be subject to the copyright law."* That's why every library posts notices by their photocopiers. The law doesn't specify photocopiers, luckily, but says "reproducing equipment" (see below the fold for the law itself). Libraries should display these same notices by any reproducing equipment, say, computers and printers.

I don't believe the law contemplates the boasting infringing patron who borrows the library's DVDs to make copies using patron-supplied-equipment. So I turn the question back to you, dear readers... for your thoughts.

Library Stuff

Steven M. Cohen

www.librarystuff.net

"The library weblog dedicated to resources for keeping current and professional development" (Figure 2.10).

Social Software in the Enterprise

There's a mini-essay in EContent by David Meerman Scott about blogs and wikis in the enterprise that is worth a few minutes of your time. From the piece:

"On one side of the corporate fence, the legal eagles are worried about secrets being revealed by their employees as they create content on blogs and wikis. And on the other, there's the feeling that so much of the information being created today is just not to be trusted. Corporate nannies want to make certain that their naïve charges don't get into trouble in the big scary world of information."

"Well, duh. We're talking about people here. Employees do silly things. They send inappropriate email (and blog posts too) and they believe some of the things on TV news. The debate should be centered around people, not technology. As the examples of previous technology waves should show us, attempting to block the technology isn't the answer. Blogs and wikis, like PCs, the public Internet, and email in previous decades are like chewing gum in your hair—they're easy to get into an enterprise, but impossible to remove without some ill-fated hair pulling."

This morning, I spoke to about 100 law librarians at a PLI event (presentation here). I took my usual poll of the group, asking how many use blogs internally in their firm. Only a few hands went up. I wasn't surprised to see that, considering Scott's argument above. Liability issues abound, even in corporate intranets, where control is not easily given over to front end staff. Getting buy-in is also tough because blogs, wikis, and other social web applications can be scary. That doesn't mean that we shouldn't continue to push the corporate envelope.

One piece of advice that I give is to not present ideas, but something more tangible. Instead of talking about creating a blog, create one. Then, show the people in charge how they work and what they can do for your company. Show and tell is easier digested than just tell.

Library Web Chic

Karen A. Coombs

www.librarywebchic.net

"Resources for librarians who are interested in the application of web design and technologies in libraries" (Figure 2.11).

Open Source Federated Search Tools

I've been really interested in trying to incorporate federated search and federated search results into the Libraries website and have been looking at different tools which I might use to do this. In my search I discovered several open source federated search tools. dbWiz and Keystone DLS are both provide open source federated searching. I haven't really learned a lot about either of these products yet. However, volume 23 issues 4 of Library Hi Tech has a good article on dbWiz that explains what the software does and how it was created. One of the things that caught my eye in the article was the "it is also possible to embed a dbWiz search box directly into any web page". The article talks about doing this on subject guide pages which is something that I've been thinking about doing for more than a year.

Truthfully, I'd like to take it further than this and have the results returned on the libraries site. I also would like to be able to construct collections to be federated searched on the fly. I don't know if this will be possible in the near term but is definately something I'd like to work on down the road.

A Library Writer's Blog

Corey Seeman

librarywriting.blogspot.com

"Have writer's block? Hopefully this resource will help librarians identify publishing and presentation opportunities in library & information science, as well as other related fields. I will include calls for papers, presentations, participation, reviewers, and other notices that I find on the web" (Figure 2.12).

Call for Book Reviewers: Journal of the American Studies Association of Texas

JASAT, the publication of the American Studies Association of Texas, is a peer-reviewed journal that exists

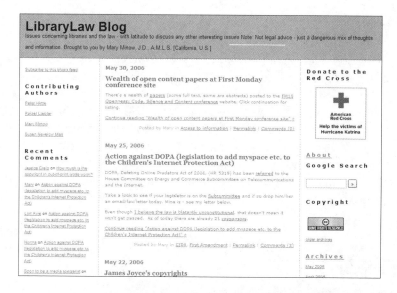

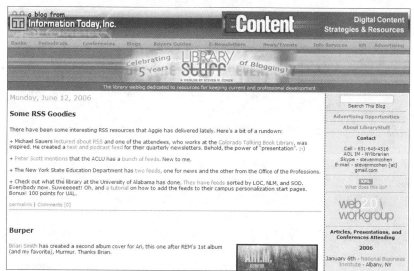

Figure 2.6   Librarian's Rant (left, top)

Figure 2.7   librarian.net (left, middle)

Figure 2.8   Librarian in Black (left, bottom)

Figure 2.9   LibraryLaw Blog (above, top)

Figure 2.10 Library Stuff (above, bottom)

to focus interdisciplinary attention on thematic, methodological, and pedagogical issues in American culture. Each annual issue includes short reviews (approximately 400 words) of books relevant to scholarship in American Studies, with emphasis on Texas, Southern and Southwestern United States, and/or Northern Mexico.

If you are interested in reviewing for JASAT, contact Steven Schroeder, Book Review Editor, at steven_schroeder_at_earthlink.net Please indicate the title you'd like to review and briefly outline your qualifications. Deadline for review submissions is 1 July 2006. A list of books available for review, updated regularly, is online at: http://home.earthlink.net/~shschroeder/ 2006jasatbooks.htm

LibraryTechtonics

Andrea Mercado
www.librarytechtonics.info
"A librarian riding the shift" (Figure 2.13).

China Day 4 (and 5ish): Beijing to Kunming, Yunnan University Library

I'm currently sitting in a meeting in the Yunan University Library in Kunming, the capital of the Yunnan province where we'll spend the remainder of our trip. Just for kicks, I enabled the wifi on Carol's laptop to see if I could get a connection, and I did, so I'm taking this quick opportunity to post. Perhaps I can post a quick summary of this current meeting before we leave the library. Go go gadget free university wifi!

The delegation hopped a 3-hour flight from Beijing to Kunming yesterday morning. We were finally settled into our hotel around 3:30P or so, then spent some time walking around Kunming before dinner at a local famous restaurant.

Kunming is *beautiful*. There just aren't enough words to describe it. Even just sitting in a conference room at Yunnan University Library, warm, spring sunlight streams through a wall of windows, and you can see the green grass, budding trees, and beautiful flowers everywhere. I'm jealous of the students and staff here!

We have 2 professional meetings today, the current one at Yunnan University Library, and an afternoon meeting at Yunnan Provincial Library, which is the local version of a public library.

LISNews

Blake Carver

www.lisnews.com

"LISNews is a collaborative weblog [aka blog] devoted to current events and news in the world of Library and Information Science. A dedicated team of authors scours the Web to find stories they find interesting. You'll find links to interesting stories and Web sites, along with original stories, interviews and reviews. LISNews is updated frequently around the clock, usually 7 days a week. We are a non-commercial site, supported by our users" (Figure 2.14).

News For Library Geeks: Amazon and Google and Librarians, Oh My

Imagine a reference librarian who, when asked for books on abortion, responds, "Do you mean adoption?" Up until recently, a keyword search on Amazon for "abortion" did just that. Conspiracy theories aside, this is because a number of people presumably searched for abortion books and then ended up clicking on a few adoption titles. So the suggestion was, as the Google News page excuses it, "determined automatically by a computer program."

Speaking of Google, they are being sued, again, this time for lowering the results ranking of a company's site (presumably just because the site became less popular), thereby depriving them of business. Technology is an essential tool for what librarians do nowadays, but cases of skewed reviews are becoming more prevalent. What do these stories say about how people understand the role of computers in the search process, let alone how machines will mediate library services in the future?

Lorcan Dempsey's weblog (OCLC)

Lorcan Dempsey

orweblog.oclc.org

"On libraries, services, and networks" (Figure 2.15).

The simple search box and the rich texture of suggestion

I have been in a couple of meetings recently where people have been talking about the attraction of the simple, single box search as the ultimate goal. To this, my response is 'yes, and what else?'. In Google's case, pagerank has been the principal 'what else'. Going forward they have interesting questions to face about how to rank materials which do not fit the web-page model. The improvement of search, and the improvement of ad placement, are a major focus for them, as indicated in the much discussed Google analyst day presentation [pdf]. A simple box is one part only of their formula: good results and good ads are necessary for them.

Interestingly, in Amazon's cases their results **are** their advertizing. Each result represents a potential purchase. This is one reason that it is useful for them to make APIs to their results available. And it is one reason that their presentation strategy is to offer a rich texture of suggestion on their results pages. You are hit with many hints about potential items of interest, and this data is created in multiple ways (mobilizing the edge of reader contributions, mining the 'intentional' data from user purchase and browse patterns, mining the text of books). An Amazon page has many 'suggestions', using a variety of approaches.

I think we will see more 'simple search' but supported by smart results and rich browse. Whenever somebody says that people need a simple single box to search, try asking 'yes, and what else?'.

Open Stacks

Greg Schwartz

openstacks.net/os/

"Promoting information access and literacy for all" (Figure 2.16).

Library-branded podcatcher

Kelli Staley IMed me this evening to let me know about her library's shiny new branded, preloaded version of the Juice podcatcher. So if patrons download the Lansing Public Library branded Juice, they get an aggregator with all four of LPL's podcast feeds preloaded and a shiny LPL logo staring them in the face. Talk about presence - even if you unsubscribe from the feeds, the logo remains! How completely overdue.

Search Lounge

Chris Fillius

searchlounge.org

"Welcome to the Search Lounge with your host Chris. Here in the lounge you'll find original reviews, interviews, and articles about Internet search engines and search related topics" (Figure 2.17).

Tagging and Meta-Search

Tagging systems are segmented by media. You can tag photos on Flickr, web pages on Furl, del.icio.us, Yahoo!'s My Web, videos on YouTube, your book collection on LibraryThing, and so forth and so on. But why should my video tags be different from my photo tags? There might be one-off situations, but generally my tags should follow me rather than me having to follow my tags around from search box to search box.

I want one search box or tag cloud to give me access to all of it. At times I may want to limit my search or browse by media (as in tabbed searching for local vs. news vs. images, etc), but often I'll want all relevant results regardless of media type.

Tag Central does this, but it lists results by source rather than integrating them together with a ranking algorithm. But it's fun to play around with.

Has anyone built a meta-search engine or a widget of some sort that actually integrates and ranks the results across tagging systems?

The Shifted Librarian

Jenny Levine

www.theshiftedlibrarian.com

"Shifting libraries at the seed of byte!" (Figure 2.18).

OPAC Tagging - Who's It?

There's an interesting discussion about tagging and OPACs over on the WEB4LIB mailing list. Start here and work your way through the thread (so far the subject line hasn't changed so it should be relatively easy). Some interesting comments and pointers to the PennTags project at ~~Penn State~~ the University of

Library Web Chic

Resources for librarians who are interested in the application of web design and technologies in libraries

Protected RSS feeds, web-based news aggregators, and user convience

June 6th, 2006 6:28 am

Sometimes you sit down and plan something only to discover that all the desired traits make things impossible under current technologies. This seems to be the case for our ongoing internal blog projects. These blogs (and their RSS feeds) are password protected because the content on them is really part of our intranet. In order to view them from an non-library IP address people have to authenticate using the computer username and password. Additionally, we do the authenticate over SSL in order to make sure the username and password are encrypted.

This all is sound in theory except for one *big* problem. None of the current web-based news aggregators (Bloglines, Rojo, etc) support authenticate RSS feeds over SSL. So essentially people can't subscribe to the RSS feeds unless they use a desktop aggregator, which none of them have or want to have. Sigh.. Its a vicious chicken/egg cycle that has had my head spinning for a week. At the moment the organization is f...

Search

Home

About

Articles and Presentations
» Upcoming Presentations

Contact Me

My Blogroll

My FURL Archive

Stories - Tutorials & Code Demonstrations

Archives
» June 2006
» May 2006
» April 2006

Blogger | SEARCH THIS BLOG | SEARCH ALL BLOGS | BlogThis! | GET YOUR OWN BLOG | FLAG? | NEXT BLOG»

A Library Writer's Blog

Have writer's block? Hopefully this resource will help librarians identify publishing and presentation opportunities in library & information science, as well as other related fields. I will include calls for papers, presentations, participation, reviewers, and other notices that I find on the web. If you find anything to be posted, please drop me a note. thanks -- Corey Seeman, University of Michigan(cseeman@bus.umich.edu)

Links

- NEW -- RSS Site Feed (XML) -- Cut and Paste this URL - http://librarywriting.blogspot.com/atom.xml - into your RSS Reader
- Corey Seeman's Home Page
- H-Net Call for Papers
- Beyond the Job Blog
- ALA New Members Round Table Writers Information (great resource & email list)
- The Researching Librarian

Subscribe to **A Library Writer's Blog**! (powered by Bloget)

[ ] subscribe

Thursday, June 08, 2006

Call for Posters: Michigan Library Association Academic and Research Library

LibraryTechtonics
A librarian riding the shift

June 06, 2006

It's easy to get lost in an install

My apologies if this post reads poorly, my brain is stuck in productivity mode, with communication leaping out in fits and spurts...

After my test run with WordPress, I decided that if I was going to have the PLA Blog ready for ALA later this month (or for my OPAL presentation on conference blogging this coming Friday), it was time to dive in and get a move on.

I started Sunday (I was on the desk all day Saturday), and I was able to get a significant amount of work done after the truly 5-minute install, and the super easy import from Blogger (way easier than the outdated documentation on the WordPress site). Most of what's taking so long is porting over the static content, and configuring the blog to do everything it should upon release to the world (WP plugins "rawk", and I would even venture to say they're a bit addictive).

Blogger is really, really bare bones. Yes, you can do some interesting things with Blogger tags and what have you, but it's nothing like what you can do with apps like Movable Type or WordPress. Due to the limitations of the current PLA Blog, there's a lot to be done with getting the content situated in WordPress. My biggest issue right now is categories and tagging, since Blogger doesn't really support it (you can add tags, but they're kinda hacked into the HTML). Unfortunately, with the latest release of WP, the nifty batch-categories plugin no longer works, so all tagging needs to be done by hand.

The PLA Blog currently has about 564 posts. That's a lot of hand-tagging. For now, I'm focusing on the conference posts, since by tagging the conference posts, I can generate a link to all of the posts for a given conference. Since we've lived this long without categories, we can live a little longer, I'm sure, and I may have some volunteers lined up to help with the rest of the hand tagging. Unless someone can work some magic and make the batch-categories plugin work with WP 2.0.3, I'd

SEND ANDREA TO CHINA IN MARCH

What's this about?

LINKS

About the author
Send me email
Read my Bloglines blogroll
Free stuff to do in Boston
Technorati Profile

2006
NANOWRIMO
PARTICIPANT

10093 / 50000 words

FEED FLAVORS:
SUBSCRIBE!

RSS 1.0

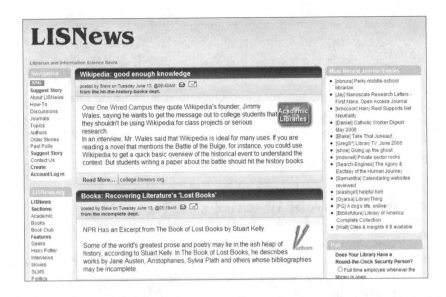

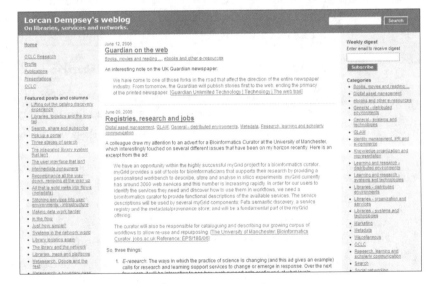

Figure 2.11   Library Web Chic (left, top)

Figure 2.12   A Library Writer's Blog (left, middle)

Figure 2.13   LibraryTechtonics (left, bottom)

Figure 2.14   LISNews.com (above, top)

Figure 2.15   Lorcan Dempsey's weblog (above, bottom)

Pennsylvania, which I didn't realize incorporated tagging into the catalog. Rock on, Michael Winkler and ~~Penn State~~ UPenn!

In addition, make sure you stay current on what Davey P. is doing with his OPAC, in particular the pewbot which provides Amazon-like suggestions (read more about it here and here).

Earlier this year, John Blyberg did a great job surveying some of the really great experimenting we're seeing with taking OPACs to the next level. Could 2006 be the year the OPAC finally begins to truly evolve? Let's hope so.

Tame the Web: Libraries and Technology

Michael Stephens

www.tametheweb.com/ttwblog

"The Tame the Web Blog is written by Michael Stephens, a librarian, technology trainer and writer living in Northern Indiana. ... The blog includes topics such as current and future technology uses in libraries, training tips, staff development and various other interests concerning library settings" (Figure 2.19).

Ten Ways to Lose Your Techie Librarians (Updated)

On page 67 of the January/February *Public Libraries* magazine is one of the HOTTEST numbered lists I've read in a long time: "How to Lose Your Best People" is authored anonymously by "several seasoned librarians." Points like "Nitpick the dress code - because socks are essential for good public service" are not only humorous but very telling in some libraries.

So with apologies to the Seasoned Anonymous Writers, let me offer up:

Ten Ways to Lose Your Techie Librarians

1. Dismiss blogs/wikis/RSS as just for the geeks not library users

2. Plan technology projects without involving them until the wheels are in motion/contracts are signed

3. Appoint a technophobe librarian to manage the techies

4. Allow barriers to exist that make it difficult for IT staff and librarians to plan and collaborate

5. Bog down their projects in red tape and approvals that take weeks or months to get

6. Send your seasoned librarians to conferences instead of mixing up seasoned folks & your techies to a variety of association and professional meetings, including tech-based conferences

7. Plan project timelines that extend so long the planned service or tech innovation is out of date before it launches

8. Pooh Pooh the idea of the Emerging Technology Committee, the library is doing just fine without it

9. Make your library Web site an afterthought not a "cyber branch" location

10. Always ensure that non-technical people make the important technical decisions

BONUS: Never Dream. Never innovate. Never think outside the Box.

Travelin' Librarian

Michael Sauers

www.travelinlibrarian.info

This is my blog. It tends to cover more personal than work related topics but I'm not afraid to dive into opinion and controversy when it comes to library and technology issues (Figure 2.20).

Library WiFi access issue

I've now published two articles on policy issues for public libraries when offering WiFi to the public. I though I'd thought of everything. I should have known better...

Yesterday one of my students from a WA small public library mentioned that they require a library card number (or other temporary id number) to access the library's WiFi connection. This caught me off guard as I'd never heard of this being done before. Granted, many libraries require some sort of login for the library computers for timing software purposes and/or to have a basic tracking system in case there is damage to the equipment. However, I'd never heard of requiring a login for the WiFi when the patron is using their own equipment.

I discussed it briefly with the librarian and she was unable to offer an explanation beyond the fact that since they did it with

OPEN STACKS
Promoting information access and literacy for all.

June 06, 2006

Presentation crib sheets

Christine Brown attended both of the SirsiDynix presentations that I recently gave and posted fairly comprehensive summaries of both. So if you're interested, the links follow:

Part 1 - The Listener's Guide

Part 2 - The Creator's Guide

Comments?
Posted by Greg at 06:26 AM |

CONTACT
Contact Form

SOME OPTIONS
Carnival of the Infosciences wiki
Carnival of the Infosciences @ Blog Carnival
Blogs For Libraries
Cooking the Books (my personal cookbook project)
Indiana Blogs!
My Amazon Wish List (you never know)
My Bloglines subscriptions
My Listology

June 05, 2006

Lazy link dump

Travelin' Librarian reports that the Colorado Talking Book Library has adopted RSS, providing feeds for their quarterly newsletters, including a podcast feed for the audio version. I've talked about using podcasting to extend services to your visually impaired community, but haven't had a great example to point to before now.

From the current AALL Spectr
Rutgers Law Library is doing s
points of contention with the c
it apart point-by-point. I can o
for my take on podcasting and

SearchLounge.org

5/9/2006

Yahoo! Cool Thing of the Day
Filed under: General — Chris

True to its name, every day the writers (who are Yahoo! employees) of Yahoo! Cool Thing of the Day publish something interesting to be found in the Yahoo! universe. Recent posts have included tips for using Yahoo! Maps, Open Shortcuts, Yahoo! Travel Tips, etc.

It's great to see these lesser known features and products being publicized.

Comments (0)

5/8/2006

Digforit - Meta-Search Engine for Sale
Filed under: General — Chris

Digforit.com is for sale on eBay. Check out the auction. As of the morning of May 8 the top bid is $15,000, and the auction ends on May 14.

For web search, Digforit uses GYM, though it's more focused on Google. For other types of search, such as Audio, Blogs, Video etc. the engines vary. Digforit has built in a query refinement feature that pops up after you type in your query.

Back in October, Jux2.com, another meta-search engine, sold for

welcome to the search lounge
with your host chris. here in
the lounge you'll find
original reviews, interviews,
and articles about internet
search engines and search
related topics.

recent posts
  yahoo! cool thing of the
  day
  digforit - meta-search
  engine for sale
  keotag
  guest obituary for zeal.
  by alice swanberg
  zeal.com, r.i.p.

links
  about me
  news and blogs i read

categories:
  general
  interviews
  natural language engines
  clustering engines
  search engine reviews
  visual engines

the *shifted* librarian
Shifting libraries at the speed of byte!

My name is *Jenny*, and I'll be your information maven today.

◻ **Thursday, June 8, 2006**

Second Life Library .20

"Cypress Barrett told me that a resident volunteered to donate land in Caledon for a library branch. If you have not been to Caledon, please go. It is a new sim and is a nineteenth century atmosphere. There are people walking around in clothing from the nineteenth century and all the houses and shops must have this look too. I have a friend who recenty rented a house there - and there were people waiting in line to buy land and rent there. It is very charming.

This is the challenge: how would you build a nineteenth century library in a twenty-first century digital world?

I think this is fascinating - but I need to work on getting our main library up and running. Is there anyone or any group that would like to work with this concept as a branch? Let me know." [An email to the Second Life Library Google Group]

I'm having trouble keeping up with all of the great stuff happening in the Second Life Library project because there's just so dang much of it. The international collaboration, community, and conversation that is building around this is phenomenal. Besides the pure people aspect of it, the fact that Ebsco, OCLC's QuestionPoint, and TechSoup are all experimenting with the group signals how much gaming has hit the library world over the last year. It's fascinating to watch, and I hope it continues. I couldn't see the images in this video, but I'm guessing it gives a good summary of what has happened in just one month.

I hope to start joining in the fun in a couple of months when my travels slow down a little for me. It's been a grueling year so far; Michael Stephens and I counted up dates yesterday, and we think we'll each have given 28 presentations/talks in the first six months of this year. One of my goals at this point is to relax a little after June and have some fun playing in Second Life by just hanging out in the public library there!

Meanwhile, if Lori's challenge sounds interesting, be sure to contact her!"

June 2006

Sun	Mon	Tue	Wed	Thu	Fri	Sat
				1	2	3
4	5	6	7	8	9	10
11	12	13	14	15	16	17
18	19	20	21	22	23	24
25	26	27	28	29	30	

TSL Archives

Blogroll (Sites I Read in My Aggregator)

Mobile Blogroll (Sites I Read on My Treo 600)

◻ Check box to open links in new windows

Search TSL

Spreading the meme:
Why You Should Fall to Your Knees and Worship a Librarian

About Jenny
Chicago Sun-Times article
What is a Shifted Librarian?
A Shifted Reading List
Presentations and Articles
The Shifted Librarian Moblog!

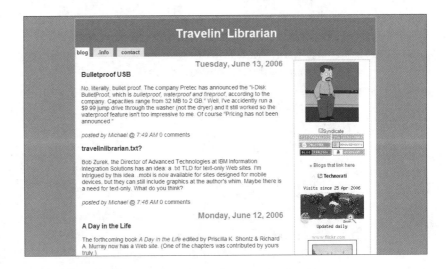

the library computers, they decided to do it for any computer that used their connection.

I thought about this overnight, and here's my opinion:

1. As a patron with a laptop, the last thing I want to do is to have to walk into the library and have to enter my library card number to use my laptop.

2. As a visitor to a library with my own laptop I don't want to have to ask for a temporary card to use my laptop.

3. As a staff member of a library that received a lot of tourists (as is the situation at the library in question) I don't want to have to give out temp ID cards to a large number of patrons whom will never get a library card since they're not residents.

Am I off base here? Do other libraries do this and I'm just unaware of it? What do you think? Please leave a comment and let me know.

Travels with the State Librarian

Christie Brandau

ksstatelibrarian.blogspot.com

"The thoughts and travels of the State Librarian of Kansas" (Figure 2.21).

Continuing the Tour!

On August 23, the Governor's tour continued, with a visit to the Sullivan Elementary school library in Ulysses. Mrs. Mitchell, the school librarian, showed us around the library and explained some of the creative programs and outreach done to instill a love of reading and learning in their students.

The next library stop was in Lakin where the Governor read to children at the Kearny County Library and we talked with library staffer Patty Timm and director Richard Brookman. If you want to know anything about graphic fiction or non-fiction, Richard is the librarian to ask!

We had a wonderful surprise when we walked into the Hamilton County Library in Syracuse as the library staff there had created a ten-foot replica of the last page of the book *No Matter What* by Debi Gliori! The Hamilton County Library Board president introduced Governor Sebelius and gave warm words of praise for the One Book, One State project. The Governor then read to a group of preschoolers assembled to meet her.

When at Syracuse, I had a chance to talk with some of the area librarians, including the new director of the Southwestern Kansas Library System, Emily Sitz. Emily is on the far left in this picture next to the Governor, Denise Smith (Stanton County Library Director), Joyce Armstrong (Hamilton County Library Director) and me.

It was a great tour, and we visited some outstanding libraries. I love the western side of Kansas with its rolling hills and wide open areas. As I was driving back to Topeka, I saw my first field of sunflowers and just had to take a picture!

Walt at Random

Walt Crawford

walt.lishost.org

"Libraries, music, net media, cruising, policy, and other stuff not quite ready for Cites & Insights" (Figure 2.22).

Fair use: A brilliant comic book!

If you care about balanced copyright, fair use, and real creativity (which almost always means creating new works based in part on existing works), you really should go look at *Tales from the Public Domain: Bound by Law?*.

It's a 70+-page comic book (color covers, b&w interior), with the first and last pages done in "Tales from the Crypt" style, and it tells an interesting and difficult story–and does so about as fairly and clearly as I've ever seen the story told.

It's from Duke University's Center for the Study of the Public Domain. You can view it online, download it, or buy print copies.

What can I say? I'm impressed. I'll certainly revisit it when I get around to a big C&I piece on balanced copyright. (This is important: The comic book is not an attack on copyright or a claim that everything should be up for grabs–but it also doesn't buy into the "permission culture" where every use of every artifact, no matter how fleeting, requires rights clearance.)

Figure 2.21   Travels with the State Librarian

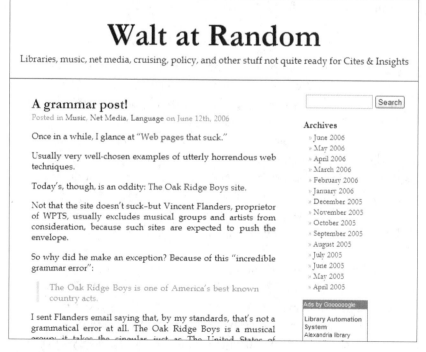

Figure 2.22   Walt at Random

Library Blogs

As I write this, there are still relatively few libraries using blog technology to enhance their Web sites. (I hope there will be at least one more by the time you finish the book!) Of the libraries that adopted blog technology early on, here are some of the best blogs; one or more of them might prove useful as a model for your own library blog. This is by no means an exhaustive list, though I have attempted to represent a useful range of library types and blog purposes.

Ann Arbor District Library

www.aadl.org

What makes this one of the best examples online today is that this blog is also the library's home page! These librarians don't have a Web site and a blog, the blog is the Web site (Figure 2.23).

Tax forms and more, at the Ann Arbor District Library

All outlets of the Ann Arbor District Library are once again distributing federal and State of Michigan tax forms. In addition to the basic forms and instruction booklets, each outlet also has notebooks of reproducible forms.

To supplement your tax form needs, the Library has a link on its website that gathers together dozens of useful links to help you through this annual adventure. Our tax information page has links to the IRS and the Michigan Department of the Treasury where you can find all the tax forms and publications on line. We have a list of places in Ann Arbor where low income residents and senior citizens can receive free tax help. You can also find links to tax forms from the other states and to the City of Detroit.

PaperCuts (Topeka and Shawnee County Public Library)

papercuts.tscpl.org

"Cutting Edge Library News, Reviews and Events" (Figure 2.24).

What Every Good Citizen Needs to Know ...

Throughout the years our government has protected, prepared and educated us for numerous different disaster scenarios. From attacks from Native Americans, the British, our own citizens, the Germans, the Japanese, the Russians, poxes, plagues, influenzas, nuclear bombs, the year 2000, natural disasters and terrorists, the United States government has kept us on our toes, making sure we know what to do when we are in the face of disaster as well as protecting us from these foes. Looking back on some of these potential threats, they seem laughable, although at the time they were not and some of the actions that the United States government and its citizens took in dealing with these threats were anything but hilarious. I have to say, though, for the most part, I'm mostly pleased with our government and how they've handled our national security. We now have the formidable Department of Homeland Security watching out for us, making sure that we can all sleep soundly at night not having to think about terrorist threats. But are we really sleeping that soundly?

The one thing our government has never prepared us for is attack from zombies. That's right, zombies. The potential threat of widespread zombification and attack on normal brains has been around for centuries, yet we know nothing on how to protect ourselves or where we should go in case of attack. Are there emergency routes for zombie attacks similar to those emergency snow routes? Will we be informed of imminent brain eating by the Emergency Alert System? What are the best tools for "killing" zombies? If a zombie scratches me, does that mean I'll become a zombie too or does it have to bite me? Can my pet cats be zombified? Is it possible to reverse zombification or teach zombies how to live amongst us? What are the answers to these questions? Our government is extremely lax and negligent in protecting us from zombies or even formulating a plan on how to fight zombies (at least they haven't divulged one).

Luckily, citizens, we have a knowledgeable zombie expert among us: Max Brooks. Max, the son of famous director Mel Brooks, tells us all we need to know in his book The Zombie Survival Guide: Complete Protection from the Living Dead. You'll learn how to identify your enemy, what best to use in "killing" zombies, the different classes of outbreaks, and what causes zombification. I highly suggest that you check out this title today in order to prepare yourself for the inevitable. Max Brooks knows what he is talking about and he cares for your safety. Brooks has another zombie title coming out this September, World War Z. Be sure to put yourself on hold for it as soon as we get it ordered.

Even though these following titles are "fiction" I suggest that you check these out as well so that you can see what a zombie attack might look like and get some ideas on how you can protect yourself from the undead.

"Shaun of the Dead"
"Land of the Dead"
"28 Days Later"
"Day of the Dead"
"Night of the Living Dead"
"Resident Evil"
"Dawn of the Dead"

From the Director ...

ofldirector.blogspot.com

"New and views from the Director of the Ogden Farmers' Library" (Figure 2.25).

Popcorn ... Yummmm

Our very first film program was over about an hour ago, and I've just now finished vacuuming our meeting room, which was — literally — one big sea of popcorn. I am so happy and content, words just cannot express!

Last December, the Sickelco Family gave the library a lovely donation that allowed me to buy a digital DVD projector. Around the same time, I bought a subscription that allows us to show films produced by nearly all the major motion picture studios.

So today, we showed Madagascar to **52** little kids and their parents.

Members of our Junior Friends group made several batches of popcorn in our great big, wonderful popcorn maker, which made the library smell like a theater, and we opened the doors to the little ones. Can I just say....

S-U-C-C-E-S-S!

What I find somewhat amusing about all this is that film programs are nothing new for libraries. I used to show 16mm films when I was a page at the Gates Library back in 1978 and those programs were always well-attended. I think film programs went by the wayside when videotapes became the rage and 16mm went away. But now they're back....with a vengeance! And everything old is new again.

Utah State Library—Utah and National Library News

library.utah.gov/library_news/
"The latest library news from Utah and National news sources" (Figure 2.26).

CriticasMagazine.com Wins min Award for Best Companion Site

Launched in August 2005 as the companion site for Críticas Magazine, published by Library Journal, and its free, monthly newsletter Críticas Connection, CríticasMagazine.com, won min's Best of the Web Award in the B2B Companion Site category. Library Journal, March 17, 2006

Got Firefox? Library Link to Google Book Search Now Available

You can't easily find a library link using Google Book Search, as LJ pointed out earlier this year... Library Journal, March 17, 2006

Phasing out librarians helps Provo schools balance books

The school district continues to replace its degree-bearing librarians with lower-paid and lower-skilled employees, but some parents have a suggestion for the cost-cutting move: Shelve it. Salt Lake Tribune, March 17, 2006

Georgia State University Library's Public Health Blog

www.library.gsu.edu/news/index.asp?typeID=60

"A weblog featuring news, events, and resources from the Institute of Public Health and Georgia State University Library" (Figure 2.27).

Older Americans and Mental Health Month

From MedlinePlus:
The month of May has been designated Older Americans Month and Mental Health Month by the Center for Mental Health Services.

Pre-Issue Publication from PLoS Medicine

Ezzati M, Vander Hoorn S, Lawes CM, Leach R, James W, et al. (2005). Rethinking the "Diseases of Affluence" Paradigm: Global Patterns of Nutritional Risks in Relation to Economic Development. PLoS Med 2(5): e133

Cardiovascular diseases, traditionally thought of as diseases of affluence, are likely to become a substantial public health [issue] in low-income and middle-income countries.

Off the Shelf

www.readingpl.org/weblog/offtheshelf.htm
"A weekly newsletter from the Reading [MA] Public Library" (Figure 2.28).

Older Active Adults Day

The aging of the baby-boomer generation and longer life expectancies are fueling growth in the number and percent of older Americans who are active, healthy and eager for community engagement. These adults are a great resource for our communities, and we hope that the Library can also be a great resource for them! The Reading Public Library in conjunction with the Burbank YMCA will be presenting a free information fair for people age 55 + on Thursday, May 26.

This event will be held at the Library from 9:00- 12:00 a.m. and will feature refreshments, door prizes, and lots of great information! Are you looking for educational opportunities? New employment? Or the chance to give back through volunteerism? Come chat with representatives of a wide variety of organizations including Elderhostel, the YMCA, Winchester Hospital, the U.S. Food and Drug Administration, and many

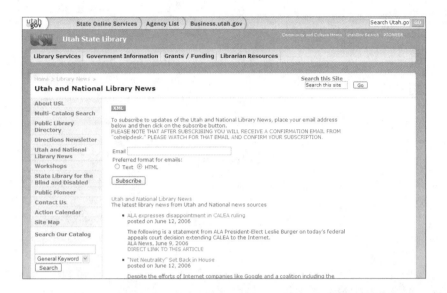

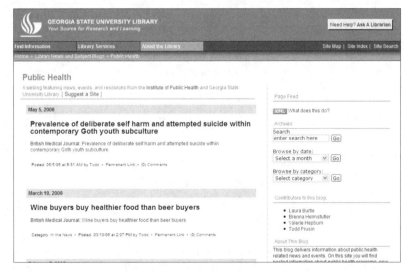

Figure 2.23   Ann Arbor District Library (left, top)

Figure 2.24   PaperCuts (left, middle)

Figure 2.25   From the Director… (left, bottom)

Figure 2.26   Utah State Library—Utah and National Library News
             (above, top)

Figure 2.27   Georgia State University Library's Public Health Blog
             (above, bottom)

more. Find out what's new in educational, volunteer, recreational and health information.

It's fun and it's free! Follow it up with a free Open Swim at the Burbank YMCA. For more information call the Reading Public Library, 781-944-0840, and ask to speak to Lorraine Barry, Head of Information Services.

New Slackers Title Announced: The Buffalo Soldier by Chris Bohjalian

This month, Slackers Book Club provides its members with a novel of both love and loss. The Buffalo Soldier is the story of the aftermath of a tragedy in small-town Vermont. Laura and Terry Sheldon lose their twin daughters when the river that divides their town pours over its banks. Two years later the now childless couple decide to adopt, and a young black boy named Alfred is placed with them. Alfred is a troubled child: wary, distant, and acutely aware of his status as the only black child in the almost all-white world of Vermont.

As Laura takes the first tentative steps to becoming a mother again, Terry finds it impossible to form a relationship with the boy whose background and interests are so different from his own. Feeling alienated and excluded, he falls into an affair with a young woman—and gets her pregnant. Meanwhile, Alfred's adjustment is eased by his friendship with an elderly neighbor—and inspiration in the story of the buffalo soldiers, the black cavalrymen of the old West.

Out of the entwining of these complicated lives, The Buffalo Soldier creates a suspenseful, moving portrait of a family. There is much to think about in this novel as the main characters attempt to come to terms with issues of interracial adoption, infidelity, and grief. Copies of the book and comment cards for Slackers Book Club members are located on the Main floor near the Information Desk. For a reading group guide to accompany this book, go to http://www.readinggroupguides.com/guides3/buffalo_soldier1.asp

Liblog: A Library Weblog (Redwood City [CA] Public Library)

www.rcpl.info/services/liblog.html

"Welcome to Liblog—a weblog of current web sites and stories dealing with the interface between technology and libraries. Sometimes the connection to the sphere of the library is tenuous ... but in today's world, *everything* has an impact on libraries, on librarians ... and on library users" (Figure 2.29).

FORTUNE: Trapped in cubicles

A look backwards at why the "cubicle" was created, and why it prospered - as well as a look ahead to how office space seems to be changing. Or rather, how work is changing so the office is becoming less important.

Good Morning Silicon Valley: New from Google Labs: Microsoft Office Live

Google purchases Upstartle, the company behind Writely, a web-based word processor. Put that together with Gmail (email/instant messaging.2.5 GB of storage), and the recent testing/announcements of an html editor, calendar program, and a universally accessible network drive.... It doesn't seem like a challenger to Microsoft Office is very far away.

Old Bridge Library Weblog

obpl.blogspot.com

"A regularly updated listing of news and events for patrons at the Old Bridge, NJ Public Library" (Figure 2.30).

The Old Bridge Central Library will be hosting a display of artwork from the Old Bridge High School entitled Visions Of Our Creativity from May 1st - 30th. The artworks were created by a selection of students from various visual art classes offered at the High School. The exhibit is an excellent survey of techniques, media, and themes in which these developing artists have demonstrated a degree of enthusiasm and excellence. Faculty and students will be hosting a reception for the artwork which is open to the public on Thursday, May 5 from 6:00 - 8:00 p.m. For more information, please contact the Library, (732) 721-5600 ext. 5033 or e-mail Tim

Miscellaneous Blogs

While the blogs listed in this section are not created by librarians or libraries, they are of potential interest to those in the LIS world. Some of them are technical; some of them are more issue-based. Take a look. Chances are you'll find one or two that will pique your interest.

Gizmodo

Joel Johnson

www.gizmodo.com

"Gizmodo is a fast-growing web magazine, dedicated to everything related to gadgets, gizmos, and cutting-edge consumer electronics. Our influential audience stops by frequently to check out the latest news, reviews and recommendations for products including laptops, cell phones, PDAs, digital cameras, home entertainment and more" (Figure 2.31).

Samsung SH-B022 Blu-Ray Burner Reviewed (Verdict: You Might Want to Wait a Bit)

We're already over three months into 2006, the year that high definition and next generation DVDs are set to make their big splash. The gang over at The Register got their hands on Samsung's SH-B022, the company's Blu-Ray disc burner and gave it a thorough testing. The overall impression of the drive appears positive, but it's not without its faults. For starters, the drive uses an IDE interface, a technology that Intel will drop support for with its South Bridge chipset. A single 12.7GB file took 25 minutes to burn, which translates to whole disc burning clocking in at around an hour. The drive also didn't burn any other type of media, such as CDs or regular DVDs. Then there's the price: It's not official, but Register estimates that it will cost $800-$900. So if you've got the money to spend on a drive that produces discs that only it and a handful of other drives can read, jump right in. You may just want to hold out a bit longer to wait for the price to drop and for the Blu-Ray technology to gain more of a foothold in the marketplace.

Google Blog

www.google.com/googleblog

This is the official blog from Google. Here's where you can get all the up-to-the-minute news of what's going on in the company (Figure 2.32).

A real find

As a librarian and a Googler, I love the "Find it in a library" links we've added to many — but not yet all — of the titles in Google Book Search. While we work on getting these links rolled out for the rest of the books, at least one user has taken matters into his own hands: "Superpatron" Edward Vielmetti has written a Greasemonkey script for Firefox that enables him to see which books are available at his local library.

Since Google Book Search is all about helping you discover and locate books you never knew existed, it's especially gratifying to see people like Ed embracing and extending this mission.

IEBlog—Microsoft

blogs.msdn.com/ie
"The Microsoft Internet Explorer Weblog" (Figure 2.33).

Application Compatibility Logging In IE7

As Rob pointed out in his last blog post on security and compatibility in IE7, one of the biggest challenges in software development is making the software secure and compatible at the same time. In IE7, we have many new security features that help protect users against various attacks by blocking certain content, but as a consequence, some web applications may no longer work as they used to. To help web developers and IT professional find such compatibility issues, IE7 offers an application compatibility logging feature. When the feature is enabled, the user is notified by an icon in the status bar. Thereafter, if one of the new security features blocks certain content, information about the security feature and the blocked content is created in the Windows Event Log.

At the RSA conference, I talked to a customer who reported that one of his pages no longer worked correctly and showed a security warning. He was frustrated that he was seeing this warning that he did not see on IE6 SP1. He did not know what was causing this issue. We found that the warning was due to

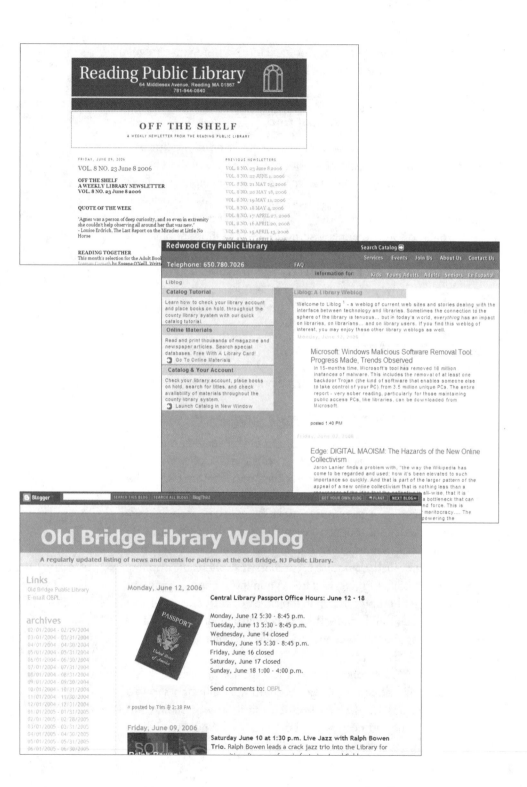

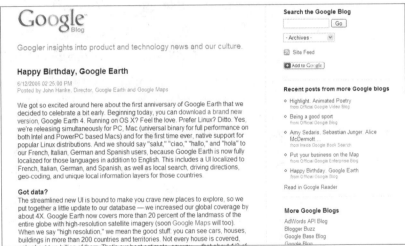

one of the new security features (local machine zone lock down) first introduced in XPSP2. The Application compatibility toolkit is designed to help you diagnose such issues. When you use this toolkit while viewing your website/web application in IE7, the relevant event log entries are displayed in the toolkit to help you find compatibility issues.

A new article on MSDN named Finding Security Compatibility Issues in Internet Explorer 7 describes how to download and use the toolkit.

Lessig Blog

Lawrence Lessig

www.lessig.org/blog

Lawrence Lessig is "Professor of Law at Stanford Law School and founder of the school's Center for Internet and Society" (Figure 2.34).

And a HUGE victory for the Stanford CIS

So it's Saturday morning here in Australia, and I'm reading my email in reverse order. First the fantastic news about PublicKnowledge. Now this: The Stanford Center for Internet and Society has won an important case about anonymous speech. An anonymous participant in an online chat posted comments critical of Ampex and its chairman. They sued for defamation. The poster sued under the California anti-SLAPP (strategic lawsuit against public participation) statute. Ampex tried to dismiss and run away. The Court of Appeals ruled at first that there remained anti-SLAPP jurisdiction. The District Court then refused to award fees. The Court of Appeals has now reversed the District Court and ordered fees. The case was argued by a law student. It will have an important effect in stopping the abuse of process against online critics.

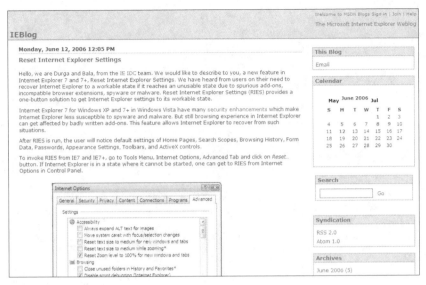

Figure 2.33   IEBlog

Figure 2.34   Lessig Blog

Chapter 3

The Library Blogosphere, Part 2: The Bloggers

Through my work and at conferences—notably Computers in Libraries and Internet Librarian—I've met many librarians who blog. Some of the most informative and creative among them were also very generous in taking time to be interviewed for the book. Relying mainly (but not solely) on e-mail, I asked each individual to share his or her insights and experiences as a librarian blogger and also to tell us something about the person behind the blog. I hope you will find this behind-the-scenes look as interesting and inspiring as I did.

Christie Brandau

Travels with the State Librarian
ksstatelibrarian.blogspot.com

Tell us a little about yourself, Christie.

I am a native Iowan, born on a farm to Swedish immigrants. I attended Wartburg College in Waverly before transferring to Iowa State University, where I received a BA in political science. I received an MLS from the University of Iowa in 1988.

I worked in public, special, and system libraries before accepting the position of Assistant State Librarian of Iowa in 1991. I went on to become State Librarian of Michigan in 2000 and State Librarian of Kansas in 2005.

I am married to John Brandau, and we have three children and five grandchildren.

Why do you blog?

To share information and opinions.

53

What got you started blogging?

I was visiting some great libraries on my trips around the state and wanted to share a little about them with other librarians. Plus, I love to try new things and had not done a blog before.

How would you describe your blog? (personal, professional, mix, etc.)

Professional, because I focus on libraries and library-related activities.

What do you see as blogging's greatest strength?

It's a quick, informal, and fairly non-technical way to share information. I don't have to know HTML or wait for someone's permission to post to the blog.

What do you see as the greatest problem with blogs?

People don't know how to access them, or how to use an aggregator for reading their favorites.

Why should someone start a blog and what advice would you give him or her?

People are surprised when I tell them that they can create a blog in five minutes by themselves! It is the content that takes time to create, and I spend much more time on that than launching the blog.

What are your top five favorite blogs to read?

- The Shifted Librarian, theshiftedlibrarian.com
- Free Range Librarian, freerangelibrarian.com
- LutheranChik's "L" Word Diary, lutheranchiklworddiary.blogspot.com
- Daily Kos, dailykos.com
- Library Crunch, librarycrunch.com

Steven M. Cohen
Library Stuff
www.librarystuff.net

Tell us a little about yourself, Steven.

I am Senior Librarian at Law Library Management, Inc., in New York. I also contribute content to Resourceshelf.com [and] am the co-manager for the PLA Blog (www.plablog.org), and, of course, Library Stuff is still my baby.

Why do you blog?

I usually tell people that I blog because it keeps me off the streets. It has come so engrained in my life that I don't see it as work anymore (although I am one of the only librarians who gets paid to blog). I don't feel like my day is complete unless I have posted to my Weblog.

What got you started blogging?

Library Stuff was launched in August 2000, but I was posting to LISNews in 1999 (I still do, but very rarely).

How would you describe your blog?

Library Stuff is 97 percent professional and 3 percent personal. Every so often, I will post personal information. Ironically, it's the personal posts that elicit more commentary.

What do you see as blogging's greatest strength?

For the blogger, it's a way of expressing one's thoughts and emotions in a public forum so feedback is theoretically instantaneous. It also allows anyone to publish to the Web without having to know any coding languages.

For the reader, it's the ability to read about anything from anybody and not having to rely on MSN for commentary and news. Blogs allow for that even playing field.

What do you see as the greatest problem with blogs?

The power wielded by blogs sometimes gets to people's heads. There is a very big ego problem in the blogging world.

Why should someone start a blog and what advice would you give him or her?

Professionally, librarians should start a blog to get their ideas out there for consumption and commentary. Networking is very important in our profession and I've had the fortunate opportunity to travel and speak to thousands of colleagues because of my blog.

What are your top five favorite blogs to read?

- The Kinky Librarian, kinkylibrarian.blogspot.com
- Blog of the Bookslut, www.bookslut.com/blog
- Catalogablog, catalogablog.blogspot.com
- Search Engine Watch Blog, blog.searchenginewatch.com/blog
- Conversational Reading, esposito.typepad.com/con_read

Karen Coombs

Library Web Chic
www.librarywebchic.net

Tell us a little about yourself, Karen.

I have an MLS and an MS in information management from Syracuse University. I serve as the head of Web services at the University of Houston Libraries. My duties there include development and maintenance of the libraries' Web site and electronic presence.

Prior to working for the University of Houston Libraries, I worked as the electronic services librarian at SUNY Cortland. My duties there included development of the library Web site, design and maintenance of the library's Web catalog, development and maintenance of the library's Web-based systems, maintenance of electronic resources, and a host of other duties as assigned. I have had articles published in *Computers in Libraries, Journal of Academic Librarianship,* and *Library Hi Tech.*

Why do you blog?

I blog because it gives me a chance to express my opinions and share what I am working on with others. It is nice to get a wider range of feedback about my work than just the people who are in my library. In addition, blogging is a way for me to keep up with what is going on in the library world and to sharpen my writing skills. I have had blog posts turn into articles. Blogging helps me to capture "idea seedlings" down in an informal format. I can then use these seedlings as the basis for writing formal articles.

What got you started blogging?

In the spring of 2003 I met Steven Cohen and Jenny Levine at Computers in Libraries and they were really promoting blogging. I really liked the idea and thought a lot about putting a blog together and what it would be called. A year later I saw them again and Steven kind of gave me the "whatever happened to that blog you said you were going to have" speech. So, less than a month later I started writing Library Web Chic. I wasn't sure if it would be successful so I only registered the domain name for a year. Well, nearly two years and more than 400 posts later I can't imagine not having a blog as part of my life.

How would you describe your blog?

My blog is mostly professional. As the About page says, the site is meant to be a resource for librarians who are interested in the application of Web design and technologies in libraries. Additionally, I wanted it to be about my experiences working as a female librarian doing technology stuff. Occasionally I will talk about my personal life if it in some way relates to the work I am doing or if my work and personal life become intertwined like they often do when I go to conferences.

What do you see as blogging's greatest strength?

The greatest strength of blogging is the fact that you don't have to wait months to go through a peer-review process to share what you are doing and get feedback on your work. People read your blog and they comment on both the content and occasionally the writing. You find out much more quickly who is doing similar things and get to network and collaborate. Additionally, with technology changing so quickly, blogging is the best way to disseminate "new" information.

What do you see as the greatest problem with blogs?

The greatest problem with blogs is that people have such different perceptions of them. Some people take them very seriously and expect them to be very much like traditional publications. Other people don't take them seriously at all. To add to this problem, not all blogs or bloggers are the same. Therefore, the quality and tone of the information you receive from blogs is going to vary greatly. This variation in tone and quality and the opinion aspect to blogs often gets them criticized. I don't believe that these are fatal flaws for Weblogs. The solution to these problems is for people who want to use blogs as information sources to critically evaluate the information they obtain from them like any other source.

Why should someone start a blog and what advice would you give him or her?

There are a multitude of reasons why someone should start a blog. First, a blog is a great way to keep track of professional development. You can track what projects you have worked on over the year, new skills acquired, papers written, conferences attended, etc. Second, a blog is a great way to plant "idea seedlings." You can write a short post or posts about a project you are working on or an idea you have, and later use that material for an article. Third, if the traditional publication and peer-review process frightens you, a Weblog is a great way for you to develop your voice as a writer before you have to send something off to be peer-reviewed. The biggest advice I would have for someone starting a blog is just try it for a month. You don't need a domain name. Just get a free account and commit to posting for a month. I would strongly suggest that you blog about the things that interest and have meaning to you. Don't worry if anyone will read it. You may gain an audience without knowing it.

What are your top five favorite blogs to read?

These are in no particular order of preference:

- Blyberg.net, www.blyberg.net – John Blyberg's exceptionally thoughtful blog that talks about the intersection of technology and libraries in a public library setting.

- Tame the Web, www.tametheweb.com – Michael Stephens's blog takes a look at libraries and technology from the public library perspective.
- The Distant Librarian, distlib.blogs.com/distlib – Paul Pival's blog talks about tools for reaching library users at a distance. Great information on screencasting and Web-based tutorials.
- TechCrunch, www.techcrunch.com – The blog to read if you want to keep up with the latest developments in Web 2.0 and social software. Great software reviews and sneak peaks, including screenshots.
- A List Apart, www.alistapart.com – A great site that discusses topics of Web design: CSS, Web accessibility, usability, and designing with Web standards.

Walt Crawford

Walt at Random
walt.lishost.org

Tell us a little about yourself, Walt.

I have been involved in aspects of technology in libraries over five decades, as a programmer, analyst, designer, writer, and speaker. [I have also been] active in LITA (one-time president). "Day job" activity has ranged from early MARC-based projects through user interface design to report generation and statistical analysis. Writing and speaking began with a focus on library automation, expanded to aspects of technologies and media in libraries, and has broadened further to the intersections of technology, policy, media, and libraries.

Why do you blog?

Because there are some things I feel like writing about that don't fit neatly into other outlets or benefit from the immediacy and casualness of blogging.

What got you started blogging?

A combination of peer pressure and annoyance at some "anti-blogging" comments.

How would you describe your blog?

Mix of personal and professional, perhaps more the former than the latter.

What do you see as blogging's greatest strength?

Transparency: Ease of use, immediacy, and lack of rules allow the writer's motives and thoughts to show through with little filtering.

What do you see as the greatest problem with blogs?

Urgency: The sensed need to keep blogging even when there's nothing to say, and to spend time on blogging that might better be spent on other things.

Why should someone start a blog and what advice would you give him or her?

Start a blog because you want to and you feel you have something to say that works well within this casual, reverse chronological medium. No other motive is really needed. Don't feel bad about pausing from time to time or stopping completely: Real life should always trump blogging.

What are your top five favorite blogs to read?

I don't have a top five; my preferences shift too often.

Lorcan Dempsey (vice president of programs and research & chief strategist, OCLC)

Lorcan Dempsey's Weblog
orweblog.oclc.org

Tell us a little about yourself, Lorcan.

I am a librarian who moved into R&D [Research and Development]. I'm currently the VP of research for OCLC. I oversee the work of OCLC Research and participate in OCLC's Strategic Leadership Team and was named OCLC Chief Strategist in March 2004. I am very excited by the recent combination of RLG and OCLC; one of my roles will involve bringing together OCLC Research activities and the new RLG-Programs unit within OCLC.

I joined OCLC in the summer of 2001. Before this I worked in the U.K. as, at times, director of the U.K. Office for Library and Information Networking (UKOLN), founding co-director of the Resource Discovery Network (RDN), and director of the Joint Information Systems Committee's Distributed National Electronic Resource (JISC/DNER).

Why do you blog?

The blog began as an internal activity, as a way of communicating with colleagues. After a while we decided to externalize it as much of the material on it was general.

How would you describe your blog?

My blog is largely professional with the occasional personal tinge. I like the way in which you can note something that interested you alongside some editorial, as well as be more reflective about particular issues.

What do you see as blogging's greatest strength?

My favorite blogs are those with a "voice," where you become interested in a particular person's perspective on things, whether or not you agree with it. I suppose I prefer "thinkers" over "linkers." The benefit is that you can follow developments from several perspectives.

What do you see as the greatest problem with blogs?

There are two. We are still in early days when it comes to RSS readers. It does become tedious and time-consuming to read a lot of feeds. (Self-aggrandRSSment is the tendency by some to talk about all the feeds they subscribe to ;-) The second is redundancy among the linkers: The same stuff crops up in various places.

What are your top five favorite blogs to read?

I find that interest comes in waves. I will tend to track a particular blog for a while and then move on to another one. Here are a couple that I check out at the moment:

- Catalogablog, catalogablog.blogspot.com—Good for tracking stuff relevant to work.
- Rough Type: Nicholas Carr's blog, www.roughtype.com— Somebody to make you think, even when you don't agree.

Sarah Houghton
Librarian in Black
librarianinblack.net

Tell us a little about yourself, Sarah.

I am the Information and Web Services Manager for San Mateo County Library. I also work as a consultant for the Infopeople Project, am on the LITA Top Technology Trends Committee and the California Library Association's Assembly, and am President of the California Library Association's Information Technology Section. I chose the "Librarian in Black" moniker because I am 100 percent goth on the inside, and usually on the outside. I live in San Rafael, California with my partner (also a librarian) and our cat, Torin.

Why do you blog?

I blog because I like to share information—that's what made me become a librarian in the first place. I got sick of wading through oodles of information—newspaper articles, blog posts, Web sites, etc.—just to find those few gems of info that pertained to me. I decided to try to save others some work and post what I found, adding my (sometimes useful) commentary to go with it.

What got you started blogging?

I really started blogging because I saw other people doing it in the LIS world, and it looked like something I could handle technologically. I have two unused advanced degrees in English, so I figured I had the writing part of the process in hand as well.

How would you describe your blog?

I would describe my blog as largely professional (for techie librarians) with some personal-interest stuff thrown in there for good measure every once in a while.

What do you see as blogging's greatest strength?

Blogging's greatest strength is the ease with which folks with something important to say or share with others—but not necessarily with the technical skills required to Webify their words, sounds, or images—can publish online and share their thoughts with potentially millions of people.

What do you see as the greatest problem with blogs?

The biggest problem with blogs is their undeserved bad reputation. A lot of early blogs were of the "I ate a grilled cheese sandwich for lunch" variety. As a result, many people began to associate the word "blog" with "uninteresting personal journal." There are so many quality information blogs out there, but I think people's initial prejudices have prevented them from taking this form of publishing seriously.

Why should someone start a blog and what advice would you give him or her?

Someone should start a blog if (s)he feels (s)he has something to say. If you don't have something to say, don't start a blog. Please. I'm begging you. I've seen too many blogs start off well, and then linger on and on in an anorexic state for months. If you do have something to say, keep at blogging for six months with daily entries, and see if it's still something you want to do. But you do have to make time in your schedule to blog—otherwise you just won't do it. You'll sit in front of the television and watch *Greg the Bunny* episodes instead. I would.

What are your top five favorite blogs to read?

My top five blogs to read (all LIS related; I'm boring):

- Librarian.net, www.librarian.net
- ResourceShelf, www.resourceshelf.com
- Tame the Web, www.tametheweb.com
- The Shifted Librarian, www.theshiftedlibrarian.com
- Walking Paper, walkingpaper.org

Jenny Levine
The Shifted Librarian
www.theshiftedlibrarian.com

From *LibraryJournal.com:*

"My name is Jenny, and I'll be your information maven today." That's the first thing you see on Jenny Levine's well-known Weblog, "The Shifted Librarian." How well-known? Until recently, if you went to Google and typed "Jenny," her site was the top search result.

Levine has come a long way since 1992, when, after getting her MLS, she had to have a friend type her resume in

WordPerfect because she didn't know how to use the word processor.

She became a convert to the Net in that same year, when a patron in her public library asked for a recipe for Irish soda bread; Levine couldn't find it in her library's collection, but she found one on CompuServe. She went on to teach the whole staff to use e-mail, gophers, telnet, and CompuServe.

When the World Wide Web came along, Levine was one of the first librarians out there, finding the good stuff and sharing it with her colleagues in training sessions. In 1995, she created the Librarians' Site du Jour Web site, where she reviewed a reference Web site in detail every day, to convince librarians that the Web was extraordinarily useful for everyday reference and to give them a reason to make visiting the Web a daily habit.

When she became technology coordinator at Grande Prairie Public Library District, in 1996, she created and maintained its Web site. Thanks to her leadership, Grande Prairie became the first public library in Chicago's south suburbs to offer public Internet access.

In her current job, providing "vision and leadership regarding emerging technologies ... and their integration into library environments" is actually the first item in her job description. Among her many accomplishments, Levine has launched quarterly "technology summits" to keep library system members up-to-date, created user documentation packages and manuals, organized and led a user group on Web authoring, and initiated and carried out a grant project to teach Web authors about accessibility issues.

But she didn't create her blog for the glory. Levine has one simple goal: to help us librarians become as technologically adept as our users are so that we can deliver services to them when and where they wish to use them and in their preferred medium and platform. On her blog, Levine regularly posts information about "cool tools," along with comments about how librarians could use them in their daily tasks. Her blog also links to her Power Point presentation explaining the "shifted librarian" concept. [Excerpted from LibraryJournal.com, March 15, 2003; see www.libraryjournal.com/index.asp?layout=article&display=LJMS&articleid=CA281672&pubdate=3%2F15%2F2003&publication=libraryjournal]

Jenny, how would you describe your blog?

That's a tough question, because TSL is very much a personal blog, but the main thrust of it is professional. I don't think it's black and white enough to say one or the other; can a librarian blogger be anything other than a mix?

What do you see as blogging's greatest strength?

Efficiency and voice. There's just no other way to get your information/thoughts/whatever out into the ether faster or easier. I encourage libraries to blog in "the key of we," which means using that efficiency to create an authentic voice for what has traditionally been a faceless, inhuman institution. Instead of always saying, "The library did this ..." or "The library will do that ...," *we* need to start putting a human face out there. We're bad enough at "telling our story" and translating the fun and interesting life within a library, but our Web sites are even worse. They're staid, often unattractive, and aesthetically neutered. Blogs can help change that, especially by letting a more informal voice come through, as well as the opportunity for actual conversation.

What do you see as the greatest problem with blogs?

Coming at this from an institutional point of view, the biggest problems are fear and resources. I've heard story after story about administrations that are too scared of implementing blogs because someone *might* say the wrong thing sometime someday. They have no trust or faith in their employees, and they're too short-sighted to risk that chance against the incredible payoff (of conversation, inbound links, and efficiency) that blogs can provide.

Conversely, there are organizations that are able to move past the fear, but they don't have enough resources to maintain a blog. Staff are already wearing five different hats, and after the initial adrenaline rush, the blog decays because no one has the time to post anything. We have to treat our blogs like we do our newsletters and devote specific resources to them (in this case, staff time).

Why should someone start a blog and what advice would you give him or her?

I think that individually, you already have an inkling if you should start a personal blog, so I tend to focus on how blogs can help libraries. In that vein, your library should start a blog if you have a "What's New" page on your Web site. It's the ideal candidate: It will make your work life much easier, and you'll get the automatic RSS feed. Advice for libraries:

- Find the people who pass around all of the links or are always saying, "Did you see that article about ...?"
- Post at least once a week; keep your posts short and sweet.
- Treat the commitment the same way you do your newsletter.
- Send your PR (blog URL, VR services, etc.) to local bloggers.
- Make sure your whole staff knows about the blog and encourage them to read it.
- "Tell your story"—don't be afraid to highlight your services and write in "the key of we."
- Show the fun side of your library.
- Informality is the key to "voice"—HUMANIZE your library!

What are your top five favorite blogs to read?

More than five, but the LIS ones are pretty obvious:

- Boing Boing, boingboing.net
- MetaFilter, www.metafilter.com
- LISNews, www.lisnews.com
- Engadget, www.engadget.com
- Weblog-ed News, www.weblog-ed.com
- Library Stuff, www.librarystuff.net
- Tame the Web, www.tametheweb.com
- Walking Paper, www.walkingpaper.org

Andrea Mercado

Library Techtonics
www.librarytechtonics.info

Tell us a little about yourself, Andrea.

Currently, I work as the Reference and Techie Librarian (that is, indeed, my real title) at Reading Public Library in Reading, MA, as well as managing the PLA Blog: The official blog of the Public

Library Association (www.plablog.org). I received a Bachelor's degree in English from Wesleyan University in 1996, and a Master of Science from the Simmons College Graduate School of Library and Information Science in May 2004. My past life is in technology, working as a Web developer, technical writer and editor, project manager, and technical support specialist. I've always been an information junkie, and after a stint as a research intern at the American Museum of Natural History, I was hooked on the idea of working with information, technology, and people, so library science is definitely the right direction for me.

Why do you blog?

To share my thoughts on librarians and librarianship, to practice communication through writing, and to self-publish conveniently and immediately.

What got you started blogging?

I began blogging at the urging of other librarian colleagues who blog. At first I didn't really know how I could differentiate myself from the many other blogging librarians online, or how I could possibly keep up with consummate bloggers who are on the bleeding edge of information and articles online. But there seemed to be enough people interested in my thoughts and ideas in everyday conversations that a blog seemed like a good way to share my thoughts and promote myself at the same time, especially while I was looking for a job that first year after library school.

How would you describe your blog?

I post bits about articles, other blog posts, TV shows, conversations (with permission, as necessary), conference presentations, random references, and projects related to libraries, librarians, and librarianship, so it's mostly professional. Even when I discuss what might be considered more personal subjects, like job hunting or what I'm reading, I try my best to ensure that it relates it back to librarianship.

What do you see as blogging's greatest strength?

Anyone can set up a blog, so there's inherently a huge variety of perspectives. Blogs are as easy to set up as signing up for an account on Blogspot or as complex as highly customized templates with a package like Movable Type, and the diversity of authors and perspectives is enormous.

What do you see as the greatest problem with blogs?

Anyone can set up a blog. The Internet is a very anonymous-friendly place. Add them together and the resulting environment is one where the issue of authoritativeness becomes fuzzy. Whether it's because a blog author has good information from good sources, but doesn't cite them properly or at all, or the author doesn't provide information linked to their blog as to who the author is and what makes them an authority on any subject, or a hack masquerades as someone he's not, it's hard to tell what's good stuff on the Internet. Internet users are increasingly interested in the quick answer, even if it's not exactly correct, so "bad" blogs, not-so-substantiated blogs, have the potential to undermine the notion of authoritative information on the Internet.

Why should someone start a blog and what advice would you give him or her?

The real success of a blog depends on three things: timeliness, authoritativeness, and personality. If you're willing to update your blog regularly (daily, weekly, monthly, whatever), use good sources and cite those sources, and find a good niche for yourself as a writer, by all means, start a blog. Learn from other blogs—good and bad, high and low readership, those you agree with and those you don't. Find mentors to help you out. And if at some point you can't keep up with it anymore or it's not your bag, know to gracefully close up shop.

What are your top five favorite blogs to read?

- Boing Boing, www.boingboing.net
- Not Too Late to Change the Name, www.englishmajor.com/babble.html
- Librarian.net, www.librarian.net
- Popgadget: Gadgets, Culture, General Neophilia, www.popgadget.net – For and by women.
- Lifehacker, www.lifehacker.com

Aaron Schmidt

Walking Paper

www.walkingpaper.org

Tell us a little about yourself, Aaron.

I'm the reference librarian at a medium-sized public library in Illinois. I'm in charge of reference [and] technology, and assist with about a million other things.

Why do you blog?

Two main reasons. First, and most importantly, I love libraries and want to share my thoughts with people. I think I have some contributions to make, and publishing to the Web through a blog is an easy and effective way to do it. It has been gratifying to hear of libraries directly benefiting from things I've discussed on my blog.

Second, and less importantly, blogging is a good career move. Not only have I been able to further develop my thoughts on LIS issues (which always helps on the job) but I've been recognized for my blogging, which is very cool. Without my blog, fewer people would know who I am, and I wouldn't have received as many invitations to present ideas at conferences.

What got you started blogging?

I was maintaining a number of personal blogs (seems like ages ago) that Jenny Levine read. I occasionally posted about libraries, and she liked it. So she bugged me for about six months, then I gave in.

How would you describe your blog?

Many blogs cycle links and make some commentary on them. While I do a bit of that, I try to place an emphasis on original content. This means that my posts are less frequent and a bit longer than others in the library blogosphere. I write when something strikes my interest (and I have time).

What do you see as blogging's greatest strength?

Speed! Think of how behind we'd all be if we only read print publications!

What do you see as the greatest problem with blogs?

There aren't too many inherent problems with the blogging format. There are problems with certain blogs because they aren't interesting or good, but I don't know if I see any problems with blogs in general. We could discuss the effects of blogs on journalism, authority of Web sites, and so forth, but this probably isn't the place. The library blogosphere can be a bit incestuous at times, which can be annoying, but that also might be another story.

Why should someone start a blog and what advice would you give him or her?

When talking about starting with blogs, I use Walt Crawford's line, "First have something to say." People should start blogs if they're interested in the technology and want to see what it is like firsthand, but they should probably have some topics, and original perspectives on these topics, if they want to have fun with a blog.

What are your top five favorite blogs to read?

Looking at my feeds in Bloglines (just reduced to 88 feeds), I would like to mention two that I really like. As if these aren't standard enough, the rest seem either very standard or way too specialized.

- Metafilter, www.metafilter.com
- Kevin Kelly's Cool Tools, www.kk.org/cooltools

Michael Stephens

Tame the Web
www.tametheweb.com

About Michael from his page:

Holding an MLS from Indiana University, Michael Stephens has spent the last fifteen years working in public libraries as a reference librarian, technology trainer, and manager of networked resources and training at the St. Joseph County Public Library, South Bend, Indiana. His most recent position in the public library setting was as Special Projects Librarian, focusing on technology, policy, and planning. Beginning in the fall of 2006, Michael will be joining the Graduate School of Library and Information Science at Dominican University, River Forest, Illinois, as an Instructor.

In 2004, he was awarded an Institute of Museum and Library Services-funded fellowship for the University of North Texas IMLS Distance Independent Information Science PhD Cohort Program to study libraries, librarians, and social software. He is currently writing his dissertation.

Active in the American Library Association, he has presented at library conferences locally, nationally, and internationally as well as at leading workshops for libraries and library associations across the country. The Social Technologies Roadshow, a workshop he teaches with Jenny Levine (Internet Development Specialist and Strategy Guide at the ALA), is making stops in Illinois, the Netherlands, and London before the end of the year.

In 2001, Stephens published The Library Internet Trainer's Toolkit, a series of technology training modules on CD-ROM, with Neal-Schuman Inc. in North America and in 2002 in the U.K. with the British Library Association. In 2005, he was named a *Library Journal* "Mover and Shaker," and he served as a Scholar at the Chicago Public Library's Scholar in Residence program. He has written for Public Libraries, Library Journal, the OCLC Newsletter NextSpace, and SirsiDynix's UpStream, co-authors a department in *Computers in Libraries* with Rachel Singer Gordon, and currently writes for the ALA TechSource Blog (www.techsource. ala.org/blog) as well as his own blog, Tame the Web (www.tametheweb.com). His library technology report Web 2.0 & Libraries: Best Practices for Social Software was published by ALA in July.

He resides in Mishawaka, Indiana and Oak Park, Illinois and spends as much of the summer as possible in Traverse City, Michigan.

Why do you blog, Michael?

I blog because I was inspired by all of the blog discussions at Computers in Libraries 2003—I wanted to share some of the things I was working on and the "tips and tricks" that seemed to work at SJCPL for technology training and Web development. I blog first for myself, to remember a link, a thought, or an event. I blog a "Top Ten" for folks who might be reading as well and maybe something there will inspire them to do some training, add a blog to their library site, check out RSS, or propose a session at a conference.

If posts like these—www.tametheweb.com/2004/05/10_things_a_library_can_do_to.html or www.tametheweb.com/2004/05/ten_tips_for_technology_traine.html—help one or two librarians, I've succeeded!

How would you describe your blog?

Tame the Web is for librarians and other interested folk. It is a "professional" blog because I have others on my site for the personal: Traverse City, iPod, and Dreaming On. I have found that since I started school, I mainly focus my blogging energies on TTW because it is my favorite.

What do you see as blogging's greatest strength?

Blogging allows someone to participate in a community. It gives them a voice amid many other voices. It allows someone to speak his or her mind, share something, or just journal. My favorite blogs are those that not only give me great info and resources but I get a good idea of *who* the person is on the other side of cyberspace.

What do you see as the greatest problem with blogs?

Libraries and librarians have to be very careful: If you start a blog, make the commitment. If it doesn't work out, post that and leave it as an archive or take it down. Nothing pains me more than a library-related blog that hasn't seen a post in months … still up and inactive.

Why should someone start a blog and what advice would you give him or her?

Start a blog because you have something to say. Make the commitment!

Ten Things a Blogging Librarian Must Do (an exercise in common sense):

1. Cite your sources.

2. Post often but have something to say. However, make the commitment to follow through.

3. Post about what you're passionate about and don't be afraid to say what you think!

4. And share yourself.

5. Never miss an opportunity to show your administration how well an external library blog is working.

6. If you are doing a personal blog, don't do it on your library's dime.

7. Blog unto others as you'd have them blog unto you.

8. Read other blogs for inspiration and AHHA moments. Chime in. CITE!

9. Learn all there is to know about your blog app and make use of its features.

10. Have FUN!

(Excerpted from www.tametheWeb.com/ttwblog/archives/000255.html)

Ten Guidelines for Developing Your Internal Blog

1. Involve appropriate staff.

2. Utilize software that's free and easy.

3. Test for usability and staff buy in.

4. Technical enhancements count.

5. Utilize categories and archives effectively.

6. Breadcrumb your navigation.

7. PDFs and Word documents rule.

8. Collaborate!

9. Train staff.

10. Promote and celebrate.

(Excerpted from www.tametheweb.com/2004/10/ten_guidelines_for_developing.html)

For more on internal blogging, see Stephens's article, Tech Tips for Every Librarian: How and Why to Try a Blog for Staff Communication, *Computers in Libraries*, February 2006.

What are your top five favorite blogs to read?

It's hard to choose just 5 biblioblogs! I am very pleased with the number of librarians who have started blogging in the last couple of years. More voices with more viewpoints and experience to draw from make this pool of knowledge and conversation so rich and diverse. I tell my workshops: Find 5 or so voices that really speak to you and your heart and follow those and the links they provide. Find 5 or so library blogs as well, especially if you are a library Weblog author, and follow the conversations and look for the voice. It'll inspire you.

Jessamyn West

librarian.net
www.librarian.net

Tell us a little about yourself, Jessamyn.

I'm currently working with librarians in central Vermont to help them with their technology problems. I also teach e-mail and other computer skills to older people. I was an ALA Councilor from 2003–2006. I got my library degree back when it was called an MLib and have gone back and forth between working in the tech industry doing support and maintenance, to working in the library world doing reference and outreach. I maintain a Weblog called librarian.net, which was arguably one of the first library Weblogs on the scene. My dream is to be a live-in librarian in some bucolic rural setting.

Why do you blog?

Because I don't talk to many librarians in my day-to-day interactions and I come across a lot of information that I think they would like. I also think that people don't really understand what librarians do—though they do more now than when I started in 1999—and my blog helps outline some of the issues that I think are relevant to the library world today. I have a personal blog as well and that's mostly just a way to touch base with people I don't see too often and as a little online notepad for tracking what I'm up to on a regular basis. Both blogs keep me writing, which is useful.

What got you started blogging?

I found the domain was free and I snagged it and then thought, "Hmm, what can I do with this?" At the time I was getting disenchanted with ALA because they were having Colin Powell speaking at their conference, which I thought was borderline inappropriate. I was reading about it online, as well as a lot of other librarian news and I thought, "Hey, I could make a blog out of this!" It was a chance for me to experiment with the form in a non-personal setting and learn about coding. Over time, I've learned RSS, CSS, XML, and a bunch of other acronyms just by keeping it updated and current.

How would you describe your blog?

Librarian.net reflects my professional interests and my personal opinions, though I try to keep it from being too polemical, more reflective. My personal blog is a lot more staid, either you're interested in what I've been up to or you're not. If you're not, you probably wouldn't want to read it.

What do you see as blogging's greatest strength?

Giving people a way to interact with what we commonly think of as "the news" in a more personal fashion, both as creators and as readers. Giving people a chance to interact with a community that they may not be physically close to. Creating serendipitous connections between interesting things.

What do you see as the greatest problem with blogs?

The same problem as you see with other online interactions: People can hide behind personas and as a result can be less civil to each other than they would have to be if they had to interact with people in real life. Plus, not everyone has something to say, so there are a lot of people who heard that blogs were interesting and got one, but then didn't know what to do with it. I had content first and a blog second, which I felt was the way to go. On the other hand, blogs are so ubiquitous now that it's pretty easy to connect with the ones you feel strongly about and ignore the ones you don't.

Why should someone start a blog and what advice would you give him or her?

I feel like people know if they should start one; there's nothing inherently built into the online world that means everyone needs to blog. I'm wary of all the blog boosterism that in some ways seems to be supplanting people's knowledge of the technology behind the tools. My advice is the same as it is for people getting into tech in general: learn the tools; learn to troubleshoot; you are responsible for what you do and say, so act appropriately; think about your audience; and of course, first have something to say (thanks to Walt Crawford for that line; I use it often). Some people will always love what you do, some people will probably always hate it. With a blog, you're making a decision to have an online persona; whether it jibes with your actual self is up to you, but it's as hard to take back something you do or say online, as it is in person, sometimes harder.

What are your top five favorite blogs to read?

This week it's ...

- Metafilter (particularly ask.metafilter.com), www.metafilter.com
- RandomWalks, www.randomwalks.com
- Boing Boing, www.boingboing.net
- Library Autonomous Zone, gort.ucsd.edu/mtdocs/laz
- Copyfight, www.corante.com/copyfight

These change all the time, though. I also have favorite skimmers including Gary Price's ResourceShelf and LISNews.com.

Chapter 4

Creating a Blog

If you want to create a blog for your library, I suggest first creating one for yourself. You don't have to keep it up, or even tell anyone about it, but you can use it to experiment, to learn (and play) without your mistakes or missteps having any permanence or public repercussion.

Why Blog?

Almost everyone seems to have something to say, yet many people either don't know how to express themselves or lack an appropriate forum. A blog offers an informal means for expressing your ideas in public without the pressures typically associated with public speaking.

Blogs help you stay on top of events. This is a reason not only to read other people's blogs, but also to create your own. In order to post to your own blog regularly, you'll have to stay current on your subject.

Unfortunately, most libraries are not promoted effectively to their respective communities. A blog offering new and interesting information on a regular basis is a great way to promote your library and encourage repeat visits to its Web site.

Blogs are cheap, fast, and easy. In this chapter, you will learn how to set up a blog in less than five minutes without any budget impact other than a minimal staff investment. Posting to a blog takes no more technical know-how other than typing.

Once you've decided that a blog is the right medium for getting your ideas across, you'll want to keep the following guidelines in mind:

- *Have something to say.* In Chapter 3, you'll find profiles of some LIS bloggers. When asked what advice they would give to a novice blogger, the most common response was, "Have something to say." Sarah Houghton (Librarian in Black) may have said it best: "If you don't have something to say, don't start a blog. Please. I'm begging you."

- *Have something to say **regularly***. A blogger has an idea brilliant enough to think everyone should know about it. He posts it on his blog and then disappears. This happens all the time, and it doesn't encourage readers to return. If you don't post on a regular basis, no one will read your blog. Blogs need to be updated often and regularly.

- *Have something to say **responsibly***. Blogging has raised issues of free speech when it comes to the relationship between bloggers and employers. There are documented cases of individuals being fired for the content of their blogs. If you're going to blog, especially about work-related activities, talk to your immediate supervisor or even your library director first. Make sure they're aware of what you're planning to do and why. You may not need supervisory approval for an individual blog, but it can't hurt to check first.[1]

Michael Stephens offers two excellent posts on his blog "Tame the Web: Libraries and Technology" on issues relevant to library bloggers. The first, "Ten Things a Blogging Librarian Must Do (an exercise in common sense)" (www.tametheweb.com/ttwblog/archives/000255.html), focuses on librarians interested in creating individual blogs. The second, "Ten Guidelines for Developing Your Internal Blog" (www.tametheweb.com/ttwblog/archives/000422.html), should be read if you're considering creating a blog to represent your library.

Methods for Creating Your Blog

There are several methods for creating your blog. You can use a Web-based service, server software, or client software. Each has its unique advantages and disadvantages.

Web-based services have the advantage of being accessible from any Internet-connected computer. Because I travel a lot and may use as many as three different computers in a single day, the flexibility of using the same service from any location makes Web-based service my choice. The most popular Web service, Blogger.com, is free to use and offers free hosting space on its server. (You may, however, choose to store your blog on any server to which you have access.) A disadvantage is that Web-based services typically lack some of the advanced features that are available with server-based packages or client software.

Server-based packages are software programs you can download and install on your Web server. Since the software resides on a server, this blogging method is similar to a Web service in that it is accessible from any Internet-connected computer. MoveableType (www.movabletype.org), TypePad (www.sixapart.com/typepad), and WordPress (wordpress.org) are some of the more popular programs. These programs offer a number of additional features—such as displaying an interactive calendar-based view of posts—not available in free Web-based services. Significant disadvantages are that the software is typically not free and requires a certain level of technical expertise to be installed on a server. Bloggers on a budget or those who lack technical expertise tend not to invest in this method of blog creation—at least not for personal or small library blogs.

Client software is similarly downloaded and installed, but on a client computer rather than a Web server. As with the server option, client software has the advantage of additional features not found in Web-based services. Although the technical know-how needed to install this kind of software is not as great as for server software, using client software remains more complex than the Web-based service option. Additionally, this software is generally not free and you're immediately locked into posting to your blog from a single computer (the one on which you installed the software). Radio's UserLand software (radio.userland.com) is a leading example of this type of blogging software.

Because the main purpose of this book is to help you master the basics of blogging and RSS without considerable expenditure or technical knowledge, we'll focus on Blogger.com for the rest of this chapter. Even if you switch later to a different service or to a software product, this coverage of Blogger.com will provide you with a useful grasp of the basics.

Blogger.com, or simply "Blogger," includes excellent help files for bloggers who want to use the service. Due to potential changes in the service, its help files will be more up-to-date than the instructions supplied here.

Creating Your First Blog

Creating a Blogger Account

To get started, open your Web browser and go to the Blogger Web site (www.blogger.com). On the right side of the page is a big orange arrow labeled "Create Your Blog Now." Click on that arrow to create your Blogger account (Figure 4.1). You will not need to repeat this step in the event that you decide to create additional blogs.

The following steps are required to create your account:

- *Choose a username.* Enter the username you want to use for your account. You may need to choose an alternate if your choice is unavailable.

- *Enter a password.* Choose a password for your account. Passwords must be at least six characters long.

- *Retype password.* Type the password again. This is to confirm that you typed the desired password correctly the first time.

- *Display name.* Choose the name you want displayed to your readers. Typically, individuals use their real names but it's up to you. Some use a nickname; others use pseudonyms to obscure their identities.

- *E-mail address.* Enter your e-mail address. This is to allow Blogger to contact you with updated system information. In the 3+ years I've been using Blogger, I can remember receiving only a few e-mails from the service. So unless there is a drastic change, there's no need to worry about your inbox being flooded with spam.

- *Acceptance of Terms.* Check this box to accept Blogger's terms of service. (You can read the terms by clicking on the "Terms of Service" link to the left.) If you do not accept, your account will not be created.

Once you've answered all six questions, click on the "Continue" arrow.

After you've created your account, you will begin the setup process for your blog. Here you have to answer a variety of questions depending on where your blog's files will be stored. The "Basic" option will host your blog on blogspot.com, Blogger's free hosting server. Use "Advanced Setup" if you want to host your

Figure 4.1   Creating a Blogger account

blog's files on your own server. (This is not something I recommend for your first blog. Wait until you're comfortable with Blogger before you try getting it to work with your own server. You can always move your files later.)

Basic Setup

If you select the Basic setup (Figure 4.2), you'll need to provide the following information:

- *Blog title*. You may name your blog whatever you want. My blog is named "TravelinLibrarian.info" since that's also the name of my domain. Give your blog a name that indicates who you are, where the blog is located, and/or the blog's purpose. If this is a blog for your library, the library's name is an appropriate choice.

- *Blog address (URL)*. Since you'll be hosting your blog on Blogger's server, you don't get to build the complete URL, but you do get to pick the first part. In the example shown in Figure 4.2, I've named my blog "Blogging and RSS: A Librarian's Guide" and chose http://bloggingrssalibrarians guide.blogspot.com as the URL. This URL field cannot contain special characters, punctuation, or spaces. If you pick a URL that's already in use, you'll be asked to pick another.

Figure 4.2   Blogger's basic setup

- *Word verification.* Here you'll need to type in a series of letters that appears above the field ("rpiae" in Figure 4.2). This is an extra security feature used to "prove" the user is a human and not a computer attempting to automatically create multiple accounts.

Advanced Setup

Advanced setup (Figure 4.3) is for bloggers who want to host a blog on their own server/domain. For this setup, you'll be asked to provide the following information:

- *Blog title.* As with the Basic setup, you may name your blog whatever you want. Give your blog a name that indicates who you are, where the blog is located, and/or the blog's purpose. If this is a blog for your library, the library's name is an appropriate choice.
- *Listing.* If Blogger were to host your blog, it would automatically be listed in the Blogger directory. In this case, as Blogger will *not* be hosting it, you have the option of having your blog listed or not listed.

Figure 4.3   Blogger's advanced setup

- *FTP server.* Enter the name of the FTP server where you want the files to be sent. Do not include ftp:// or http:// as this will prevent your blog from publishing.
- *Protocol.* Choose either FTP (File Transfer Protocol) or SFTP (Secure File Transfer Protocol). If you're not sure which your server supports, try the FTP option first.
- *FTP path (optional).* This is the path on the server to the directory in which you intend your blog's files to be placed. Leaving this information out will send your files to server root.
- *Blog filename.* Enter the filename of your blog's home page.
- *Blog URL.* Enter the full URL of your blog. This is the address that you will be giving out so readers can access your blog.

If you are not the server administrator for the domain in which your files will be hosted, you may need to coordinate with that person to set the blog up correctly.

Choosing a Template

Whether Blogger is hosting your blog or it is being hosted on another server/domain, the next step is to choose a template for your blog (Figure 4.4). There are 12 different templates to choose from. If you don't prefer any of them, pick the one you dislike the least for now. You'll have the opportunity to choose from a larger list of templates or to modify the template once this process is complete. (We'll cover this later in the chapter.)

Once you've chosen a template, click the orange "Continue" arrow at the bottom of the page. Blogger will take just a few moments to create your blog and will notify you when it's done. Click next on the "Start Posting" arrow (Figure 4.5).

Using the Blogger Dashboard

After clicking on the "Start Posting" arrow in the last step, you should now see a Posting interface (Figure 4.10 later in this chapter). From here, click on the "Back to Dashboard" link in the upper-right corner of the screen. This brings you to Blogger's Dashboard page. The main section of the dashboard is labeled "Blogs," and it contains a list of blogs you have access to and a button that allows you to create a new blog associated with your existing account. The example shown in Figure 4.6 (from my actual account) shows that I have access to many different blogs. You can create as many blogs as you like without having to create multiple accounts, and all the blogs you have access to are listed in alphabetical order. You are also provided with links that allow you to create a new post and change settings, the date of the last post, and the total number of posts in the blog. (You may notice that not all of the blogs I've created have posts. Some are old blogs that I no longer actively post to but have kept in order to retain control of their titles and URLs.) Take a closer look at the "Second Life Library 2.0" blog listing and notice that the "Change Settings" link is not active. This is because I am not the owner of this blog, though I do have the rights to post to it. If your library creates a blog, you can set only one person as the blog's administrator. By giving other staff members their own Blogger accounts, you enable them to post to the library's blog but only the assigned administrator will be able to change the blog's settings. Additionally, posts by individual users will be marked with the name of the user.

Figure 4.4   Choosing a template

Figure 4.5   Your blog has been created!

Below the Blogs section is the Blogger News area. This section changes often and includes important news and updates from the Blogger system. I advise checking these news items regularly, as system problems and changes in features will be reported here.

On the right, you'll find links to access your account profile and password. I've added a photograph to my profile. We'll discuss profile options in the next section of this chapter.

Also on the right are links to "Blogger Help" and "Blogs of Note." "Blogger Help" provides links to the Blogger knowledge base. The "Blogs of Note" area, which changes often, features blogs chosen by the staff at Blogger as worthy of attention.

The last section on the right is titled "Recently Updated." This section is automatically updated by the Blogger system and lists blogs that have recently added posts. This section changes every few minutes, and like the Blogs of Note section, can be a great source of useful or interesting blogs.

Managing Your Profile

Let's now focus on the Profile section of the Dashboard. You have three options: "Edit Your Profile," "View Your Profile," and "Change Your Password." Take a moment to view your profile. Since you've just created your account, there won't be much to see at this point, but it will grow over time. Because I have been posting to my blog for several years, I have a relatively lengthy profile (Figure 4.7).

The "Edit Profile" link will lead you to the Edit User Profile interface (Figure 4.8). Complete the fields as you see fit. Beyond the first two sections, all the information requested is optional. If you feel that you need to be anonymous in your blog, leave the Name field blank or provide a pseudonym for public viewing. If left *unchecked*, the first option, "Share My Profile," will prevent people from viewing your profile even if you have supplied information. Even if you choose not to share your profile, information such as your name will automatically be attached to your posts, so be sure to fill in that part appropriately. When you've completed the form, click the "Save Your Profile" button at the bottom of the page. If you don't follow this step, your changes will not be saved.

The "Change Password" link opens a new page that allows you to change your account password (Figure 4.9). As with many systems, Blogger requires you to key in your current password once and a new password twice to make sure you haven't made a typing error.

Creating a Post in Blogger

Now that you've familiarized yourself with the Dashboard and completed your profile, you're ready to create your first post.

Figure 4.6   The Blogger Dashboard (top)
Figure 4.7   Author's Blogger profile (bottom)

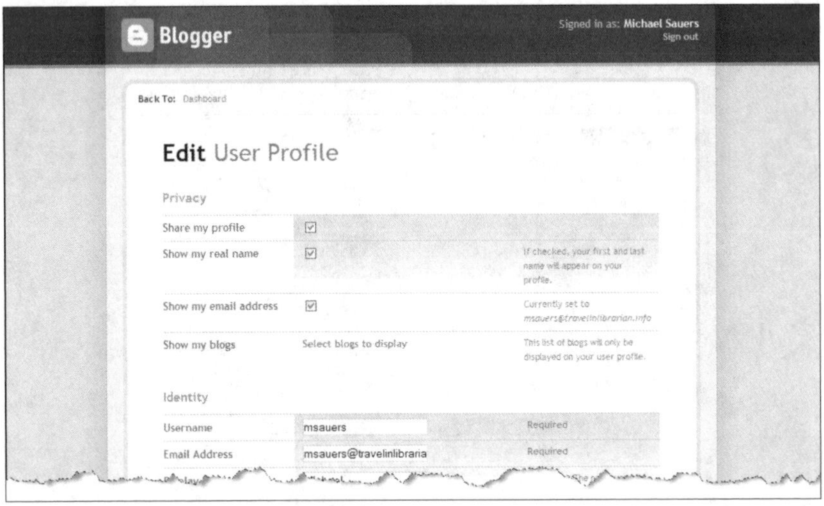

Figure 4.8   Edit your profile

Figure 4.9   Change your password

While in the Dashboard, click on the "New Post" link (green "plus" icon) to the right of your blog's title. You will be taken back to the Posting/Create interface for your blog. Notice there are four major sections available in the Blog interface—Posting, Settings, Template, and View Blog. These are represented by four tabs under your blog's title.

By default, you are in the "Edit XHTML" (eXtensible HyperText Markup Language) version of the Create page (Figure 4.10). (This version of post creation assumes that you have a working knowledge of XHTML.) Here you are presented with a Title field and a large Composure field. Options relating to comments and date/time settings can be found by clicking on the "Post and Comment Options" link below the Composure field. To create a post, first fill in the title of the post, and then type the content of the post into the larger Body field. The buttons above the Body field let you select text and add formatting (bold and italics), insert a hyperlink, quote text, perform spell-check, and insert images without using XHTML. These buttons will place the appropriate XHTML code into your post automatically, or you can type code into both the Title field and the Body field.

The "Comments" option lets you decide whether readers may post comments in response to your post and directly into your blog. (Here you're allowed to decide on a post-by-post basis.) Later in this chapter, I will show you how to turn off comments altogether should you decide not to support them in your blog.

The Date and Time fields are set, by default, according to when you started creating the post. You can change these values by selecting the appropriate dropdown menus (Figure 4.11).

If you don't have a working knowledge of XHTML, select the "Compose" tab (above the upper-left corner of the Body field), and you will be taken to a WYSIWYG (What You See Is What You Get) interface for creating posts (Figure 4.12). Here there is no assumption of or need for XHTML knowledge. You can create your posts as if you had written them in a standard word processing program.

Editing options in the Compose interface include basic font control (face, size, color, bold and italics), hyperlink insertion, text alignment, numbering, adding bullets or quotation marks, image insertion, and format clearing.

If you need more time to compose your post or want to finish it at a later time, click the "Save as Draft" button. This will save but not publish (i.e., make public) your post. You can return to your post at a later time to either finish or delete it.

When you have finished writing your post, click on the "Publish Post" button to instruct Blogger to make your post public. Depending on the size of the post and whether you're publishing your blog on Blogger or another server, publishing a post can take anywhere from a few seconds to a few minutes. While your post is

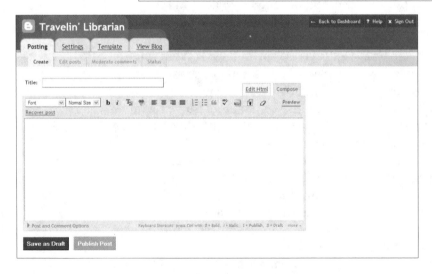

Figure 4.10   XHTML interface for creating posts (top)

Figure 4.11   Comment and Date/Time fields (middle)

Figure 4.12   WYSIWYG interface for creating posts (bottom)

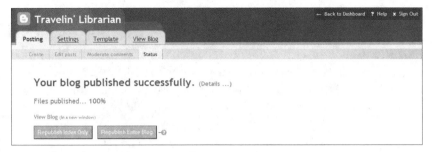

Figure 4.13   Notice of successful publication

being published, you will see a status screen showing the progress of the publishing. You will be notified on screen when the publishing process has been completed successfully (Figure 4.13). If the publishing mechanism encounters any errors, you can click on the "Details ..." link for more information.

The two buttons presented to you on the Details screen— "Republish Index Only" and "Republish Entire Blog"—are typically used only if there is a temporary error and you want to try again. In such cases, republishing just the index, the first page of your blog, will usually suffice. Republishing the entire blog, especially if you've been running it for any considerable period of time, is only necessary if you've made a global change to your blog (for instance, changes to the template). Larger blogs will take a while to republish; for example, my blog, with almost 2,000 posts, takes about 30 minutes to republish in its entirety.

If you're done publishing and have no errors to correct, you can proceed to any of the other sections of the Blogger interface available via the links on the page. Don't forget that you also have the option of clicking the "View Blog" link if you want to see your blog live, including your new post.

To create another post in the same manner, click the "Create" link under the "Posting" tab at the top of the page.

Using Alternate Posting Methods

Blogger offers three alternate methods for creating new posts. These methods do not require you to be on the Create page in the Blogger system. You may find that one of the alternate methods is more effective for you.

Blogger for Word

In August 2005, Blogger released the Blogger add-in for Microsoft Word (buzz.blogger.com/bloggerforword.html). Once this add-in has been downloaded and installed, you can create and edit your Blogger posts using Microsoft Word. The add-in installs an additional toolbar in Word with buttons labeled "Blogger Settings" (to give Word access to your blog), "Open Post …" (to display a list of posts from your blog so you may choose which to edit), "Save as Draft …" (to save the current document as a draft post), and "Publish …" (to publish the current document as a live post).

The advantage of using the Blogger add-in is that you have all of the editing capabilities and tools of Word available to you, thereby extending your options well beyond those of Blogger's built-in Editing interface.

BlogThis!

BlogThis! is a bookmarklet available from Blogger that allows you to automatically create a new post linking to the Web page you are visiting at the time. The bookmarklet can be found by going into "Blogger Help" and selecting the "Posting & Editing" link and then "What is BlogThis!?" By installing the bookmarklet, you create a new bookmark that, when selected, will open a new window that contains a Create New Post form. The post's title will be automatically filled in with the title of the Web page and the post's body will include a link back to that page; the post is now ready for you to add whatever additional text you'd like (Figure 4.14). (If you are not logged into your Blogger account, you will be asked to enter your username and password before the form is presented to you.)

The upper-right corner of the "Blog This!" window contains a dropdown list of the blogs you have access to from your account. If you only have one blog, this is not an issue. If you have multiple blogs, as I do, be sure the blog you want to post to is selected before you click the "Publish" button. More than once I've created a post using the "Blog This!" method, only to discover I've published it to the wrong blog.

"Blog This!" uses by default the WYSIWIG version (labeled "Rich Text" in this window) for editing the new post. If you'd rather use the markup-editing version, click on "Rich Text" and change to "Edit HTML." BlogThis! will remember which editing format you choose so that next time you will be presented with that version first.

"BlogThis!" is also available as part of the Google Toolbar in Internet Explorer. Instructions for installing the Google Toolbar (along with turning on its "BlogThis!" button) are available on the same page as the bookmarklet.

Posting Via E-mail

Sometimes you may not have Web access but you can send e-mail (for example, you do not have Internet access on your cell-phone, but you can send e-mail from it). As long as you can send e-mail, you can create a blog post.

To turn on e-mail posting for your blog, select the "Settings" tab in your blog and then select "E-mail." From the two settings available, select "Mail-to-Blogger Address." (We'll discuss the other setting later in this chapter.) You will be prompted to enter a secret word of at least four characters into the field (Figure 4.15). Enter your secret word and click "Save Settings." You are now ready to post via e-mail. Whatever you put in the subject line of the e-mail will be the title of the post, and the body of the message will become the body of the post. The post may include XHTML, but if you don't include any markup when e-mailing, you can always log in and enhance your post later.

The "Publish" checkbox on this page tells Blogger either to automatically publish e-mailed posts (checked) or to save them as drafts for later editing and publishing (unchecked).

Posting Via Phone (Audio Posts)

If all else fails and you have no Internet connectivity and absolutely must post something now, you can use the telephone. By signing up (in advance) for Audioblogger (www.audioblogger. com), you can dial a phone number, enter your blog's PIN, and record a post. The post will be published to your blog as a button (Figure 4.16) that users can click to hear your audio recording in MP3 format.

Blog Options

Now that your blog is up and running and you've created a post or two, let's take a walk through Blogger's built-in options (accessible by the four tabs at the top of the main posting page).

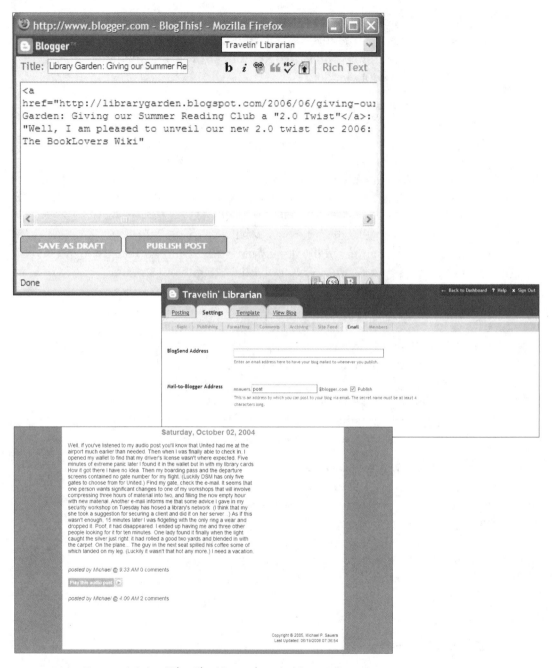

Figure 4.14 "BlogThis!" window (top)

Figure 4.15 Setting up e-mail posting (middle)

Figure 4.16 Posting via phone (audio post) (bottom)

Figure 4.17   Edit Posts screen

Posting

The "Posting" tab offers four options: Create, Edit Posts, Moderate Comments, and Status.

Create

The Create screen (see "Creating a Post in Blogger" earlier in this chapter) is the main interface for creating a new post or editing an existing post.

Edit Posts

The Edit Posts screen (Figure 4.17) displays a list of the most recent posts to your blog and the status of these posts. The screen shows, by default, the 25 most recently created posts regardless of status. You have access to all of your posts through the "Show" and "from" dropdown lists and the "Search" box.

The "Show" dropdown list lets you see 5, 10, 25, 50, 100, or 300 posts at a time. Using the "from" dropdown list, you can then specify that you want to see all posts, only drafts, only the most recently published posts, or future posts (those with future dates and times). To change the posts shown, choose the appropriate choices from the two dropdown lists and click the "Go" button.

The "Search" box allows you to perform a keyword search of all of your posts, published and drafts, and display only those posts.

Figure 4.18   Delete confirmation

For example, searching on "holiday" would display only your posts that contain the word "holiday."

Also on this screen is a "Create New Post" button, which will take you back to the Create screen.

The rest of this Edit Posts screen displays the posts that you have requested. Each post shows the date of the post, the post's title (with a triangle icon immediately to its left—more on this shortly), the name of the user who created the post, and links for "Edit," "View," and "Delete." The "Edit" button will take you to the Compose screen, but the Compose fields will be pre-populated with the information from that post. This gives you access to edit an existing post. The "View" link opens a new window and shows you a post as it will be seen by your readers. The "Delete" link allows you to delete a post from your blog. You will be asked to confirm that you want to delete a post or to cancel the deletion request (Figure 4.18).

The small triangle to the left of a post's title allows you to view the text of a post without leaving this screen (Figure 4.19). Clicking on the triangle toggles between viewing the post and hiding it. If you have any images in your post they will not be displayed in this view.

Moderate Comments

At this point, clicking on the "Moderate Comments" link brings up a screen stating you have not turned on comment moderation. This screen will only offer options once this feature has been turned on in your blog. This feature will be covered in more detail under the Settings heading later in this chapter.

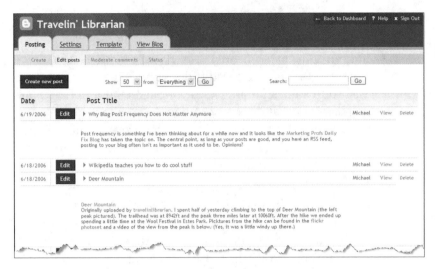

Figure 4.19   Edit Posts screen with two open items

Status

The Status screen tells you if your post has published success-fully. This is the same screen that appears after you've published a post (see Figure 4.13 earlier in the chapter).

Settings

The "Settings" tab contains most of the settings needed to cus-tomize your blog (without needing any XHTML knowledge) and contains eight sections: Basic, Publishing, Formatting, Comments, Archiving, Site Feed, E-mail, and Members.

When you change an item in the Settings section, the change will not be permanent until you click the "Save Settings" button. Even after you save your changes, they will not be seen on your live blog until you republish it.

Basic

The Basic screen (Figure 4.20) has six settings you can change:

- *Title*. This field contains the name of your blog as displayed at the top of your blog's pages. Initially, this field will contain the text that you entered when you set up your blog.

- *Description*. This field, which is not required, should contain a brief narrative description of your blog and its purpose. The content of this field will be displayed under the blog's title if you are using any of the standard Blogger templates.

- *Add your Blog to our listings?* The Blogger system has a directory of all the blogs created from within Blogger. Answering "yes" to this question indicates your agreement to have your blog listed in that directory, and will also allow your blog to appear on your user profile page should your profile also be public. Answering "no" will prevent your blog from being listed in either location.

- *Show Quick Editing on your Blog?* Answering "yes" to this question will add an "Edit" link (pencil icon) after the title of each individual post (Figure 4.21). This link allows you to select a post from your blog and go directly to the editing screen for that post. This link will only appear for individuals that are logged into Blogger at the time and have permission to post and edit that blog. No one else will see this link.

- *Show E-mail Post links?* Answering "yes" to this question adds another link (an envelope icon) after the title of each post that allows your readers to automatically e-mail the content of a post to themselves or someone else (Figure 4.22). When the link is clicked, the user will be asked to enter his name and e-mail address, the intended recipient's e-mail address, and a note; the post will then be e-mailed directly to the specified recipient (Figure 4.23).

- *Show Compose Mode for all your blogs?* On the Create screen, we know there are two compose options: an Edit XHTML version and a WYSIWYG version. Answering "no" to "Show Compose Mode…" will turn off the WYSIWYG version. The key difference in this option compared to all the others on this screen is that this selection affects *all of your blogs* in the system, not just the one you're currently working on.

Lastly, there is a "Delete This Blog" button on the lower left of the Basic screen. If you decide that you no longer want to have this blog on the system, this button will do the job. You will be asked to confirm your decision and, if you answer "yes," the blog and all of its content will disappear. Keep in mind that deleting a blog puts its blogspot.com URL and title back into the pool for others to use.

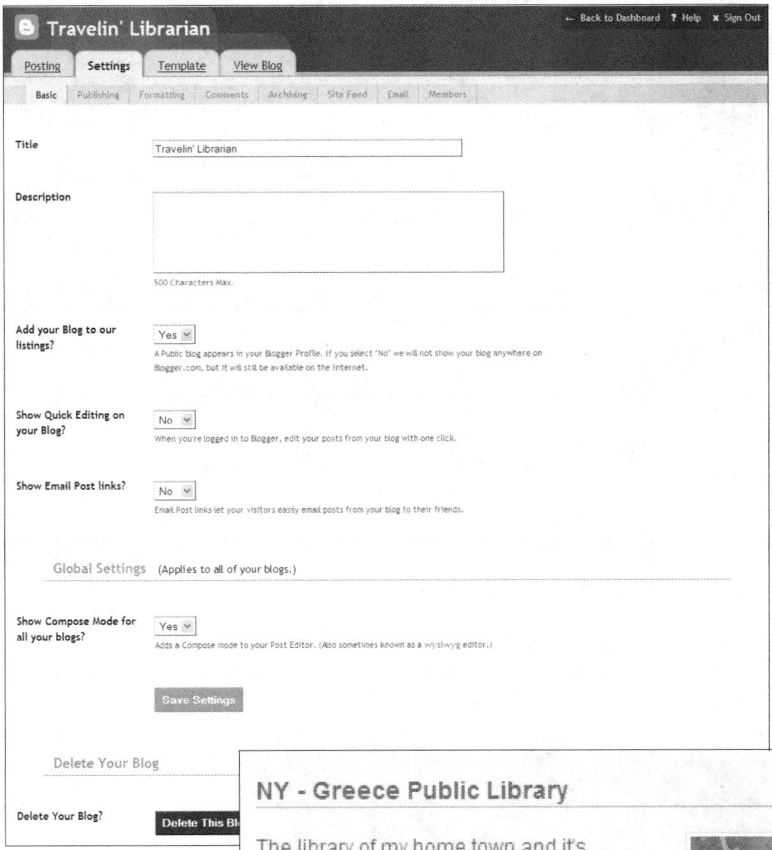

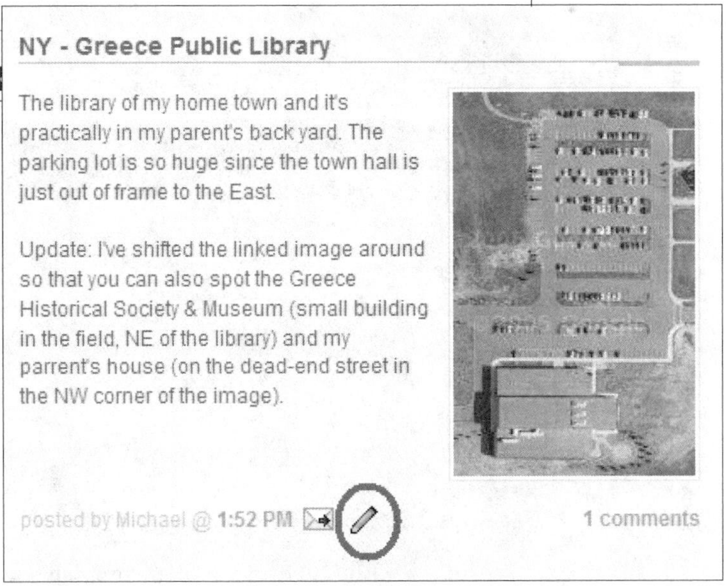

Figure 4.20   Basic screen under the "Settings" tab (top)
Figure 4.21   A blog post showing the "Edit" link (bottom)

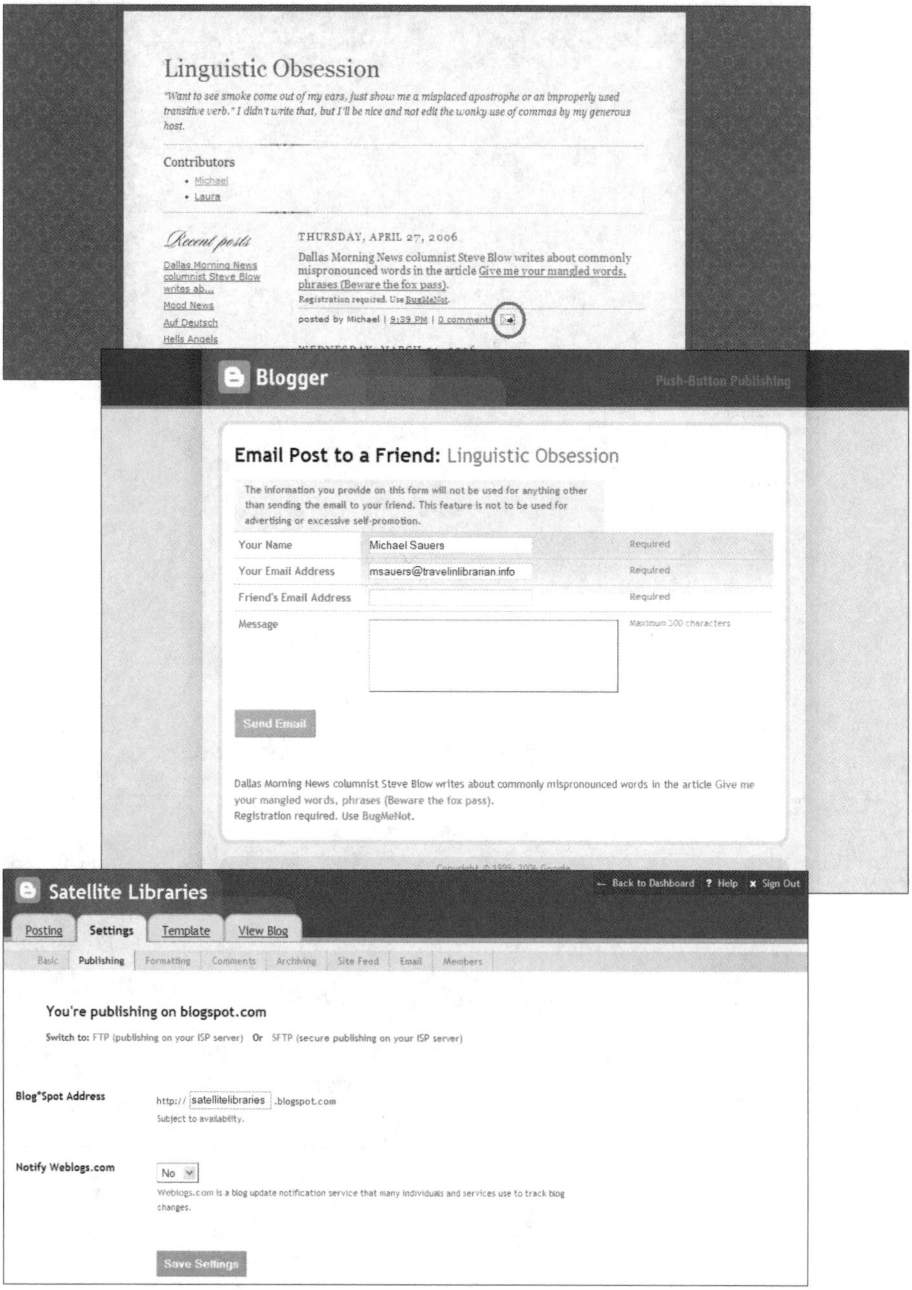

Figure 4.22 A blog post showing the "E-mail" link (top)

Figure 4.23 E-mail Post interface (middle)

Figure 4.24 Publishing on blogspot.com (bottom)

Publishing

The Publishing screen has three versions, depending on where and by which method you're publishing your blog. The blogspot.com screen is for those publishing their blog on Blogger's free hosting domain. Authors publishing to their own Web server will see either the FTP (File Transfer Protocol) screen or SFTP (Secure File Transfer Protocol) screen depending on which they are using.

On the blogspot.com screen (Figure 4.24), there are only two settings: the name of the sub domain in which you want to publish (originally set up when you created your blog) and a choice of whether or not you wish to "ping" Weblogs.com. Weblogs.com is a service that some people use to keep track of when and if blogs have been updated. If you answer "yes" to the ping question, Weblogs.com will be notified whenever you publish a new post and will then notify its subscribers that your blog has been updated. With the advent of RSS, I am not aware of anyone still using the Weblogs.com service. While it doesn't hurt to have this feature turned on, it is no longer a necessity.

The same questions are asked on the FTP (Figure 4.25) or SFTP (Figure 4.26) screens. The only difference is the method in which your blog will be published to your server (via standard FTP or secure FTP [SFTP].) You'll need to provide the following information:

- *FTP Server.* The domain name of your FTP server. Do not include ftp://.
- *Blog URL.* The URL of your blog as you'll be supplying it to your readers.
- *FTP Path.* The path to the directory into which you'd like your files placed. In most cases, this will be the path based on your home directory. In some cases, it may be the path from server root.
- *Blog Filename.* The filename for your blog's first page, typically *index.html*.
- *FTP Username.* Your username for your FTP server.
- *FTP Password.* Your password for your FTP server.

Formatting

The Formatting screen (Figure 4.27) allows you to control the look and feel of your blog (beyond the issues of the physical layout,

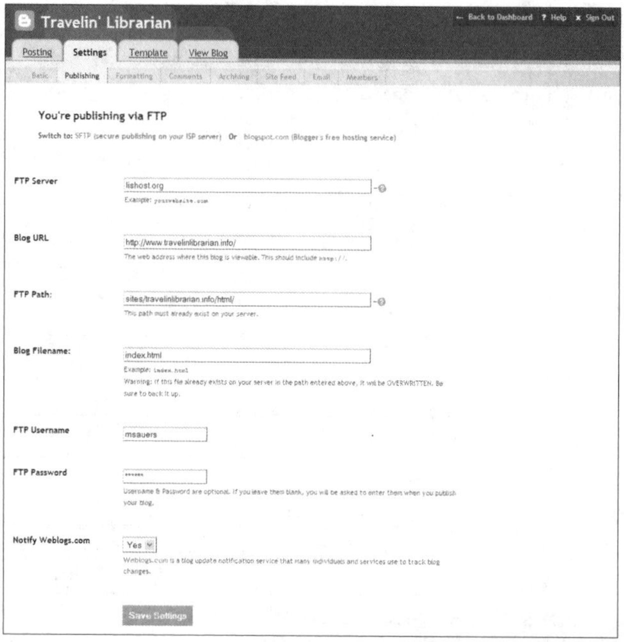

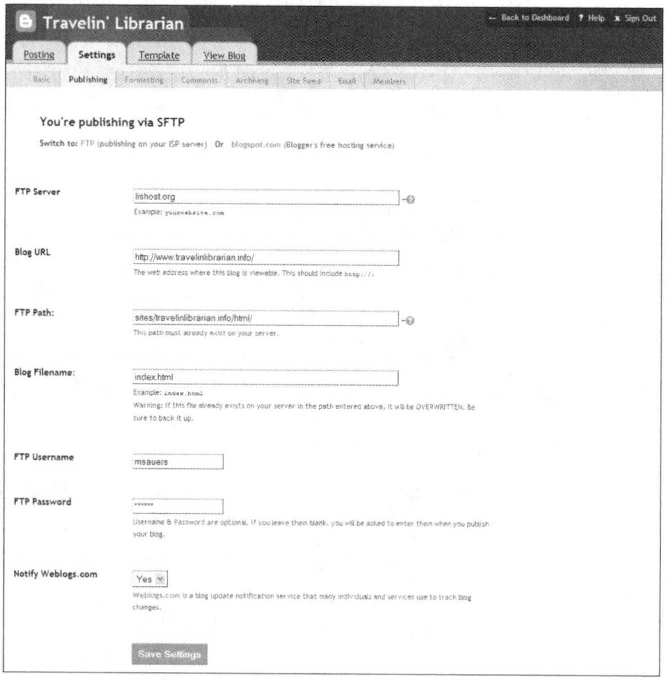

Figure 4.25   FTP interface (top)
Figure 4.26   SFTP interface (bottom)

which is controlled by the Template, covered later in this chapter). The Formatting screen features the following settings:

- *Show*. This allows you to set the number of posts to be displayed on your blog's home page. You can set it to show between one and 999 of either days or posts. (There is a limit of 999 posts; if you set this to the past 100 days, but that includes 1,000 posts, only the first 999 will be displayed.) The typical setting for "Show" is the past seven days.

- *Date Header Format*. Your posts are automatically grouped by day. The date header format is how you want the heading for each day to look. You have 13 different formats from which to choose (Figure 4.28).

- *Archive Index Date*. This setting controls the format of dates for the links to your blog's archive (archives are covered later in this chapter). You have 14 different choices for how this date may be displayed (Figure 4.29).

- *Timestamp Format*. This setting controls the date and time displayed on individual posts. You have seven different choices as to how this information may be displayed (Figure 4.30).

- *Time Zone*. This setting tells Blogger which time zone your blog is located in. All of your timestamps, by default, will be based on the time zone you set here. For example, while at a conference in Washington, DC, I created a post at 8 A.M. local time, but as my time zone is set for Mountain Time, the post displayed the time of 6 A.M. instead (Figure 4.31).

- *Date Language*. Your date/timestamp for individual posts may be displayed in any of almost 100 different languages. Choose which language you'd like from the dropdown list (Figure 4.32).

- *Encoding*. The encoding scheme of a document specifies which *character set* is being used in the document, not which language the document is written in. For example, English, German, French, Italian, and Spanish all use the same character set, while Hebrew, Russian, and Japanese use different character sets. The "Encoding" setting (Figure 4.33) specifies which character set to use. Assuming you're using English (or another language with the same character set), "Universal (Unicode UTF-8)" is your best choice, as it offers the greatest

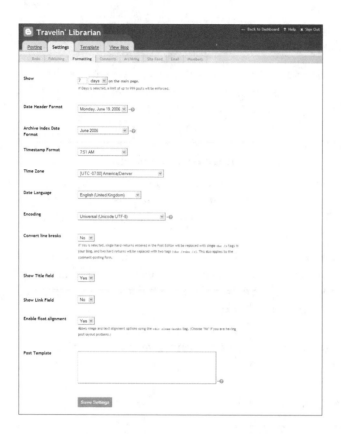

```
6/19/2006 07:51:37 AM
Monday, June 19, 2006
6/19/2006
7:51:37 AM
07:51
19.6.06
7:51 AM
```

```
[UTC -08:00] PST
[UTC -08:00] PST8PDT
[UTC -08:00] Pacific/Pitcairn
[UTC -08:00] SystemV/PST8
[UTC -08:00] SystemV/PST8PDT
[UTC -08:00] US/Pacific
[UTC -08:00] US/Pacific-New
[UTC -07:00] America/Boise
[UTC -07:00] America/Cambridge_Bay
[UTC -07:00] America/Chihuahua
[UTC -07:00] America/Dawson_Creek
[UTC -07:00] America/Denver
[UTC -07:00] America/Edmonton
[UTC -07:00] America/Hermosillo
[UTC -07:00] America/Inuvik
[UTC -07:00] America/Mazatlan
[UTC -07:00] America/Phoenix
[UTC -07:00] America/Shiprock
[UTC -07:00] America/Yellowknife
[UTC -07:00] Canada/Mountain
```

```
Danish (Denmark)
German (Austria)
German (Switzerland)
German (Germany)
German (Luxembourg)
Greek (Greece)
English (Australia)
English (Canada)
English (United Kingdom)
English (Ireland)
English (India)
English (New Zealand)
English (South Africa)
Spanish (Argentina)
Spanish (Bolivia)
Spanish (Chile)
Spanish (Colombia)
Spanish (Costa Rica)
Spanish (Dominican Republic)
Spanish (Ecuador)
```

Figure 4.27   Formatting screen under the "Settings" tab (left, top)

Figure 4.28   Date Header format choices (left, middle)

Figure 4.29   Archive Index Date format choices (left, bottom)

Figure 4.30   Timestamp format choices (above, top)

Figure 4.31   Time Zone choices (above, middle)

Figure 4.32   Date Language choices (above, bottom)

number of characters to work with. The question mark to the right of this field is a link to further information.

- *Convert Line Breaks.* If this is set to "no," any use of the Enter key will be ignored when you are creating a new post. If set to "yes," when you use the Enter key while creating a post using the Compose Version, an XHTML <br/> will be added to the post.

- *Show Title Field.* Changing this to "no" removes the Title field from the Post Creation interfaces. Typically this is used by bloggers with extensive XHTML knowledge who want more precise control over how their blogs are presented. For most bloggers, there is no reason to ever change this setting.

- *Show Link Field.* When changed to "yes," this option adds a new field named "link" to the Post Creation interfaces (Figure 4.34). This allows bloggers with little to no XHTML experience to insert a URL that will automatically associate itself with the post's title, creating a hyperlink to another Web page.

- *Post Template.* This field is for those folks who always insert the same bit of markup or content into every post. By placing such information into this field, it will automatically show up in the Body field when a new post is created. For example, in Figure 4.35, I've placed the following text into the "Post Template": & copy; 2006, Michael Sauers. In Figure 4.36, that text automatically appears when I create a new post.

Comments

Comments allow readers to add responses to your postings. This is a great option, but automatic posting of outside comments will not be appropriate for every blog. If the blog is your own, whether personal or professional in nature, reader feedback may be welcomed and appreciated. For a blog representing activities in the library, however, comments may not be appropriate.

In addition, there is the growing problem of "comment spam"— the posting of advertisements rather than legitimate commentary. In spite of this, many bloggers allow comments to be posted, only disabling the feature if comment spam becomes a problem.

The Comments screen (Figure 4.37) has the following settings:

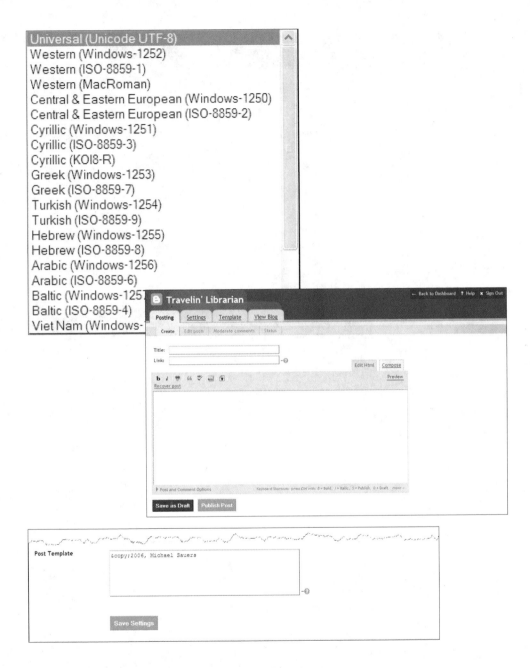

Figure 4.33   Encoding choices (top)

Figure 4.34   Compose interface with Show Link Field turned on (middle)

Figure 4.35   Post template (bottom)

Figure 4.36   Creating a post with a post template (top)
Figure 4.37   Comments screen (bottom)

- *Comments.* This setting basically turns comments on or off. If you decide to hide comments, existing comments are not actually deleted; they are just not displayed to your readers.

- *Who Can Comment?* This option lets the blogger specify who is actually allowed to post comments to the blog. The three options are "Anyone," "Only Registered Users," and "Only Members of this Blog." "Anyone" allows literally anyone to post a comment to your blog. Although this does allow for the broadest range of comments, it also significantly increases the risk of comment spam.[2] "Only Registered Users" means that an individual must be registered with Blogger to comment. Although this seems like it might be a good choice, I wouldn't personally want to register for the service for the sole purpose of commenting on someone's blog. Lastly, "Only Members of this Blog" limits your blog to comments only from individuals who are allowed to post to the blog. Although this will completely eliminate the chance of comment spam, it severely limits who can comment. If you have a blog solely for exchanging information among your library's staff, this would be an appropriate option.

- *Comments Default for Posts.* This option's default allows people to comment on all your posts. If you feel that the majority of your posts do not need to allow for commenting, then change this setting to "New Posts Do Not Have Comments."

- *Backlinks.* These are links from other Web sites to your posts. By displaying backlinks, your users will see what sites are linking to your posts. If you decide later to hide backlinks, they will not be deleted, just hidden from view.

- *Backlinks Default for Posts.* This option allows you to decide whether you want backlinks turned on by default for individual posts. This assumes that backlinks are being shown.

- *Comments Timestamp Format.* This option gives you an extensive list of choices for how the date/time appear on comments.

- *Show Comments in a Popup Window.* When a user clicks on the "Comments" link for a post, this option gives you the choice to have the comments displayed in the same window (answer "no") or in a new window (answer "yes").

- *Show Word Verification for Comments.* Selecting "yes" forces users to enter a string of random characters to "prove" the post is not being created by a computer. I highly recommend you turn on this feature, as it will prevent practically all comment spam.

- *Enable Comment Moderation.* Turning on this feature allows you to approve all comments before they appear on your blog for others to read. If you choose to use this feature, you will be asked to enter an e-mail address. This is the address that will be notified when a new comment is submitted and ready for approval. This reduces the need for you to periodically check for new comments by logging into your account.

- *Show Profile Images on Comments.* If the person commenting is a Bloglines user and has added an image to their profile, answering "yes" to this option will display those images along with the posted comment.

- *Comment Notification Address.* This field allows you to enter an e-mail address to which a notification will be sent whenever a new comment is added to your blog. Personally, I find this to be a handy feature.

Once you have turned on comment moderation, the "Moderate Comments" link (found under the Posting tab) will present you with additional information and options (Figure 4.38). If you have no comments waiting to be approved, the screen will say "No Unmoderated Comments Found." When there are pending comments, you will be shown a list of them. You can view the comments, select a single or multiple comments using the checkboxes on the left, and then choose whether to "Publish" or "Reject" the comments. If you publish a comment, it will appear on your blog for everyone to read. If you reject a comment, it will immediately be deleted and will not appear on your blog.

Archiving

Archiving your blog is an important concept. If posts aren't archived, new posts will continue to be added to the top of a single Web page, making it longer and longer and in turn causing increasingly long load times for readers. Archiving takes older posts and places them into their own Web pages, providing links to the older material and allowing the most current items to load

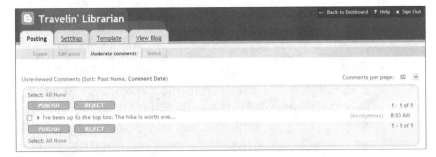

Figure 4.38   Moderate Comments screen

Figure 4.39   Archiving screen

quickly. The Archiving screen (Figure 4.39) gives the following options:

- *Archiving frequency*. You have four choices of how often old posts should be archived. "No Archive" turns archiving off. If you make this choice, old posts not displayed on your blog's home page will not be accessible to your users. The other three choices are "Daily," "Weekly," and "Monthly." Which you choose should depend on how often you post and how long those posts are. You also need to keep in mind that if you choose monthly, you'll have 12 additional links on your page after a year, one for each month. If you choose weekly, you'll end the year with 52 additional links; choosing daily will net you 365 (or 366) additional links by the end of one year. Most bloggers stick to a monthly archive and a few use weekly. The only blogs I've seen with daily archives are those for conferences in which there are a lot of posts and the event only lasts a matter of days.

- *Enable Post Pages?* If this option is set to "yes," then each post you create will not only appear on your blog's home page and in the appropriate archive, but will also have its own unique Web page containing just that post and any associated comments. Setting this option to "no" means your posts will only appear on the home page and archive pages and will not have individual Web pages. You may want to enable this option for two reasons. First, each post will have its own URL, which makes for easier bookmarking. Second, if a reader wants to print out a single post, having it available on its own page (instead of as a small part of a much larger document) makes this more convenient. However, there are downsides to enabling post pages. Having individual pages for each post considerably increases the size of your blog. Granted, server space is relatively inexpensive these days, but if you have a small server, you could use it up a lot sooner than expected. Using individual pages also affects the speed of publishing. With this feature turned on, creating a new post means publishing your blog's home page, the relevant archive page, *and* a new page for that particular post. These problems are not significant but you do need to be aware of them.

Site Feed

The Site Feed screen allows you to control whether an RSS feed is automatically created for your blog. RSS and site feeds are covered in detail in Chapters 5–8; the Site Feed screen will be covered in those chapters.

E-mail

The E-mail screen (Figure 4.40) gives you the option of using e-mail as a tool in your blog. By filling out the first field on the screen, "BlogSend Address," every time a new post is published, a copy of your blog's home page will be sent to that address. If you're the only person posting to your blog, this is not particularly helpful as you're already well aware of what you're posting. However, in the case of a shared blog in which multiple authors have the ability to post, it is handy to have the blog's administrator notified via e-mail whenever someone publishes a new post.

Filling out the second field, "Mail-to-Blogger Address," allows you to post via e-mail (see "Using Alternate Posting Methods" earlier in the chapter).

Members

The Members screen (Figure 4.41) allows you to control who may post to and administer your blog. When you first create your blog, you will be the only person listed as allowed to post and you will also be listed as the administrator since you're the creator and only member of the blog.

To add additional members to your blog, just click the "Add Team Member(s)" button and then enter the e-mail addresses of the persons you want to invite to your blog. You can also add a message to your invitation (Figure 4.42). In order to become a member of your blog, team members must either already have a Blogger account or create one for themselves. Blog members may post to a blog and edit existing posts they have created. An administrator may create, edit, and delete posts and change any of the other blog settings. Be cautious when granting administrator privileges.

Notice there is a "Remove" link that allows you to delete a person's access to your blog. As usual, you will be asked to confirm this decision.

Template

Your blog's template is the XHTML that controls the overall design of your blog. It gives a consistent appearance to all of your blog's pages including the home page, archive pages, and individual posting pages. The "Template" tab offers two options: Edit Current and Pick New.

Author's note: As I said earlier in the chapter, a command of XHTML is not required to use the book and start blogging. However, while that's true, the topic cannot be avoided completely. While the information provided in this section is not something you *must* know in order to blog successfully, you will probably find some familiarity with the topic of XHTML useful in the long run. Even readers with some Web page design experience should read this section, as it covers items specific to the Blogger system. However, understand that this is not a review of XHTML.

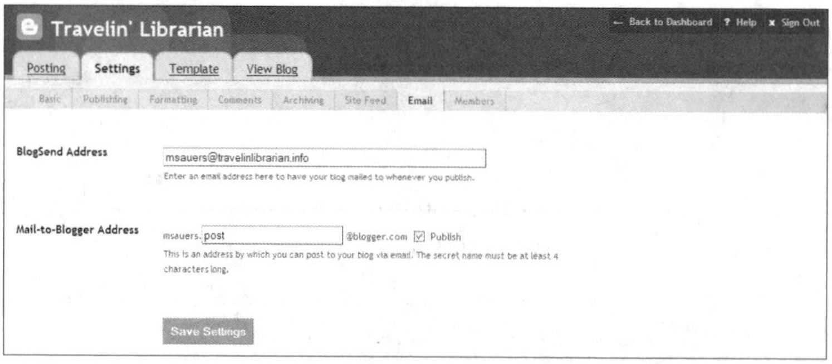

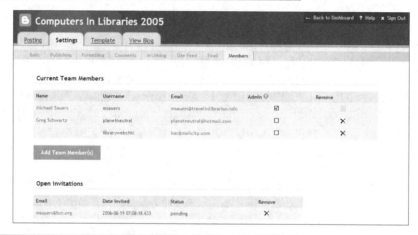

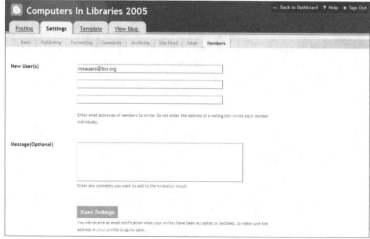

Figure 4.40   E-mail screen (top)

Figure 4.41   Current team members and invitations (middle)

Figure 4.42   Adding team members to a blog (bottom)

Edit Current

When you look at a Blogger template, keep in mind that a great deal of customization is possible. With a working knowledge of XHTML and CSS (Cascading Style Sheets), you can modify colors, change fonts, reset the margins, and much more. The XHTML-savvy blogger who doesn't care for any of the supplied templates or who needs to closely pattern a blog after the library's Web site may decide to create a template from scratch. If you have no experience with XHTML and CSS and you don't wish to learn, your best bet is to try out the various Blogger templates until you find one you can live with.

Blogger has created a set of "magic elements" unique to its system that allows your content to be presented in different ways depending upon the template you choose. (In fact, each of the major blogging systems—whether Web-based such as Blogger or software-based such as MoveableType—has its own set of such "magic elements.") These elements are bits of markup patterned on XHTML but are not in any XHTML specification. What they do is instruct the system (Blogger, in this case) to perform certain actions. Examples of these actions include "put a post here," "place the link to the archive here," and "show the post's comments here." With Blogger, the elements are known as "Blogger Tags." Table 4.1 shows a list of the more common Blogger tags and what they do. A complete list with definitions and additional information can be found on the Blogger site (help.blogger.com/bin/answer.py?answer=778&topic=39).

By moving the Blogger tags around or removing them altogether, you can easily change the look of your template and/or modify the features your blog offers.

After you've made your changes to the Blogger tags, the Edit Current screen (Figure 4.43) gives you the following options in the form of three buttons at the bottom of the page:

- *Save Template Changes*. Once you've made your changes to the template and want to make them permanent, you must click this button. Until you save the changes and republish your blog, the changes will not be live (seen by your readers). Republishing the whole blog is suggested at this stage to keep the template the same across your blog. Depending on the size of your blog, however, this may take several minutes. Republishing just the index will be faster but then your blog's

Table 4.1   Common Blogger Tags

Tag	What It Does
`<$BlogSiteFeedLink$>`	Outputs a link to your blog's RSS feed
`<$BlogPageTitle$>`	Outputs the title of your blog
`<$BlogDescription$>`	Outputs your blog's description
`<Blogger>…</Blogger>`	Contains most other Blogger Tags

`<BlogItemTitle>`
`<BlogItemURL>`
`<a href="<$BlogItemURL$>">`
`</BlogItemURL>`
`<$BlogItemTitle$></a>`
`</BlogItemTitle>`
	Outputs the title of an individual post and a link to external URLs

`<$BlogItemBody$>`	Outputs the body of a post
`<$BlogItemAuthor$>`	Outputs the post's author's name
`<$BlogItemEmail$>`	Outputs the post's author's e-mail address
`<$BlogItemDateTime$>`	Outputs the date and time of the post
`<$BlogItemPermalinkURL$>`	Outputs the URL of the individual post (a.k.a. the Permalink)

`<BloggerArchives>`
`<a href='<$BlogArchiveURL$>'>`
`<$BlogArchiveName$></a>`
`</BloggerArchives>`
	Outputs the links to the archive pages for the blog

`<BlogItemCommentsEnabled>`
`<$BlogItemCommentCount$>`
`<BlogItemComments>`
`<a name="<$BlogCommentNumber$>"></a>`
`<$BlogCommentBody$>`
`<$BlogCommentPermalinkURL$>`
`<$BlogCommentAuthor$>`
`<$BlogCommentDateTime$>`
`<$BlogCommentDeleteIcon$>`
`<$BlogItemCreate$>`
`</BlogItemComments>`
`</BlogItemCommentsEnabled>`
	Outputs any comments associated with a post

Figure 4.43   Edit Current screen under the "Template" tab

home page will use the revised template while all of the other pages will not.

- *Preview.* If you've made some changes to your template but are not sure how they'll turn out, click this button. This option will display your blog's home page in a new window using the revised template. This version is neither saved nor is it live. If you've made mistakes, you can go back and fix them before displaying them to your readers.

- *Clear Edits.* This button will undo any changes you've made to your template since the last time you saved your changes. Think of it as a giant "Undo" button.

Pick New

You can change the Blogger template at any time by selecting the "Pick New" link near the top of the page. You will be shown a list of all of the Blogger templates and be prompted to pick one. If you change your selection, all the code in the Template field will change to match your new choice. If you've already made posts to your blog, they will be reformatted into the new template.[3]

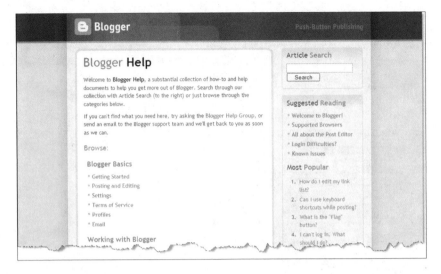

Figure 4.44   Blogger Help

Blogger Help

One final note about Blogger options: There is a "Help" button in the upper-right corner of all Blogger pages. Clicking on it will take you into the Blogger knowledge base (Figure 4.44).

Other Forms of Blogging

Now that you have set up a traditional blog, I'd like to introduce briefly two other forms of blogging: moblogging and podcasting. As these forms of blogging involve significant technical knowledge and/or computer hardware than many readers may currently possess, I will not delve into the specifics of creating such blogs. Instead I will offer a bit of background and suggest additional resources in the event you'd like to know more.

Moblogging

Mobile-blogging—moblogging for short—traditionally involves taking pictures with a camera phone (hence "mobile") and e-mailing them to a blog. Some bloggers e-mail photos as posts to their text-based blogs while others (myself included) post them to a separate blog specifically for photographs.

When moblogging, I use the service Flickr (www.flickr.com), which allowed me to sign up for a free account and then create a moblog. Once I created the moblog, I was given an e-mail address to which I can send my photos. Since my Treo600 is a camera phone and has Internet access, I can just snap a shot and e-mail it directly from my phone. The Flickr service receives the photo and posts it to my moblog (travlib.textamerica.com, Figure 4.45). I've set up my moblog to automatically display the most current photo, which is also a link to the full moblog (Figure 4.46).

Michael Stephens uses both his camera phone and digital camera to e-mail his photos to his account on Flickr, which he then makes available as the "Digital Camera Sightblog" and via an RSS feed (www.tametheweb.com/dc, Figure 4.47).

Moblogging can be a quick and simple way to promote your library by showing what's going on within minutes, if not seconds, of the event.

Podcasting

In December 2004, I started to hear rumblings about something called "podcasting." This apparently had something to do with blogging and iPods, but as I didn't own an iPod at the time I ignored it. However, two things happened in January 2005 that caused me to give the topic new consideration: First, I got an iPod. Second, Greg Schwartz—a librarian at the Louisville Free Public Library whom I had met at industry conferences—started doing an LIS-related podcast.

Without getting too technical, a podcast is a blog in which each post is similar to a mini radio show. MP3 files are created by the author and then posted as blog entries for "readers" to download and listen to via the software or hardware of their choice. (Note that Chapter 6 includes information about subscribing to podcasts.) A major misconception about podcasts is that an iPod is required to access or listen to them. In fact, you can listen to podcasts using any device or program that plays MP3 files—Windows Media Player, for instance.

Podcasts are popular because they allow you to create something akin to your own personalized radio station, listening to just the talk and music that you're interested in on the schedule you want. Podcasts are becoming so popular that "podcast" was

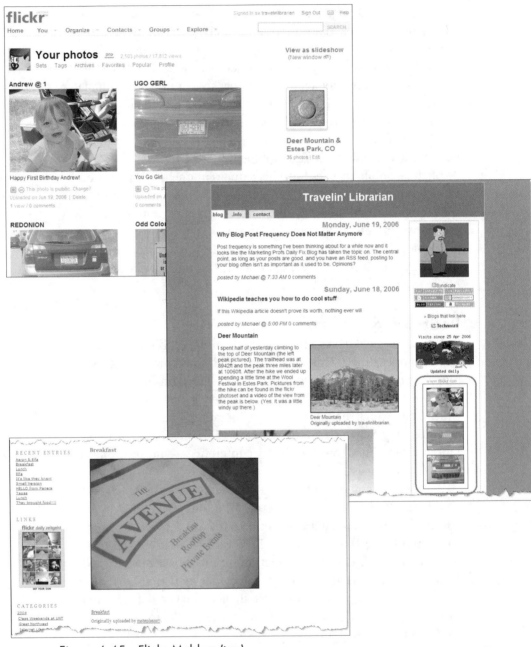

Figure 4.45 Flickr Moblog (top)

Figure 4.46 My current moblog photo as displayed on TravelinLibrarian.info (middle)

Figure 4.47 Digital Camera Sightblog (bottom)

named the 2005 word of the year by the *New Oxford English Dictionary.*[4]

If you're interested in finding podcasts to subscribe to, a number of sites/services are available:

- Apple's iTunes, www.apple.com/itunes – Contains a directory in which you can search and browse for podcasts of many different types.

- Podcast Alley, www.podcastalley.com – Contains reviews and allows users to rate podcasts.

- Podcasting News, www.podcastingnews.com/forum/links.php – A podcast directory organized into hierarchical categories.

Further information about podcasting can be found on the podcasting page in Wikipedia (en.wikipedia.org/wiki/Podcasting).

Now that you have a good grasp of blog creation and related issues, let's move on to Chapter 5, where we will take a look at the other half of the equation—RSS.

Endnotes

1. Dave Taylor's excellent blog post "Who Owns Your Words, Blogger?" (www.intuitive.com/blog/who_owns_your_words_blogger.html) contains some noteworthy points regarding this issue.
2. Comment spam is any comment posted to a blog that isn't a true comment about the content of the post but instead is an attempt to get you to click on a link to another site. (For example: "Great post. Come play online poker with me.") Comment spam can be virtually eliminated by selecting the "Show Word Verification for Comments" option on Comments screen.
3. The Blogger Templates blog (blogger-templates.blogspot.com) is dedicated to providing additional user-created templates for your Blogger-based blog.
4. "Wordsmiths hail podcast success," BBC News, December 7, 2005 (news.bbc.co.uk/2/hi/technology/4504256.stm).

Chapter 5

An Introduction to RSS

At this point we've covered what a blog is, looked at a number of interesting blogs (and bloggers), and reviewed the steps required to set up a blog. In this chapter, we move on to a new topic: RSS. As part of the RSS discussion, we'll also begin to explore the associated concepts of "feeds" and "aggregators" (covered in detail in Chapter 6).

What Is RSS?

Wikipedia defines RSS as "a family of XML[1] dialects for Web syndication used by (among other things) news websites and weblogs. ... The technology of RSS allows Internet users to subscribe to websites that have provided RSS feeds; these are typically sites that change or add content regularly ... In addition to facilitating syndication, RSS allows a website's frequent readers to track updates on the site using an aggregator[2]."[3] [*Author's note*: In the definition of RSS and elsewhere, the terms "Web site" or "Web page" and "blog" may be used interchangeably: If you remember that a blog is, in fact, a type of Web site, it should help you avoid confusion.]

Let's assume you recently started to read blogs. You have bookmarked several favorites, and are frequently discovering and adding new ones. As you check these blogs each morning, you realize that not all of them are being posted to daily, or for that matter, on any kind of predictable schedule. As busy as you are, you begin to check for new posts less and less frequently, until one day you realize you are missing out on much of the subject-specific news and commentary that inspired you to start reading blogs in the first place.

RSS addresses this situation by helping you keep up with new and revised Web-based information. It allows you to "subscribe" to a blog (or any Web resource that takes advantage of RSS syndication), letting the computer do the work of checking it regularly and notifying you when new information has been posted.

It is estimated that approximately 8.5 percent of Internet users today use RSS to access information on the Internet.[4] Although this percentage may seem small when compared to other Internet delivery methods (e.g., e-mail), about 75 million people worldwide use RSS. With this many users, RSS is a technology to watch.

Now that we know what RSS does, what exactly does the acronym stand for? Oddly enough, the answer to that question depends on whom you ask and which version of RSS you're talking about. RSS stands for "Rich Site Summary," "RDF Site Summary" (just what we need—an acronym containing an acronym!), or "Really Simple Syndication." The latter, which is the most descriptive of the three options and isn't based on a particular version of RSS, is currently favored in the LIS field.

One wrinkle in this discussion is an RSS-like language called Atom, which works the same as RSS but was developed independently. Most people think of Atom as a version of RSS, although this is inaccurate. However, for practical purposes, the distinction is unimportant: Whether you are using RSS or Atom, you are creating what is commonly known as a "Web feed" or simply as a "feed." A feed is "a document (often XML-based) which contains content items, often summaries of stories or weblog posts with web links to longer versions."[5] The feed is what the user actually subscribes to using an aggregator. In the pages that follow, when I am not specifically discussing RSS or Atom, I'll use "feed" as an umbrella term.

History of Feed Development

The history of feeds is a long and complicated one that has led to the current situation of multiple competing versions and formats. Following is a short version of the history of feeds, which is admittedly convoluted and a bit esoteric. Feel free to skip this section if you're not interested.

In December 1997, Dave Winer of Userland, a software development company, developed and released the scriptingNews format as a way to syndicate information on the Web. Not much was made of the concept until March 1999 when Netscape developed what it dubbed "RSS 0.90." Functionally similar to scriptingNews, RSS 0.90

was designed to work with Netscape's my.netscape.com portal. In June of that same year, Winer updated and released scriptingNews 2.0b1, incorporating the features of Netscape's RSS format and adding some new ones.

In early July 1999, Dan Libby at Netscape reworked RSS into version 0.91, incorporating the changes in scriptingNews in an attempt to establish a single format for syndicating Web content. By the end of the month, Userland had agreed to adopt RSS 0.91 and officially ended development of scriptingNews. The following year, company-supported development of RSS at Netscape came to an end as the company decided to remove itself from the portal business.

In August 2000, an independent group of developers, led by Rael Dornfest, from computer book publisher O'Reilly and Associates proposed what it called RSS 1.0. This product was based on the RDF metadata format[6] and modularized most of the elements of previous RSS versions but was developed independently and thus was considered an entirely new format for syndication. RSS 1.0 was not technically an upgrade of RSS 0.91 and did not supersede the "previous" version.

There were now two different tracks under which RSS was being developed. In December 2002, Userland's Dave Winer released RSS 0.92 as a follow-up to RSS 0.91. Again, this release (which was not a significant upgrade) was not technologically related to the RSS 1.0 product. Winer released a further upgrade to the program, named RSS 2.0, in September 2002. (While in development, this upgrade was referred to as RSS 0.94 but the higher number was assigned to it on release.)

By 2003, with RSS users tired of what were referred to by some as "the RSS wars," Atom (originally named Echo) was developed by a group of "leading service providers, tool vendors and independent developers."[7] Although the end result of Atom feeds is the same as that of both RSS types, Atom was developed from scratch and, unlike either of the competing products, specifically with the needs of bloggers in mind. For example, Atom feeds have made internationalization easier through additional support for non-Latin character sets.[8]

Figure 5.1 shows the history of the development of RSS and Atom.

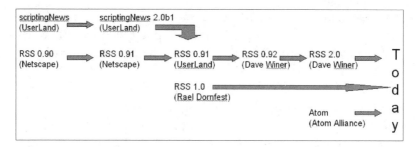

Figure 5.1 History of feed development

What's in a Feed File?

Regardless of what they are called or the version number, feeds are all XML-based languages. That is to say, they are written to conform to the rules of XML (Extensible Markup Language). For those of you familiar with HTML (Hypertext Markup Language), the structure of feeds will look familiar; only the terminology used will be different.[9]

Rather than focus on the details of the differences among the various feed versions, I'm going to walk you through one very basic example of an RSS file. Take a minute to read it and see if you can figure out what each part means. Then read the explanations following the code to see how close you were.

```
<?xml version="1.0"?>
<rss version="0.92">
  <channel>
    <title>travelinlibrarian.info</title>
    <link>http://www.travelinlibrarian.info/</link>
    <description>The blog of Librarian, Trainer, and writer Michael P.
    Sauers</description>
    <lastBuildDate>Tue, 01 Feb 2005 13:23:02 GMT</lastBuildDate>
    <docs>http://backend.userland.com/rss092</docs>
    <managingEditor>msauers@travelinlibrarian.info (Michael
    Sauers)</managingEditor>
    <webMaster> msauers@travelinlibrarian.info (Michael Sauers)</webMaster>
    <image>
      <title>Michael in Lego</title>
      <url>http://travelinlinrarian.info/blog/lego.gif</url>
      <link>http://travelinlinrarian.info/</link>
      <width>155</width>
      <height>238</height>
```

```
    <description>Michael imagined as a Lego person. Create yours at
    http://www.reasonablyclever.com/mini/</description>
  </image>
  <item>
    <title>Firefox 1.1 Delayed</title>
    <link>http://Weblogs.mozillazine.org/ben/archives/007434.html</link>
    <description>According to Ben Godger (lead Firefox engineer) version
    1.1 of Firefox has been delayed and will not be released in March as
    originally scheduled.</description>
    <category domain="http://www.dmoz.org/">Computers: Software:
    Internet: Clients: WWW: Browsers: Firefox</category>
  </item>
  </channel>
</rss>
```

Let's look at the segments of the file one at a time, with a brief description of what the code represents:

- `<?xml version="1.0"?>` – This is the XML Prolog. It indicates that the file is in an XML version 1.0 format. At this time there is only one version of XML.

- `<rss version="…">…</rss>` – This is the root element and contains the rest of the document. The version attribute specifies which version of RSS is being used.

- `<channel>…</channel>` – This is the channel element and contains information about the feed itself. Actual items are not included within this section.

- `<title></title>` – When appearing within the channel element, this is the title for the feed.

- `<link></link>` – When appearing within the channel element, this is the URL for the Web page associated with the feed.

- `<description></description>` – This element should contain a narrative description of the feed.

- `<lastBuildDate></lastBuildDate>` – This contains the date and time stamp from when the file was last updated. Aggregators use this to easily determine if new items have been posted since last checked.

- `<docs></docs>` – This contains the URL of the specifications for the RSS version being used to create this file.

- `<managingEditor></managingEditor>` – This contains the name and/or e-mail address of the person in charge of this feed.

- `<webMaster></webMaster>` – This contains the name and/or e-mail address of the Webmaster for the Web site associated with this feed. This person may or may not be the same as the managing editor.

- `<image>...</image>` – This acts as a container for the elements containing the information about the image (logo) associated with the feed.

- `<title></title>` – When this appears within the image element, this is the title for the image.

- `<url></url>` – This contains the URL of the image file.

- `<link></link>` – When appearing within the image element, this is the URL for the Web page associated with the image.

- `<width></width>` – This contains the width, in pixels, of the image.

- `<height></height>` – This contains the height, in pixels, of the image.

- `<description></description>` – This contains a brief description of the image for accessibility purposes. Should the user's aggregator not support images, the text would be displayed instead.

- `<item>...</item>` – This contains all of the information regarding a single item within the feed. An RSS <item> is the equivalent to a blog post.

- `<title></title>` – When appearing within the item element, this is the title for the individual item.

- `<link></link>` – When appearing within the item element, this is the URL for the Web page associated with the individual item.

- `<description></description>` – A narrative description of the item, this may be a summary of the item or the complete content of the item.

- `<category domain="...">`<`/category>` – This contains the category of the item. The domain attribute contains a URL pointing to the Web site that establishes the category system being used.

Keep in mind that not all of the aforementioned elements will appear in all feed types or versions, and that additional elements may appear. Detailed examples of the most common feed versions are shown in the Appendix.

While some individuals continue to code Web pages by hand, extensive knowledge of code is not required for RSS authors because, in most cases, software generates the code automatically. So there's no need to memorize what you've just read—a basic understanding of the way the code works will serve you well.

Feed Types

I've mentioned already that there are several types of RSS and Atom feeds available. Table 5.1 lists the principal attributes of each version.[10] While I have included all RSS versions in the table to show changes that have been made over time, RSS 2.0 and Atom are the most commonly used today.

You will find that some blogs and other sites offering syndication give you a choice of versions you can use to receive their feeds. I feel that this merely complicates matters for the user, especially when the choices are labeled with RSS version numbers. If given a choice, the only decision of real consequence (in my opinion) is whether to receive a summary feed (just the first few lines of a post) or a complete feed (the whole content of a post). That decision is yours to make; however, anecdotal evidence I'm aware of suggests that most users prefer full feeds to summaries when given the choice.

Identifying Feeds

Now that you have an idea of what feeds look like and how they work, how can you determine whether a site has a feed you can subscribe to? Web authors use two basic methods to indicate the existence of a feed: on screen (via hyperlinks) and behind the scenes (via HTML linking).

On-Screen Feeds

The majority of Web sites that have publicly available feeds make an effort to publicize that fact. Typically, a hyperlink to the

Table 5.1   Features of Various RSS and Atom Versions

RSS 0.90 (Superseded by RSS 0.91)	- Does not support categories on channel or item - Does not support the following elements on the channel: language, copyright, docs, lastBuildDate, managingEditor, pubDate, rating, skipDays, skipHours - Does not support item enclosures - Does not support the following elements on items: author, comments, pubDate
RSS 0.91 (Superseded by RSS 0.92, though still commonly used)	- Does not support categories on channel or item - Does not support the following elements on the channel: language, copyright, docs, lastBuildDate, managingEditor, pubDate, rating, skipDays, skipHours, generator, ttl - Does not support item enclosures - Does not support the following elements on items: author, comments, pubDate - Limited to 15 items - Channel-level metadata only
RSS 0.92 (Superseded by RSS 2.0)	- Supports categories on channel and item - Does not support the following elements on the channel: language, copyright, docs, lastBuildDate, managingEditor, pubDate, rating, skipDays, skipHours, generator, ttl - Supports item enclosures - Does not support the following elements on items: author, comments, pubDate - Unlimited number of items - Allows both channel and item metadata
RSS 2.0	- Supports categories on channel and item - Supports item enclosures - Supports all elements on the channel and items not supported by other versions - Significantly more complex than all other versions - Modularized
RSS 1.0 (Not preceded or superseded by any other RSS versions)	- Does not support categories on channel or item - Does not support the following elements on the channel: language, copyright, docs, lastBuildDate, managingEditor, pubDate, rating, skipDays, skipHours - Does not support item enclosures - Does not support the following elements on items: author, comments, pubDate - Based on RDF (Resource Description Framework) - Modularized
Atom	- Created as a "solution" to the problem of many different RSS versions - Supports all the features of RSS 2.0 but with a more highly defined structure - Automatically generated by the Blogger system - Supported by aggregators

URL of the feed is placed on the page itself. In some cases, an author will place a "syndicate" or "syndicate this site" link on the page. This link either goes directly to the feed or to a page that explains syndication and then provides links to the feeds. (This intermediary page is more typical of sites with many available feeds, such as news sites that provide different feeds for various news categories.)

In most cases, a link to a feed is provided via an orange icon. There is no standard icon, however; different people and companies have created a variety of icons to represent links to feeds. Figure 5.2 shows 25 different feed icons I've found. They're all orange (you'll have to trust me on this) but vary widely in size and visual content. Some icons specify the feed version being used, while others are based on a certain company's implementation of the technology. The key is to look for a small orange icon—if you find one, chances are it's a link to a feed.

Figures 5.3 through 5.6 show various icons and links on Web pages. The examples are circled for easier spotting. As you can see, some are text links and others are icon links, and they can appear anywhere on the page. Some offer users choices between different versions of feeds for the same content.

When it comes to dealing with all of these different feed icons, there is hope. In mid-2005, the Mozilla foundation decided on a new icon (Figure 5.7) for use in the Firefox browser to indicate that the page being viewed has an available feed. To the surprise of many in the technology field, Microsoft announced in late 2005 that it would use the same icon in its next version (version 7) of Internet Explorer. With this unexpected cooperation, a movement has begun to use this single icon as the standard for feeds of all types. More information on this standard and a downloadable collection of versions of this icon can be found on the Feed Icons Web site (www.feedicons.com).

Behind-the-Scenes Feeds

An author can also create a connection between a Web page and a feed by adding some markup in the source code of the page. I call this a "hidden feed" because there isn't necessarily any indication of the feed on the page as viewed by the user. For example, when you do a search in the isbn.nu Web site for the author "koontz, dean" you receive a page of results. What you

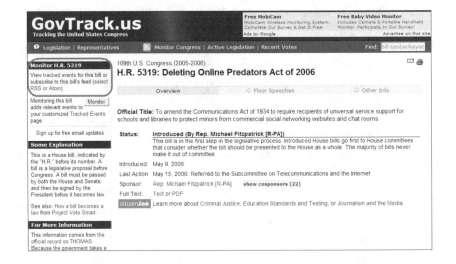

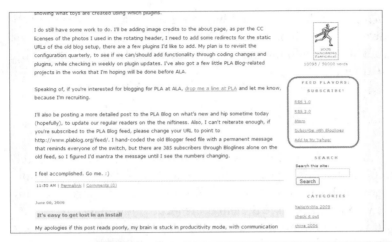

Figure 5.2   Various icons representing an available feed (left, top)

Figure 5.3   Feed link at GovTrack.us (left, middle)

Figure 5.4   Feed icons at Librarian in Black (left, bottom)

Figure 5.5   Feed links at Library Techtonics (above, top)

Figure 5.6   Feed links at Neil Gaiman's Journal (above, middle)

Figure 5.7   Proposed standard feed icon (above, bottom)

don't see is a link to a feed based on the results of that search. However, if you look at the HTML code behind the results page, you will see the following line of code near the beginning of the document:

```
<link rel="alternate" type="application/rss+xml" title="RSS
2.0" href="http://isbn.nu/xmlaisbn/koontz%20dean" />
```

This line of code indicates to the browser that there is an "alternate" view of this page in the form of an RSS 2.0 feed. Short of looking for such a line in the source code of every Web page, there are a few options available to help users locate hidden feeds.

If you're a Firefox user and you get to a page with one of these links, you'll see a small orange icon in the browser's status bar. When you right-click on that icon, you'll be given the opportunity to add this feed to Firefox (as shown in Figure 5.8). We'll discuss in some detail what this means to you as a Firefox user in Chapter 6.

If you're a Bloglines user, you can right-click on a page and select the Bloglines Toolkit, if you have installed it. If the page has a hidden feed, you'll see the option to "Subscribe to this Page" as shown in Figure 5.9. We will cover Bloglines more fully in Chapter 6.

Finding Feeds

If you've been paying attention, you now know a feed when you see one—but poking around the Web hoping to spot a feed icon is not the best use of your time. The first thing you should do is check the blogs you already read to see if they have feeds. But beyond that, let's examine some efficient methods for finding useful feeds.

Mining Blogrolls

A useful technique for finding feeds is to look through the blogrolls (listings of subscribed feeds, described more fully in Chapter 6) of the authors of blogs to which you already subscribe. Chances are that authors of blogs of interest to you are reading other relevant blogs. Click on some of the links and, if the blogs are of interest, see if they have feeds of their own.

Figure 5.8   Finding a hidden feed with Firefox

Figure 5.9   Finding a hidden feed with the Bloglines Toolkit

Searching via Syndic8 and Feedster

Syndic8 and Feedster are Web sites dedicated to indexing blogs and feeds. Syndic8 (Figure 5.10) focuses more on feeds and less on blogs and is the more searchable of the two. Feedster (Figure 5.11) is more blog-oriented than Syndic8, but has recently added a feed-specific search. Although Syndic8 has more features to help the user discover feeds using such categories as "random feeds," "sites we'd like to see syndicated," and "most popular feeds," I find Feedster to be more useful for finding feeds due to its ability to subscribe to a feed of search results. (This feature is discussed in more detail in Chapter 7.)

Figures 5.12 and 5.13 show examples of results for a search on the keyword "library" in Syndic8 and Feedster, respectively. As you

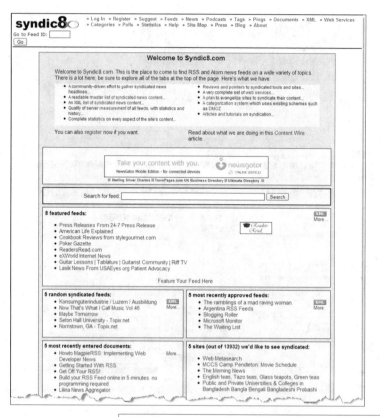

Figure 5.10   Syndic8 home page (top)

Figure 5.11   Feedster home page (bottom)

can see, Syndic8 found 740 results, while Feedster found more than 400,000.

Using a Feed

So, you've found a link to a feed—now, what do you do with it? First, click on the link to see what happens. Depending on your browser and the version of the feed you clicked on, you will see a page akin to any of those shown in Figures 5.14 through 5.17.

In Firefox and IE, when you click on a link to an RSS file, the browser displays that file (Figures 5.14 and 5.15 show the results). By default, the raw code will be displayed. This is the most common result.

In contrast, Atom feeds typically have a style sheet associated with them. This allows the browser to display the content of a feed in a more readable format (as shown in travelinlibrarian.info in Figure 5.16).

Lastly, the folks at Microsoft are hard at work integrating feeds into the next version of Internet Explorer. Figure 5.17 shows an RSS feed as displayed in IE7 beta 2. In this version, IE is automatically applying a default style sheet to any feed that doesn't already have one.

In order to truly take advantage of feeds, you must find and install a program known as an "aggregator." An aggregator will not only take the code and turn it into something more reader-friendly, it will also track a feed, alerting you to new content on a regular basis.

Let's move on to Chapter 6 where we will learn all about aggregators.

Endnotes

1. "The Extensible Markup Language (XML) is a W3C-recommended general-purpose markup language for creating special-purpose markup languages, capable of describing many different kinds of data. It is a simplified subset of SGML. Its primary purpose is to facilitate the sharing of data across different systems, particularly systems connected via the Internet. Languages based on XML (for example, Geography Markup Language (GML), RDF/XML, RSS, MathML, Physical Markup Language (PML), XHTML, SVG, MusicXML and cXML) are defined in a formal way, allowing programs to modify and validate documents in these languages without prior knowledge of

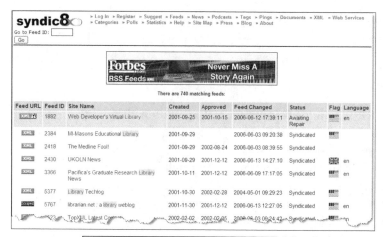

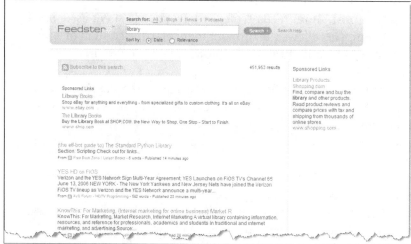

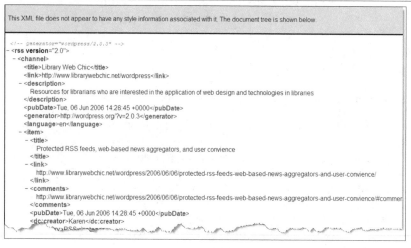

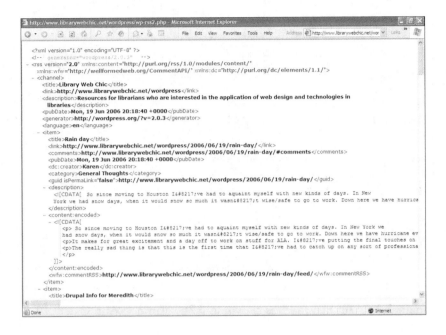

Figure 5.12   Syndic8 results for the search "library" (left, top)

Figure 5.13   Feedster results for the search "library" (left, middle)

Figure 5.14   A raw RSS feed displayed in Firefox (Library Web Chic)
(left, bottom)

Figure 5.15   A raw RSS feed displayed in IE (Library Web Chic)
(above, top)

Figure 5.16   An Atom feed with an associated style sheet
(travelinlibrarian.info) (above, bottom)

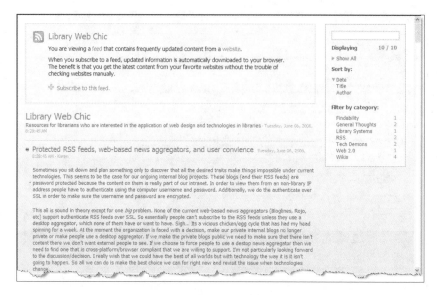

Figure 5.17 An RSS feed as shown in IE7b2 (Library Web Chic)

their form." Wikipedia contributors, 2006, XML. Wikipedia, The Free Encyclopedia. Retrieved 18:53, February 4, 2006 (en.wikipedia.org/w/index.php?title=XML&oldid=38146124).

2. "An aggregator or news aggregator is a type of software that retrieves syndicated Web content that is supplied in the form of a web feed (RSS, Atom and other XML formats), and that is published by weblogs, podcasts, vlogs, and mainstream mass media websites." Wikipedia contributors, 2006, Aggregator. Wikipedia, The Free Encyclopedia. Retrieved 18:56, February 4, 2006 (en.wikipedia.org/w/index.php?title=Aggregator&oldid=37670485).

3. Wikipedia contributors, 2006, RSS (file format). Wikipedia, The Free Encyclopedia. Retrieved 18:55, February 4, 2006 (en.wikipedia.org/w/index.php?title=RSS_(file_format)&oldid=38175285).

4. Alex Barnett. "75 Million RSS users?" June 4, 2005 (blogs.msdn.com/alexbarn/archive/2005/06/04/425277.aspx).

5. Wikipedia contributors, 2006, Web feed. Wikipedia, The Free Encyclopedia. Retrieved 18:58, February 4, 2006 (en.wikipedia.org/w/index.php?title=Web_feed&oldid=36167370).

6. "Resource Description Framework (RDF) is a family of specifications for a metadata model that is often implemented as an application of XML. The RDF family of specifications is maintained by the World Wide Web Consortium (W3C)." Wikipedia contributors, 2006, Resource Description Framework. Wikipedia, The Free Encyclopedia. Retrieved 19:06, February 4, 2006 (en.wikipedia.org/w/index.php?title=Resource_Description_Framework&oldid=38063891).

7. "What is Atom?" (www.atomenabled.org).

8. More details on the history of RSS and Atom can be found at RSS at "Harvard Law: RSS History" (blogs.law.harvard.edu/tech/rss VersionHistory), "AtomEnabled" (www.atomenabled.org), "The Great Syndication Wars" (phaedo.cx/archives/2003/07/15/the-great-syndi cation-wars), and "Six Apart: Why We Need Echo" (www.sixapart. com/log/2003/06/why_we_need_ech.shtml).

9. Those interested in more background on exactly what XML is and does should read Peter Flynn's "The XML FAQ" (www.ucc.ie/xml).

10. A more complete chart can be found on the RSS.net Web site (rss- net.sourceforge.net/documents/version_comparison.html).

Chapter 6

Using an Aggregator

As we learned in Chapter 5, a feed file is made up of a lot of code that will hold little interest for most of us. What we want is the content. Now, it's true that if you open one of these files in your browser you *will* see the content, but it will be surrounded by XML markup (see "The Code" later in the chapter for an example). Even if you are willing to try to read through this clutter, there's no way to determine what's been added since the last time you looked at the file. An aggregator addresses both of these issues, displaying readable text and alerting you to what's new. You will either need to install an aggregator or utilize a Web-based service such as Bloglines before you can start reading feeds. Keep reading to find out more about your options.

What Is an Aggregator?

According to Wikipedia, "a news aggregator is a software or a remotely hosted service that periodically reads a set of news sources, in one of several XML-based formats, finds the new bits, and displays them in reverse-chronological order on a single page." Simply put, an aggregator is what you need to read feeds.

An aggregator:

- Transforms XML markup into a readable and more visually appealing format
- Checks a feed periodically, usually once an hour, for new items
- Alerts the user when a feed has new items and, by default, displays only new items
- Provides hyperlinks to original and/or related articles as provided by the feed's author

- Allows the user to subscribe to multiple feeds, thus enabling receipt of all feed-based information in a single location with a single interface

These features are at the core of an aggregator, though some aggregators offer additional features, such as the ability to save, sort, and post via e-mail.

Types of Aggregators

Currently, aggregators are available in four different types: stand-alone clients, embedded clients, server-based, and Web-based.

Stand-Alone Clients

Stand-alone clients are dedicated feed aggregating programs that are installed on a single computer. Popular stand-alone clients today include Feedreader (Figure 6.1, www.feedreader. com), FeedDemon (Figure 6.2, www.newsgator.com/NGOL Product.aspx?ProdID=FeedDemon), and NewzCrawler (Figure 6.3, www.newzcrawler.com).

Stand-alone clients typically work in a three-pane environment as with most e-mail clients and are easy to learn. Some, such as FeedDemon and Feedreader, are free, while others, such as NewzCrawler, are available for less than $30.

There are two downsides to this type of aggregator. The first is that this is yet another program on your computer that performs just a single function. Second, this type of aggregator locks the subscriber into reading the feeds on a single computer. If you install this type of aggregator at the office, you will not have access to your subscriptions at home or on the road. (One person I know has one aggregator installed on her office computer to handle her work-related subscriptions and one on her home computer to handle her non-work-related subscriptions.)

Embedded Clients

Embedded clients also require downloading and installation on a single computer. However, unlike stand-alone clients, which are dedicated to aggregating feeds, an embedded client adds the

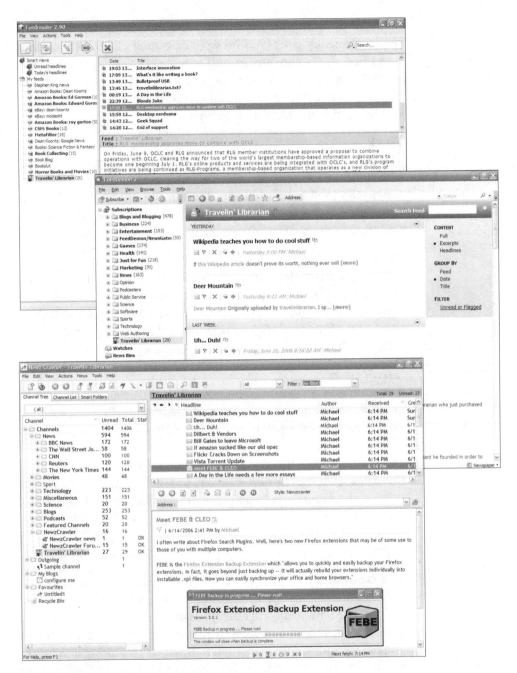

Figure 6.1   Feedreader (top)

Figure 6.2   FeedDemon (middle)

Figure 6.3   NewzCrawler (bottom)

aggregation functionality to another program you're already using—typically your Web browser or e-mail client. While many users find this a convenient option, as with a stand-alone client, you will be locked into reading your feeds on a single computer. Following are descriptions of some popular embedded clients that can be used with different programs.

Pluck

Pluck (www.pluck.com/products/rss-reader.html) integrates into Internet Explorer. Installing Pluck creates an additional button on IE's toolbar that invokes Pluck in the sidebar and gives the user full access to feeds in a standard three-pane view (Figure 6.4). For those who use IE regularly, Pluck is a great free aggregator.

Sage

Sage (sage.mozdev.org) is similar to Pluck but integrates with the Firefox browser. It installs a new button on the toolbar that invokes the program in the browser's sidebar. Sage also uses a three-pane interface (Figure 6.5). For Firefox users, Sage is currently the best free aggregator in this category.

intraVnews

intraVnews (www.intravnews.com) integrates into Microsoft Outlook, enabling the user to read feeds right alongside e-mail (Figure 6.6). Since many users view their feeds as an alternative to e-mail, integrating the two activities in a single program is an efficient option. The only significant difference from other options in this category is that intraVnews may not be free. At the time of this writing, the program is free for at-home, personal use but to use it "on a company or government PC, you need to purchase a Standard License." The per-license cost starts at $24.95 and decreases depending on the number of licenses being purchased.

Live Bookmarks

As another embedded client option, the Firefox browser now supports RSS natively. This means that Firefox allows the user to subscribe to a feed and have it placed within that user's bookmarks as a folder, with each item in the feed appearing as a bookmark. Although this option is free and very easy to use (and no discrete installation is required as with the other embedded options we've covered), experience teaches us that it is not the best solution. Integration with bookmarks means that all a user

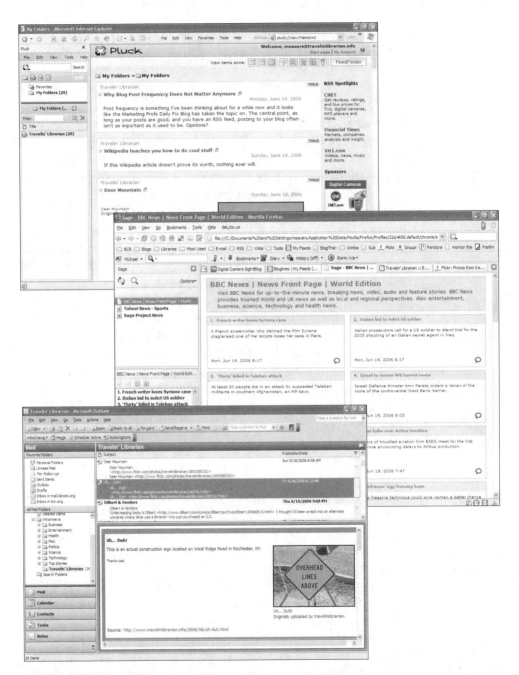

Figure 6.4   Pluck (top)
Figure 6.5   Sage (middle)
Figure 6.6   intraVnews (bottom)

will see of a particular item is its headline. To see the complete text of an item, the user must click to open it. Furthermore, when viewing the bookmarks, you are not able to distinguish between unread (e.g., new) and read items.

Server-Based

Server-based aggregators are also downloaded and installed; however, unlike the two types of client programs, server-based aggregators are installed on a Web server and then accessed via a Web browser. Server-based options, such as Feed On Feeds (minutillo. com/steve/feedonfeeds), solve the biggest problem with the client options: Since feeds are accessed via the Web, the user is no longer tied to a single computer. Once the program has been installed, all you need to do is fire up a browser from any Internet-connected computer and enter the URL of the aggregator.

The use of server-based aggregators does, however, pose some problems. First, you must have access to a server on which the program can be installed. Secondly, and perhaps more importantly, you need to have some technical expertise to install and configure such a program. Provided both these requirements are met, server-based aggregators may be your best option.

Web-Based

Although server-based options are, in fact, Web-based options, there is a key difference between them: In the case of Web-based aggregators, it is not necessary to install or configure any software. The Web-based aggregator is a service offered by a third party that allows you to subscribe to and read feeds. The most popular of this type is Bloglines (www.bloglines.com; Figure 6.7). To use this free Web-based service, the user creates an account and then logs in to perform all feed-related activities.

Services such as Bloglines, I believe, effectively address all the problems posed by the other options. First, they do not require installation of additional software on the user's computer or server. Second, unlike with server-based options, the user doesn't need any technical expertise to get the program working. Third, the work of reading the feeds is done almost completely by the servers of the service-owner's company. Finally, and most important, Web-based aggregators do not tie the user to a single computer. I have a Bloglines account myself and as long as I have an

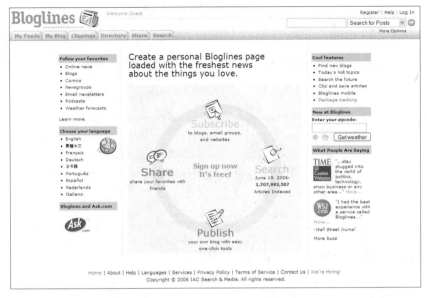

Figure 6.7   Bloglines

Internet connection, I can read my feeds. For me, this is just about anywhere, as I have a Web browser on my cellphone and regularly access my Bloglines account while at the airport waiting for a flight.[1]

As our focus in this chapter is on how to receive and read feeds with a minimum investment in time, effort, and expense, I'll direct your attention to Bloglines for the rest of this chapter. Even if you believe that one of the other options is a better solution for you, I suggest you read on or at least scan: Most aggregators work in roughly the same manner, so a tour of the Bloglines system should prove helpful regardless of your final choice.

Bloglines

As already mentioned, Bloglines is a free Web-based aggregator. It was started as an independent company several years ago and was purchased by Ask Jeeves in February 2005. Bloglines enables you to subscribe to feeds in any RSS format as well as Atom feeds with complete transparency. It includes features and options for e-mailing posts, feed organization, new item notification, and built-in blogging. In this section, I'll walk you through the process

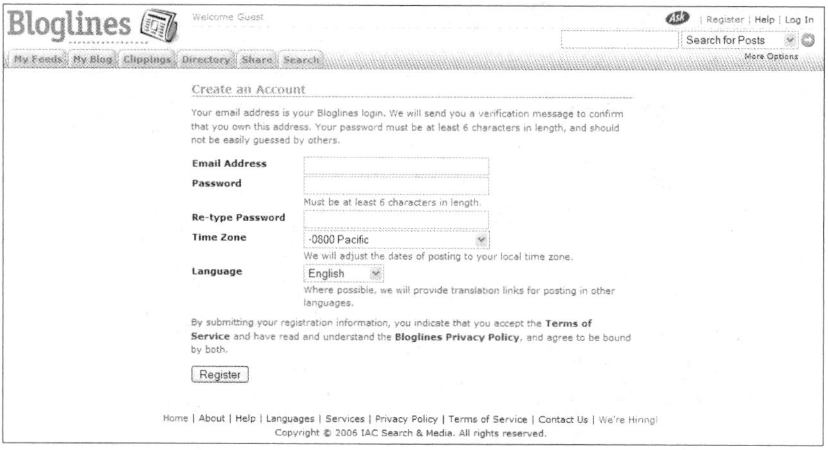

Figure 6.8   Create a Bloglines account

of setting up a Bloglines account and subscribing to feeds, and will also cover a number of useful Bloglines features.

Creating an Account

When you first enter the Bloglines site, you'll see the service's home page. All the features shown here will be available to you once you have created your account. We'll start with the "Register" link in the upper-right corner. Click on it and you'll be taken to the Create an Account screen (Figure 6.8).

In order to set up your account, you need to complete the following fields:

- *E-mail Address.* Enter your e-mail address here. This will become your "username" for logging into your account. It will also pre-set the return address on any postings you mail to others from within Bloglines.[2]

- *Password.* Choose a password for your account. The password must be at least six characters in length.

- *Re-type Password.* Type your new password again to confirm you typed it correctly.

- *Time Zone.* Choose the time zone in which you reside. Bloglines uses this information to adjust the time of postings as you receive them to match your own time zone. For example, if someone in San Francisco makes a post at 8 A.M. and you are in New York, you will see the time of the posting as 11 A.M.

- *Language.* Choose your default language from the list of supported languages. If you receive a post in another language, Bloglines may offer you a link to translate that post into your default language.

Once you have filled in all six fields, click on the "Register" button to create your Bloglines account.

Once your account has been created, Bloglines will send you an e-mail to the address you supplied. Before you may start to use your account, you must click on the URL supplied in that message to confirm you are who you say you are.

Once you've completed the confirmation, you will be presented with a list of sample feeds to subscribe to. Feel free at this time to select any that interest you. Remember, you can always unsubscribe from them later.

Subscribing to Your First Feed

As discussed in Chapter 5, there are two different ways to identify whether a site has a feed. In most cases, it's one of many different orange icons or it might be just an "RSS" or "Syndicate this site" text-based hyperlink. Once you've found a link to a feed, subscribing is easy. For your first time, though, I'll have you subscribe to the feed for my Flickr photographs.

Open a new window or tab in your browser and go to www.flickr.com/photos/travelinlibrarian. Scroll to the bottom of the page and find the syndication icon and "Feed" link (Figure 6.9). Right-click on the icon and select "Copy Link Location" (Figure 6.10). The exact wording of the selection from this menu will vary from browser to browser.

Now switch back to the window containing Bloglines and look for the blank field in the upper-right corner of the page. Paste the copied URL into that field and select "Subscribe to URL" from the dropdown list immediately to the left (Figure 6.11). Then click on the blue-and-white arrow icon to the right. The page that comes up will allow you to customize how Bloglines tracks this feed (Figure 6.12).

This first section on this page is labeled "Available Feeds." Some sites offer several versions of their feeds, such as summaries or full text. Bloglines can detect multiple versions of the same feed and

Figure 6.9   The XML icon on travelinlibrarian.info (top)

Figure 6.10   Select "Copy Link Location" from the menu (middle)

Figure 6.11   Subscribe to URL (bottom)

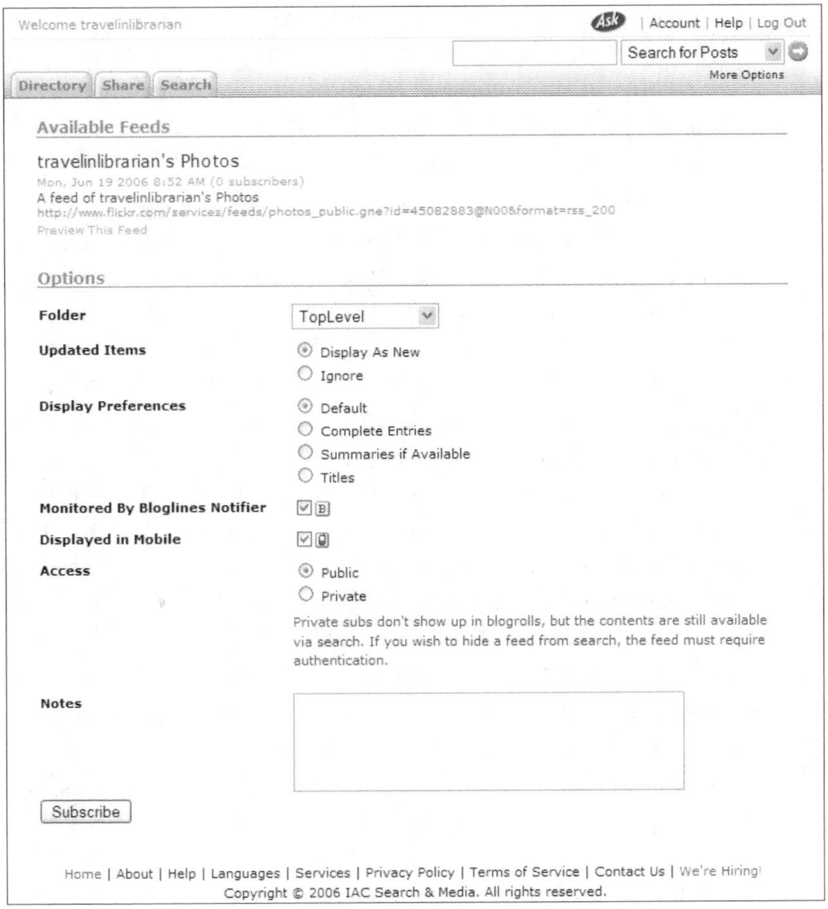

Figure 6.12   Customizing a new subscription

offers you the option to choose which one to subscribe to. In the case of TravelinLibrarian.info, there is only one version of the feed available.

The next section is labeled "Options" and contains the following choices:

- *Folder*. Bloglines allows you to organize your subscriptions into folders, similar to how you organize bookmarks in your browser. Since this is your first subscription, you only have two choices: "Top Level" and "New Folder …". "Top Level" adds the subscription to your list but does not place it in a folder. "New Folder …" allows you to create a folder that does not yet exist in your account and places the new subscription in that folder. When you create additional folders, they will also appear on this list and will be selectable for future new subscriptions. (Folders may be created and manipulated in another way that we'll be covering later in the chapter.)

- *Updated Items.* You have two choices here—"Display As New" (default) and "Ignore." "Display As New" instructs Bloglines to notify you of old postings that have been changed by their author as if they were new postings (by bolding the name of the subscription and displaying the number of new items). Setting this option to "Ignore" will prevent this notification.

- *Display Preferences.* There are four options for displaying content of individual items in this feed: "Default," "Complete Entries," "Summaries if Available," and "Titles." These options control how much of each post Bloglines will show you. "Default" instructs Bloglines to show you content based on the setting of the feed's creator. The other three options override the feed creator's settings and display the complete text, the post summaries, or just the post titles, accordingly.

- *Monitored By Bloglines Notifier.* This is a user-installed browser plug-in that will notify you of new postings in your subscribed feeds even if you are not at the Bloglines site. (We'll cover this in detail later in the chapter.) This choice allows you to decide whether or not this feed should be monitored by the Notifier plug-in. If you do not want it to be monitored, uncheck the box. Leaving this box checked, even if you do not have the Bloglines Notifier installed, will not cause any problems.

- *Displayed in Mobile.* Bloglines has a special low-bandwidth version of its service for those with small-screen mobile devices such as cellphones (www.bloglines.com/mobile). This option controls whether this feed should be displayed in the mobile version of your account. For example, I typically uncheck this option when subscribing to a Flickr feed since such feeds contain images that use much more bandwidth than text-based feeds. Podcasts are another type of feed that most people would not want sent to their cellphones.

- *Access.* Bloglines allows you to make your blogroll (the list of feeds you subscribe to, defined later under "Creating a

Blogroll") either public or private. The default is public, so if you don't want to share this information, change the setting to private.

- *Notes*. This field allows you to add your own notes about the subscription. These notes are not made public and can only be seen if you edit your subscription.

Once you've set all of the options appropriately, click on the "Subscribe" button at the bottom of the page to add the subscription to your Bloglines account. At any point in the future, you may change the choices you made, unsubscribe from the feed, or even change the name of the feed as displayed to you.

Other Methods for Subscribing

As a Bloglines user, you have two other methods available to subscribe to a feed. You may find one of these methods easier than the method just discussed.

Subscribe with Bloglines

As you start looking for new feeds to subscribe to, you'll notice a link on some pages—as text, a button, or an icon—labeled "Bloglines" (Figure 6.13). This is a special link to a site's feed that automates the process of subscribing to that feed with Bloglines. As a Bloglines user, you need only to click on the link and you will be taken to the Feed Options screen previously discussed. (If you aren't already logged into your Bloglines account when you click the link, you will be asked to do so at that time.)

If you are a blogger and want to add this feature to your own blog, you can do so by clicking on the "Get a Subscribe to Bloglines Button" link at the bottom left of the Bloglines frame. You will be asked to choose one of the pre-designed buttons, enter the URL of your blog's feed, and click the "Generate HTML" button (Figure 6.14). You can then paste that code into your blog's template wherever you want the button to appear.

Bloglines Toolkit

Also available to Bloglines users is what is known as the Bloglines Toolkit. Once downloaded and installed, the toolkit adds features to your browser that facilitate interaction with Bloglines. The features available vary from browser to browser but a common feature is the

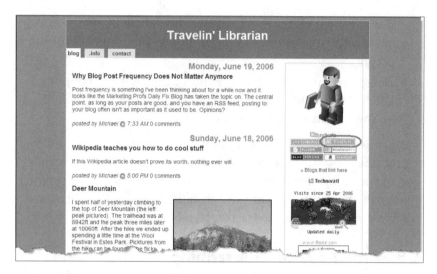

Figure 6.13   "Subscribe with Bloglines" button

ability to easily subscribe to a feed without needing to use the method described earlier.

For example, when I find a link to a feed in my browser (Firefox), I right-click on that link, select the Bloglines Toolkit, and click "Subscribe to this Link" (Figure 6.15). As with the "Subscribe with Bloglines" button, I am taken directly into the Feed Options screen within my Bloglines account. The Firefox version can be found at www.bloglines.com/help/firefox; other versions of the toolkit are available at bloglines.com/about/notifier.

Bloglines Interface

Figure 6.16 shows my view of the basic Bloglines interface. Bloglines uses a frames-based design that splits the browser window into a left pane and a right pane. (In some screenshots shown in this chapter, I've shown only one side or the other in order to focus on the topic being discussed.) The left pane shows the list of feeds you're subscribed to and any folders you may have created. The right frame displays the content of the selected feed or folder. Before you select a folder or feed to view, Bloglines will display one of several help screens.

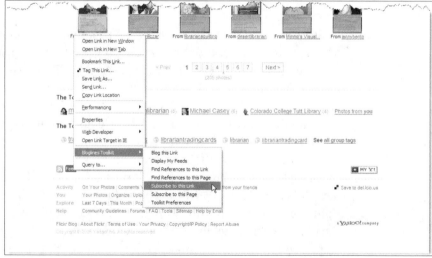

Figure 6.14   Creating a "Subscribe with Bloglines" button (top)
Figure 6.15   Bloglines toolkit in Firefox (bottom)

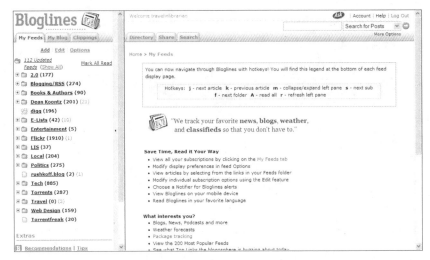

Figure 6.16   Basic Bloglines interface

Reading Feeds

Bloglines checks feeds hourly. When new items appear in a feed to which you subscribe, the name of the feed will appear bold-faced and the number of new items available will be listed to the right of the title. Most of my feeds have been organized into folders. Figure 6.16 shows 37 new items in my LIS folder, which is the total number of new items for all of the feeds in that folder.

To read the new items in a single feed, click on the name of the feed in the left frame; the new items for that feed will be displayed in the right frame (Figure 6.17). If you click on a folder, all of the new items for the feeds within that folder will be displayed in the right frame (Figure 6.18). To open and close folders, just click on the plus or minus sign to the left of the folder name. Once you have displayed new items within a feed or a folder, they are no longer considered new and will not automatically be displayed by Bloglines again.

If you select a feed that has no new items, you have the option to retrieve old posts. Figure 6.19 shows that you can display posts based on the time frame—from the last session to the last six hours to the last month—or you can display all of the items in the feed. This is somewhat dependent on the feed itself. For example, if you

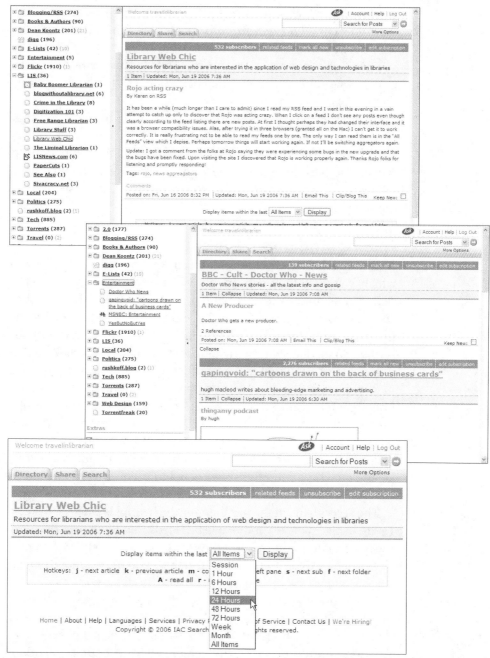

Figure 6.17   Displaying a single feed (top)

Figure 6.18   Displaying the contents of a folder (middle)

Figure 6.19   Timeframe choices for retrieving old posts (bottom)

choose to view all of the posts from the past month, yet the feed itself only contains posts from the past week, you will see only the past week's items.

There are other, more reliable methods for retrieving old posts. Check out e-mailing and clipping posts later in this chapter for further details.

The left frame will update itself periodically to show you that new posts have arrived. If you get impatient, click on the "My Feeds" tab at the top of the left frame. This will force Bloglines to refresh the left frame and report any newly available items. This tab also allows you to return to your feeds from other sections of the Bloglines system.

Finding Additional Feeds

To find additional feeds, start by clicking on one of the feeds to which you're already subscribed. When the feed appears in the right frame, notice the blue bar just above the feed's title. This bar contains two links that can assist you in finding additional feeds that may be of interest. The first link shows the number of subscribers to the feed within the Bloglines system. If you click on this link, a list of the Bloglines users that subscribe to this feed and have public profiles will come up (Figure 6.20 shows this list for the Copyfight feed). How does this help? In most cases, a user's public profile will include his or her blogroll. Click a username and you'll be taken to that user's blogroll (assuming this feature hasn't turned off). By looking at the blogrolls of subscribers with interests similar to your own, you might find new blogs you'd be interested in reading yourself.

The second link in the bar that may be helpful is labeled "Related Feeds." This link takes you to a list of feeds that Bloglines considers topically related to the feed you were just viewing (Figure 6.21 shows the related feeds for Copyfight). From here you have options to read a description, view the feed, and subscribe to the feed.

In addition to these two links, Bloglines provides a search function that allows you to keyword-search all of the feeds to which Bloglines users subscribe. To search this index, find the text box in the upper-right corner of the screen, type in your keyword(s), make sure the dropdown list to the left says "Search for Feeds," and click the blue-and-white arrow to the right of the text box. Figure 6.22 shows a search result for the phrase "public library."

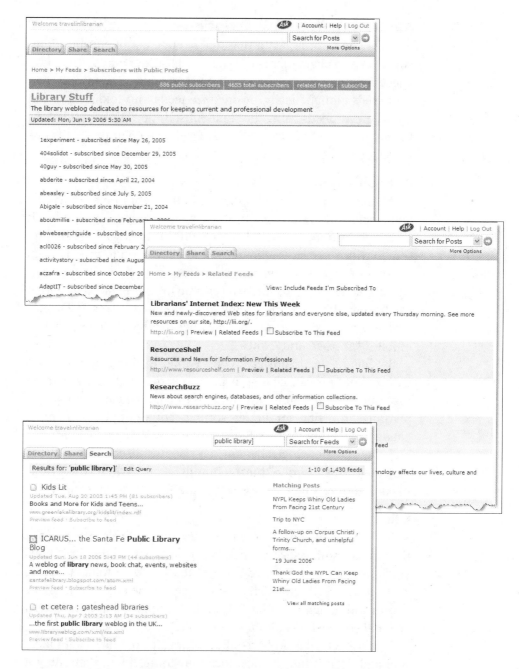

Figure 6.20   Displaying other subscribers (top)

Figure 6.21   Related feeds (middle)

Figure 6.22   Search results for "public library" (bottom)

Managing Your Subscriptions

Once you've amassed a reasonably large list of subscriptions, you'll need to begin managing your feed list. You may want to give a feed a different name (one that has some meaning to you), sort your feeds alphabetically, or organize feeds into folders. You can manage your feeds using the "Edit Subscription" link found along the top of the right frame of the My Feeds screen or the "Edit" link at the top of the left frame.

Edit Subscription

When you open a feed for display in the right frame, a blue bar appears just above the feed's title. One of the links on that bar is "Edit Subscription." When you click on this link, you will be presented with a screen (Figure 6.23) that allows you to modify eight features of that feed (seven of which you saw when you originally subscribed to the feed; see "Subscribing to Your First Feed" earlier in the chapter): "Name," "Folder," "Updated Items," "Display Preferences," "Monitored By Bloglines Notifier," "Displayed in Mobile," "Access," and "Notes."

By default, feeds are given the name assigned by the feed's author, but you can change it here to something that has more meaning for you (should the author's title not be clear enough) or rearrange the title for better sorting. For example, you might change "A Library Writer's Blog" to "Library Writer's Blog, A" so it alphabetizes more logically. You can also unsubscribe from a feed using the "Unsubscribe" button on this screen. When you're done making your changes, click the "Update" button to save them.

Edit

In the left frame of the My Feeds screen, you'll also see a bar at the top containing several links. When you click on the "Edit" link, you'll be presented with your list of feeds and/or folders (Figure 6.24). To select any item, click on it once. The selected item will be shown with a light blue background. To rename that item click it again. If you wish to edit that item's details, double-click on it.

To move a feed from or to a folder, drag it from its current location and drop it into its new location. To delete an item, drag it onto one of the trash icons located at the top and bottom of the window. To create a new folder, just click on the "New Folder" icon and name your folder.

Choose additional actions by clicking on the "Choose Operation ..." dropdown list (Figure 6.25). Select which items you would like to affect, select one of the actions from the list, and click "Submit" to perform that action. Available actions are:

- *Sort: A-Z.* Alphabetizes selected folders and feeds. Feeds and folders on the same level will be sorted as equals.

- *Sort: Z-A.* Alphabetizes selected folders and feeds in reverse order. Feeds and folders on the same level will be sorted as equals.

- *Sort: Unread.* Sorts selected folders and feeds so that those with the highest number of unread items will appear at the top of the list.

- *Sort: Oldest First.* Sorts selected folders and feeds so that those you've been subscribed to the longest are at the top.

- *Sort: Newest First.* Sorts selected folders and feeds so that those you've been subscribed to the shortest are at the top.

- *Mark Public.* Sets all of the selected feeds and folders available on your blogroll for public view. This is the default setting.

- *Mark Private.* Removes all of the selected feeds and folders from your blogroll, making them invisible to the public.

- *Notify: Off.* Instructs the Bloglines Notifier (assuming you have installed it) to ignore the selected feeds and folders. If you haven't installed the Bloglines Notifier, this option will have no effect regardless of the setting you've chosen.

- *Notify: On.* Instructs the Bloglines Notifier (assuming you have installed it) to pay attention to the selected feeds and folders. If you haven't installed the Bloglines Notifier, this option will have no effect regardless of the setting you've chosen.

- *Mobile: Displayed.* Instructs Bloglines to display the selected feeds and folders in the mobile version.

- *Mobile: Hidden.* Instructs Bloglines not to display the selected feeds and folders in the mobile version.

Once you've finished making your changes on the Edit screen, return to reading your feeds by clicking on the "(Finished)" link.

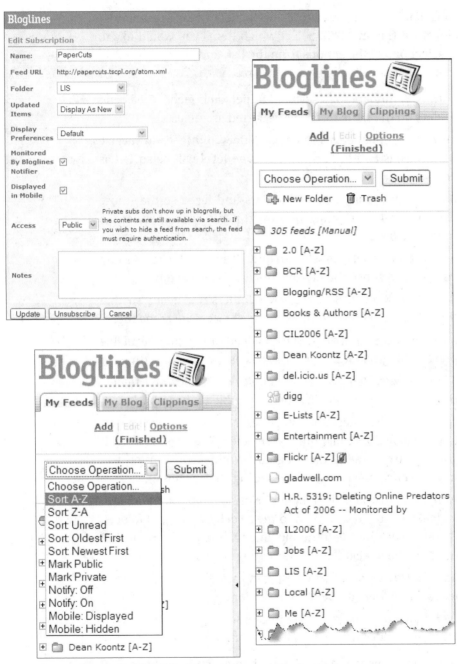

Figure 6.23   Edit Subscription screen (top)

Figure 6.24   Edit screen (middle)

Figure 6.25   "Choose Operation ..." dropdown list (bottom)

Import and Export Subscriptions

At the bottom of the Edit screen, there are two links in the Extras section labeled "Import Subscriptions" and "Export Subscriptions" (Figure 6.26).

Clicking on the "Export Subscriptions" link will open a new window in your browser containing an XML file that lists all of your folders and feeds (Figure 6.27). You can then save this file (with an .xml extension) and give it to others for importing into their Bloglines account.

Once others receive your XML file, they'll need to click on the "Import Subscriptions" link, browse for the file, and click the "Import" button (Figure 6.28). All of the feeds and folders in the XML file will appear in their account and they'll be subscribed to all of those feeds.

Exporting your feeds may not always be that easy. Problems may arise due to the fact that XML is a very specific language and one small mistake will cause the export to fail. Figure 6.29 shows an example of what happened to me when I tried to export my feeds while writing this chapter. Unless you're familiar with XHTML and XML, this error may not be clear, but it's basically telling me that the ampersand (&) in the name of one of my folders is not acceptable. (In XML, the ampersand character means something special and should never be followed by a space. "&" is the XML representation of the ampersand character.) To solve this problem, I needed to edit the name of that folder to read "Books & Authors." If you run into an error like this and can't figure out the meaning on your own, try talking to your Webmaster.

Options

The "Options" link found at the top of the left frame will open the Feed Options screen in the right frame (Figure 6.30). The fact that this page opens in the right frame and does not give you the ability to select feeds or folders means that any changes made here will affect *all* of the feeds within your account. You have the following options:

- *Open Links In.* There are three options here: "Open in New Window," "Open in Same Window," and "Reuse New Window." These options control what happens when you click on a link within a feed. When you select the "Open in New Window"

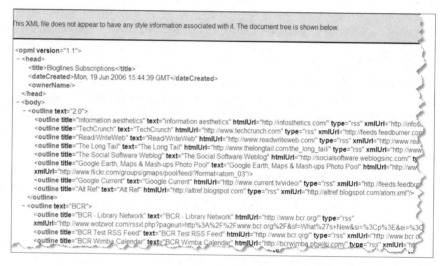

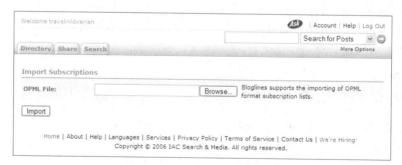

Figure 6.26   Import and export subscription links (top)

Figure 6.27   An exported subscription list (middle)

Figure 6.28   Importing subscriptions (bottom)

```
XML Parsing Error: not well-formed
Location: http://www.bloglines.com/export
Line Number 25, Column 28:

    <outline title="Books & Authors">
---------------------------^
```

Figure 6.29   An export parsing error

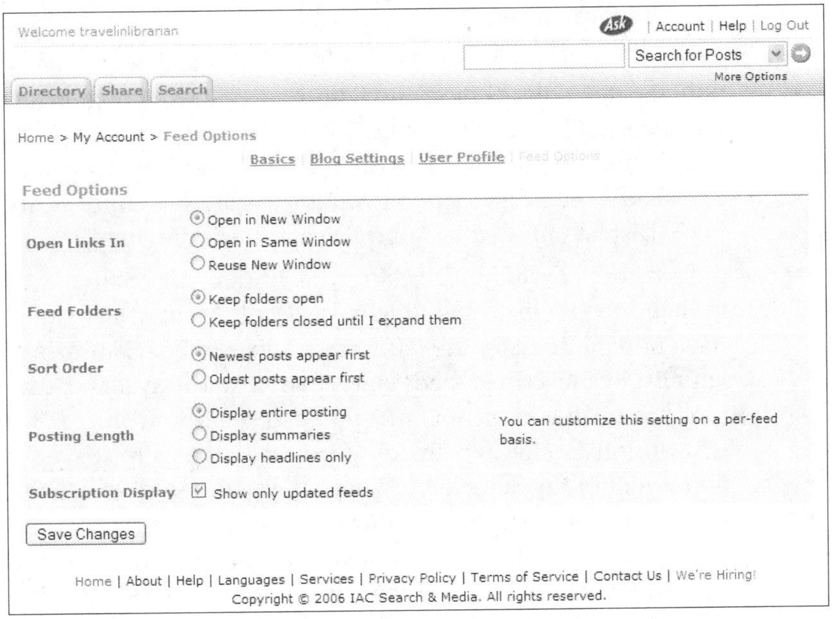

Figure 6.30   Feed Options screen

option, all links will open in their own separate window (i.e., clicking five links will result in five new windows). Selecting "Open in Same Window" will open links in the window you're currently using, overwriting the Bloglines screen. Selecting the "Reuse New Window" option causes the first link you select to open in a new window and all subsequent links to open in that same new window (i.e., clicking on five links will result in only one new window).

- *Feed Folders.* There are two options here: "Keep folders open" and "Keep folders closed until I expand them." If you choose to keep your folders open, when you refresh the left frame while a folder is open, it will stay open. Choosing to keep them closed will close all open folders when you refresh the left window.

- *Sort Order*. The two options here, "Newest posts appear first" and "Oldest posts appear first," control the order in which individual posts are displayed. "Newest posts ..." is the default and shows you posts in the traditional reverse-chronological order. "Oldest posts ..." will reverse that and show you posts in chronological order.

- *Posting Length*. Although you've already seen this setting in both the new subscription and Edit Feed screens, changing the posting length here affects all of the feeds in your account. You can change the posting length on individual feeds by accessing that feed's "Edit Subscription" options ("Display entire posting," "Display summaries," and "Display headlines only").

- *Subscription Display*. Checking the option for "Show only updated feeds" instructs Bloglines to only display feeds that have unread items in the left frame. This can be useful when your list of subscribed feeds starts to exceed the available display space on your screen. (As you can see from Figure 6.30, this option is checked in my account. I typically see only about half of my 300+ list of feeds at any time.) If you check this option, you will see a "(Show All)" link to the right of the top folder in the left pane. Clicking on this will turn off the option, showing you all of your feeds until you refresh your feed list.

Unsubscribing From a Feed

Although you won't find an unsubscribing option under the three previously mentioned links, I'm covering this here as a feed management issue. To unsubscribe from a feed, select the feed so it's being displayed in the right frame and click on the "Unsubscribe" link in the blue bar above the feed's title. You will be asked to confirm (Figure 6.31) and, on confirmation, the feed will be removed from your account.

There are many reasons for unsubscribing from a feed. For example, you may no longer be interested in what a particular blogger has to say. Other types of feeds are designed to be used only for a limited length of time. Once they have outlived their usefulness,

Figure 6.31   Unsubscribe confirmation

unsubscribing will allow you to keep your list of subscribed feeds uncluttered with useless items.

E-mail Subscriptions

Bloglines also offers the option to receive e-mail as if it were a feed. In order to do this, you must first create what Bloglines calls an "E-mail Subscription." Click on the "Create E-mail Subscriptions" link in the Extras section at the bottom of the My Feeds screen (Figure 6.32) and you will be taken to the E-mail Subscriptions screen in the right frame (Figure 6.33).

The first section on the screen explains how e-mail subscriptions work. The next section shows your current e-mail subscriptions, if you have any. The last section is what you need to fill out to create an e-mail subscription. There are five fields to complete: Name, Folder, Monitored by Bloglines Notifier, Access, and Notes. Most of these fields should look familiar since they're the same fields you fill out when you subscribe to a feed. The difference in this case is that you're asked to name the subscription. This is necessary since you're the creator of this "feed."

Once you have completed all of the fields and clicked on the "Create E-mail Subscription" button, this page will reload and update the section showing your current e-mail subscriptions. Figure 6.34 shows my results.

Use this newly generated e-mail address as you would any other e-mail address—give it to friends or use it to subscribe to an electronic mailing list. Mail sent to this e-mail address will appear in your Bloglines account just as feed items do.

For each e-mail received, you have the option to "Reply," "Forward," "Delete," or "View Headers." Be aware that any e-mail sent via these options will show your Bloglines e-mail address as the return address.

Saving Posts for Later

As previously discussed, once a feed item has been viewed, it essentially disappears from the system. Bloglines offers three ways to store particular items more permanently for later retrieval: "E-mail," "Keep New," and "Clipping."

E-mail

E-mailing a post does exactly what it implies. Bloglines takes the content of a post and e-mails it to the recipient of your choice (including yourself). By sending this e-mail you are, in effect, making a copy of the post to be stored outside the Bloglines system.

To e-mail a post, display the post and click the "E-mail This" link (Figure 6.35) just to the right of the date/time. Once clicked a new window will appear with the E-mail This interface (Figure 6.36). The From: field will be automatically filled in with the e-mail address associated with your account. The subject line will be "Bloglines –" followed by the title of the post. Complete the To: field, add a message if you'd like, and then click the "Send E-mail" button. When the e-mail has been sent, you'll be notified on-screen and may then close the window.

Keep New

The "Keep New" checkbox, located to the far right of a post's date/time stamp (Figure 6.37), instructs Bloglines to leave the post in the feed indefinitely even though you've already read it (in essence, to consider the post "new" until the box is unchecked). To keep a post new, just check the box.

Once you've instructed Bloglines to keep an item new, the number of "Kept New" items will be displayed in a light font in parentheses to the right of the feed name and the folder that feed is located in. For example, Figure 6.38 shows that I have one item that has been "kept new" in the BlogJunction feed, and therefore, in my LIS folder.

Clipping

Another way to save your posts for later is to "clip" them. The "Clippings" tab (at the top of the left frame, next to the "My Feeds" tab) is like a folder where you can store posts you want to keep, much like a file folder in which you might store physical newspaper clippings. To clip a post, choose a post from one of your feeds. At the bottom of the post between the "E-mail This" link and the "Keep New" checkbox, you'll find a "Clip/Blog This" link. Click on the link and the Clipping screen will appear (Figure 6.39).

This screen actually has two purposes: to create clippings and to post to a Bloglines-based blog. To create a clipping, make sure the dropdown list in the bottom-right corner of the window reads "Clippings folder" and click the "Save to" button. You may want to edit the item's title in case the author's title isn't clear enough. If you decide not to clip the item, click the "Cancel" button.

When you're done clipping the post, you'll be presented with a confirmation screen, which you can close. Click on the "Clippings" tab and you will see a link to the post you just saved. Under the "Clippings" tab, you'll see links for "Edit," "Reorder/Sort," and "Options." These three links work the same way they do under the "My Feeds" tab but affect your clippings instead of your feeds.

Managing Your Account

Now that you are getting the hang of using Bloglines to subscribe to, read, organize, and save items from feeds, let's talk about managing your Bloglines account. The options are broken down into these categories: "Basics," "User Profile," "Blog Settings," and "Feed Options." They can all be accessed via the "Account" link in the upper-right corner of the right frame.

Basics

The Basics screen (Figure 6.40) is made up of the following sections:

- *Change E-mail Address.* This field displays the e-mail address currently associated with your account. To change it, edit the field's contents accordingly and click the "Change E-mail" button.

- *Change Password.* This field lets you change your account password. To do so, enter your new password twice and click on the "Change Password" button.

- *Other Account Settings.* This section contains four options. Three of the four options—"Time Zone," "Language," and "Newsletter"—are fields you set when you created your account. You may change those options here. One new option

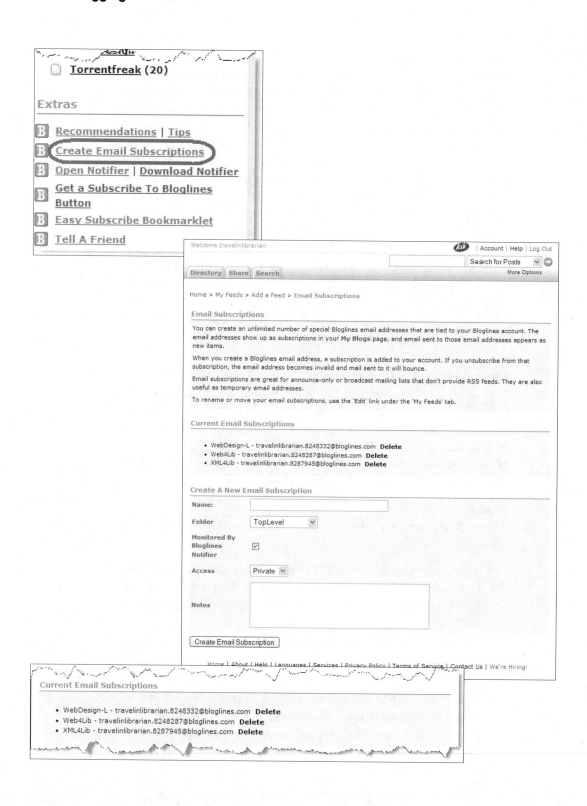

Torrentfreak (20)

Extras

Recommendations | Tips
Create Email Subscriptions
Open Notifier | Download Notifier
Get a Subscribe To Bloglines
Button
Easy Subscribe Bookmarklet
Tell A Friend

Welcome travelinlibrarian   Ask | Account | Help | Log Out

Search for Posts

Directory Share Search   More Options

Home > My Feeds > Add a Feed > Email Subscriptions

Email Subscriptions

You can create an unlimited number of special Bloglines email addresses that are tied to your Bloglines account. The email addresses show up as subscriptions in your **My Blogs** page, and email sent to those email addresses appears as new items.

When you create a Bloglines email address, a subscription is added to your account. If you unsubscribe from that subscription, the email address becomes invalid and mail sent to it will bounce.

Email subscriptions are great for announce-only or broadcast mailing lists that don't provide RSS feeds. They are also useful as temporary email addresses.

To rename or move your email subscriptions, use the 'Edit' link under the 'My Feeds' tab.

Current Email Subscriptions

- WebDesign-L - travelinlibrarian.8248332@bloglines.com **Delete**
- Web4Lib - travelinlibrarian.8248287@bloglines.com **Delete**
- XML4Lib - travelinlibrarian.8287945@bloglines.com **Delete**

Create A New Email Subscription

Name:

Folder   TopLevel

Monitored By
Bloglines   ☑
Notifier

Access   Private

Notes

Create Email Subscription

Home | About | Help | Languages | Services | Privacy Policy | Terms of Service | Contact Us | We're Hiring!

Current Email Subscriptions

- WebDesign-L - travelinlibrarian.8248332@bloglines.com **Delete**
- Web4Lib - travelinlibrarian.8248287@bloglines.com **Delete**
- XML4Lib - travelinlibrarian.8287945@bloglines.com **Delete**

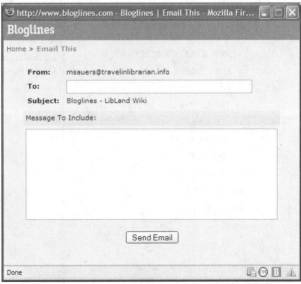

Figure 6.32   "Create E-mail Subscriptions" link (left, top)

Figure 6.33   E-mail Subscriptions screen (left, middle)

Figure 6.34   Current e-mail subscriptions list (left, bottom)

Figure 6.35   "E-mail This" link (above, top)

Figure 6.36   E-mail This interface (above, bottom)

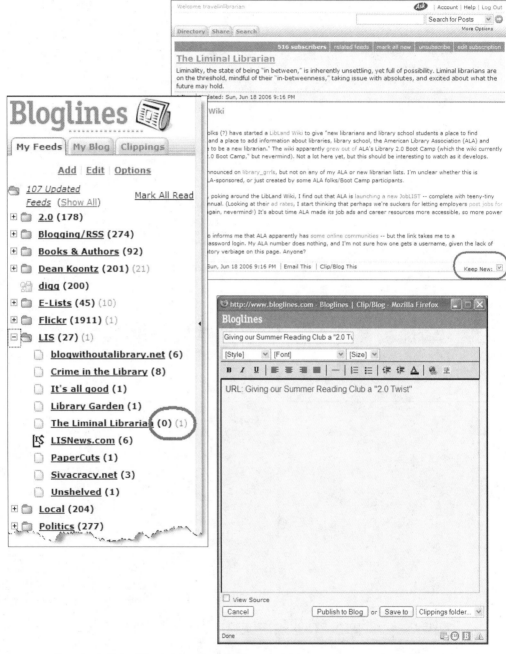

Figure 6.37   "Keep New" checkbox (top)

Figure 6.38   Display of an item that has been "kept new" (middle)

Figure 6.39   Clipping screen (bottom)

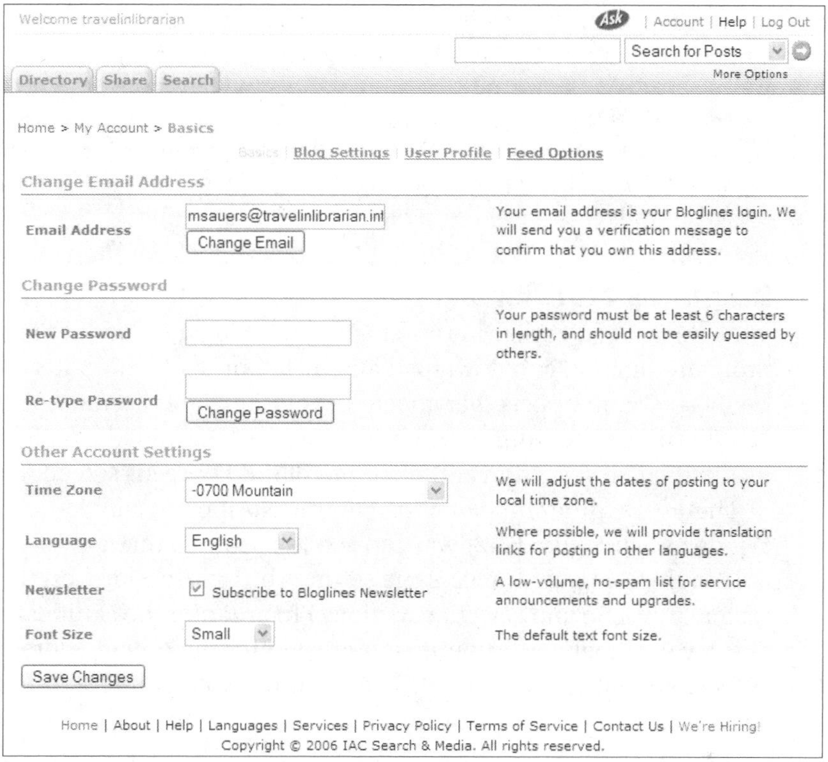

Figure 6.40 Basics screen under My Account

is "Font Size." You may choose to display Bloglines using a small, medium, or large font. You (and your optometrist) can decide which works best for you.

User Profile

All the information requested on the User Profile screen (Figure 6.41) is optional. If you decide to provide any of this information, it will be displayed in your profile, as long as you've chosen to make your profile public.

The fields here are all self-explanatory with one exception. When completing the Homepage URL field, be sure *not* to include the http:// portion of the URL. Typing that into this field would cause the resulting link to fail.

Blog Settings

The Blog Settings screen is where you can control the settings that allow you to use Bloglines for creating blogs instead of just reading feeds. (In other words, you can use Bloglines in a way that's similar to Blogger.) This will be covered later in this chapter.

Feed Options

The Feed Options under My Account are the same as those discussed earlier in this chapter. Using the "Feed Options" link under My Account is just another way to access these settings.

Bloglines Notifier

As mentioned earlier in this chapter, the Bloglines Notifier is a program that you can download and install on your computer to notify you of new posts that appear in your Bloglines account. You can download the Notifier by clicking on the "Download Notifier" link in the Extras section at the bottom of the My Feeds screen.

There are different versions of the Notifier available (i.e., Windows). In Figure 6.42, you can see the settings that are available in this program. (Access the settings by right-clicking on the system tray icon and selecting Settings.) In order for the Notifier to check your Bloglines account, you must enter the e-mail address associated with your account. Then you can make the following selections:

- *Check messages every* … Your options are 29 seconds, 1 minute, 5 minutes, 10 minutes, 29 minutes, 1 hour, 6 hours, and 24 hours.

- *Notification sound.* When this box is checked, a sound will notify you whenever new items are found. You can use the default system sound or browse for the .wav file of your choice.

- *Run program when system starts.* When this box is checked, the Notifier will automatically run when you start up your computer.

- *Uninstall.* Click this button to uninstall the program.

The Notifier periodically checks your Bloglines account to see if any new items have appeared in your subscriptions. If there are new items, you will receive an on-screen notification. Figure 6.43 shows a notification in the Windows XP version. Double-clicking on the system tray icon will take you to your Bloglines account.

To be honest, I don't find the Notifier to be particularly useful. Typically I subscribe to about 150 feeds at any given time. (In some

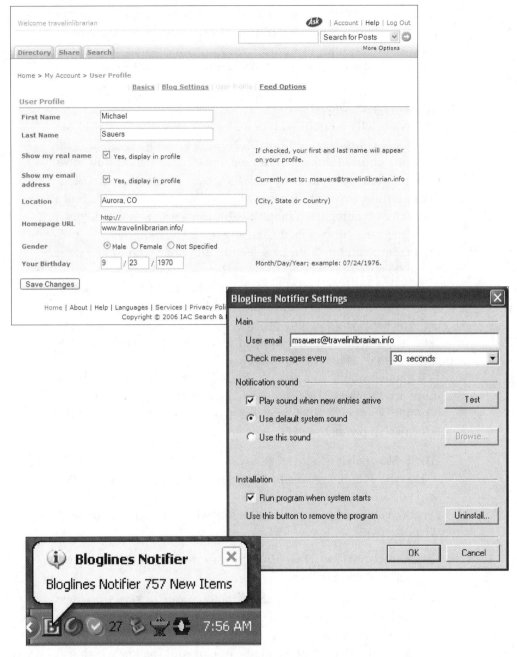

Figure 6.41   User Profile screen under My Account (top)

Figure 6.42   Bloglines Notifier settings (middle)

Figure 6.43   Bloglines Notifier (bottom)

circles that's considered a low number.) The point is that I always have new items to read; I hardly need a desktop notification to let me know. Users that subscribe to only a few feeds that do not contain new posts regularly may better appreciate notification.

Creating a Blogroll

We've briefly mentioned blogrolls previously, but now it's time for a more complete definition. According to Wikipedia, a blogroll is "a collection of links to other weblogs that are found on most weblogs" (en.wikipedia.org/wiki/Blogroll). Although your Bloglines account isn't technically a blog and not all of your feeds are necessarily coming from blogs, Bloglines uses the term "blogroll" to mean a collection of feeds that you read. The blogrolling feature of Bloglines can be found by selecting the "Share" tab in the right frame (Figure 6.44).

Before setting up your blogroll, keep in mind that a Bloglines-generated blogroll will only display links to feeds marked as "public." Any feeds you've made private will not be displayed outside of your account. Before referring others to your blogroll, be sure you've set your feeds appropriately.

Bloglines offers you two methods for creating a blogroll: the more traditional HTML method and what Bloglines calls the "/public" method. Which you use depends on how you want the information presented to other users.

HTML Blogroll

Use the HTML version of blogrolls if you want to have all or some of your feeds displayed as links within your blog. To use this version, you need to complete the following fields on the Blogroll Wizard screen:

- *Your User Name.* This should already be filled in with the user-name of your account.

- *Folder to Display.* This choice allows you to select a single folder or all folders. If you leave it blank, Bloglines will create a blogroll of every public feed in your account. Alternatively, you can enter the name of just one of your folders, which will create a blogroll of the public contents of that folder. (If you want to do this for more than one folder, you will need to create an individual blogroll for each folder.)

Figure 6.44   Blogroll Wizard

- *Link Target.* This is an HTML-related field. Leaving this field blank means that when a user clicks on a link in your blogroll, the resulting page will open in the same window as your blog. If you want the page to open in a new window, enter "_blank" (no quotes) in this field. There are other targets available.[3]

When you've completed all three fields, click on the "Generate HTML" button. You will be presented with code similar to what's shown in Figure 6.45. In most cases, you'll want to paste the first set of code into your blog's template. If your blog uses PHP, you can use the second line of code instead.

If this seems confusing to you but you still want to use the HTML method, ask your Webmaster for help. Otherwise, use the "/public" option discussed in the next section.

Figure 6.45   Blogroll code

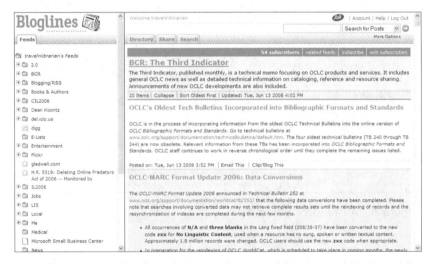

Figure 6.46   A "/public" blogroll

"/public" Blogroll

The "/public" blogroll option is very easy: You simply build a URL based on your Bloglines username. For example, my username is *travelinlibrarian*, so my URL is http://www.bloglines. com/public/*travelinlibrarian*.

When I give that URL to someone or provide it as a link in my blog, users will see the screen shown in Figure 6.46. They'll be in the Bloglines system and will be able to navigate through my subscribed (public) feeds. They will also be able to export these feeds and then import them into their own Bloglines accounts (as discussed earlier in this chapter).

The most significant difference between the view within your account and a "/public blogroll" is that items are not displayed or marked as new. This distinction is only visible to the account holder. In other words, the public will not be able to tell which items you have or have not read, only which feeds you subscribe to.

Using Bloglines to Create a Blog

Throughout this chapter, I've mentioned that you can use Bloglines to create a blog. Since Chapter 4 shows you how to blog using Blogger, I will not cover everything about Bloglines-based blogs, but I'll give you enough to get started.

Clip/Blog This

Previously, we discussed the "Clip/Blog This" link in the context of clipping a post. Now let's take a look at its other use—creating a blog post of your own.

As a reminder, Figure 6.47 shows what you see when you click on the "Clip/Blog This" link. Since you are now creating a blog post for others to read instead of clipping something for your own benefit, you'll want to add some clarifying text. Feel free to take advantage of the full WYSIWYG editing environment. If you'd rather edit the markup directly, check the "View Source" checkbox at the bottom-left corner of the window. This will show you the HTML code of the post and allow you to edit it directly.

When you're done writing your post, click on the "Publish to Blog" button at the bottom of the window. Once your post has been published to your blog, you'll receive a confirmation screen.

To view the contents of your blog, click on the "My Blog" tab at the top of the left frame. You will then see your blog displayed in the right frame along with a date-based listing of your posts in the left frame (Figure 6.48). While viewing your blog this way, you'll see the URL at the top of the right frame. This is the URL you would give to others to allow them to read your blog. If you want to see your blog exactly as a reader would, you can either paste that URL into your Web browser or you can click on the "View Blog" link at the top of the left frame. Figure 6.49 shows how a Bloglines blog looks to someone viewing it on the Web.

Blog Setting

Bloglines blogs are very easy to create and look wonderful, but they are very limited in the range of features you can change. There

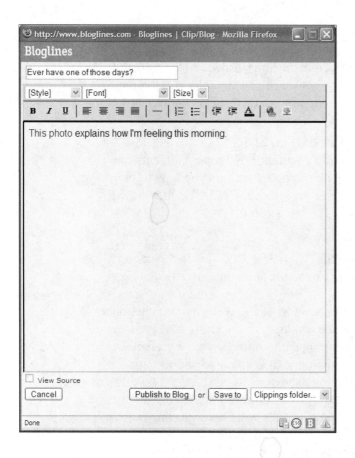

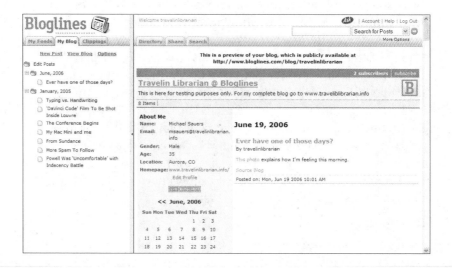

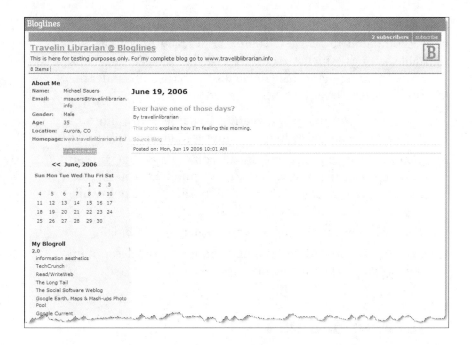

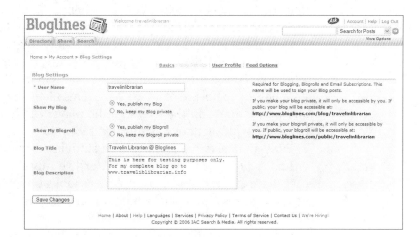

Figure 6.47 Clip/Blog This interface (left, top)

Figure 6.48 Your blog as viewed from within Bloglines (left, bottom)

Figure 6.49 Your blog as viewed from the Web (above, top)

Figure 6.50 Blog settings (above, bottom)

is no template to modify and there are fewer settings you can change compared to Blogger. There are actually only four user adjustable settings, which can be found via the "Blog Settings" link under My Account (Figure 6.50) or via the "Options" link under the "My Blog" tab. These settings are:

- *User Name.* You may choose any username you want, provided it is not currently in use by another Bloglines user.
- *Show My Blog.* You can't actually turn off the blog, but you can make it private (i.e., not available to the public). If you set your blog as private, only you will be able to view it, and only while logged in to your Bloglines account.
- *Blog Title.* This is the title you want to give to your blog.
- *Blog Description.* This field should contain a brief description of your blog's content and/or purpose.

Podcasting and RSS

In Chapter 4, I introduced you to the concept of podcasting. Now that you have a grasp of the concepts behind RSS, I'd like to follow up on podcasting with some additional technical information.

One of the features of RSS 2.0 is the ability to add "enclosures." You can think of enclosures as the RSS equivalent of attachments in e-mail. Podcasting is the creation of an RSS feed in which each item has an enclosure of an MP3 file. This file is then downloaded and played back on the user's media player of choice, the result being the equivalent of a syndicated radio show.

Early podcasts were mostly music-related—authors creating virtual radio shows of bootleg and/or live music. However, podcasts have evolved. As an example, let's look at how Greg Schwartz has turned his Open Stacks blog (openstacks.net/os) into a podcast—a radio show about the LIS world.

Here's some of the code for Greg's Open Stacks podcast feed:

```
<?xml version="1.0" encoding="iso-8859-1" ?>
<rss version="2.0" xmlns:dc="http://purl.org/dc/elements/1.1/"
xmlns:sy="http://purl.org/rss/1.0/modules/syndication/"
xmlns:admin="http://webns.net/mvcb/"
xmlns:rdf="http://www.w3.org/1999/02/22-rdf-syntax-ns#">
```

```
<channel>
   <title>Open Stacks</title>
   <link>http://openstacks.net/os/</link>
   <description>Promoting information access and literacy for
   all.</description>
   <dc:language>en-us</dc:language>
   <dc:creator />
   <dc:date>2005-02-07T06:38:07-06:00</dc:date>
   <admin:generatorAgent
   rdf:resource="http://www.movabletype.org/?v=3.14" />
   <sy:updatePeriod>hourly</sy:updatePeriod>
   <sy:updateFrequency>1</sy:updateFrequency>
   <sy:updateBase>2000-01-01T12:00+00:00</sy:updateBase>
   <item>
      <title>Enclosure handling</title>
      <link>http://openstacks.net/os/archives/000740.html</link>
      <description>Bob Jordan wrote to point out that if you are
      subscribing to the RSS 2.0 feed in a text-based aggie such
      as Bloglines or FeedDemon, you are only seeing one
      enclosure link in any given post. If there is more than
      one, the aggies seem to prefer the last one, which, in the
      case of the last post, is the podcast gif. So here's
      another post with the link you probably want. I don't
      believe this will result in a duplicate download for those
      of you with podcast aggregators, but let me know if I'm
      wrong. I strongly suggest only subscribing to the RSS 1.0
      feed in your text aggie, as this will give you all of the
      linkage properly formatted for easy digestion. RSS 2.0,
      not so much.</description>
      <guid
      isPermaLink="false">740@http://openstacks.net/os/</guid>
      <dc:subject>Podcast</dc:subject>
      <dc:date>2005-02-07T06:38:07-06:00</dc:date>
      <enclosure url="http://openstacks.net/os/os_podcast_3.mp3"
      length="8574921" type="audio/mpeg" />
   </item>
  </channel>
</rss>
```

The key segment of code in this example is the <enclosure> line, bolded in the code example. This is the link from the feed to the particular MP3 file associated with this post. If you're using a common aggregator, you'll be provided with a link to the MP3 file, which you can download and play in any MP3-supporting media player, software, or hardware.

To be very clear, you *do not* need an iPod to take advantage of podcasting—any media that plays MP3 files, such as Windows Media Player (software) or a Creative Nomad (hardware), will work (Figure 6.51).

If you *are* the owner of an iPod, you can take the concept of podcasting up one level and have the MP3 files downloaded automatically into iTunes so that the next time you sync your iPod, the new files are transferred to it. Starting with version 4.9, iTunes natively supports podcast tracking and downloading.

Before you can subscribe to a podcast, you first need to find the URL for the feed. Many sites that offer podcasts today have icons on their pages linking to the appropriate feed file.

The Coverville Web page, shown in Figure 6.52, contains three different links to provide you with multiple ways to subscribe to the podcast. The "Subscribe in iTunes" link will automatically launch iTunes (assuming it is installed on the computer) and take you to a page that will allow you to subscribe via iTunes with one additional click (Figure 6.53). The "XML" link works just as any other RSS feed link and needs to be copied into an aggregator that allows for podcast subscriptions. Lastly, the "Download and Listen" link accesses the single MP3 file for that episode, allowing you to download and play the episode on any hardware or software that supports MP3 playback.

Figure 6.54 shows the "Podcast" icon on the Open Stacks blog. However, if you are an iPod owner and would like to subscribe to the Open Stacks podcast, you must perform the process manually since an automatic link is not provided. First, right-click on the "Podcast" link and copy the link's URL. Next, open iTunes and select "Advanced/Subscribe to Podcast" from the menu (Figure 6.55). You will be shown the Subscribe to Podcast screen (Figure 6.56).

Paste the podcast's URL into the box and click "OK." The new podcast, Open Stacks in this example, will be listed in iTunes' Podcast area and will be checked for available episodes (Figure 6.57). In this example, there are four episodes available. The latest one (#15b in this example) will be automatically downloaded for

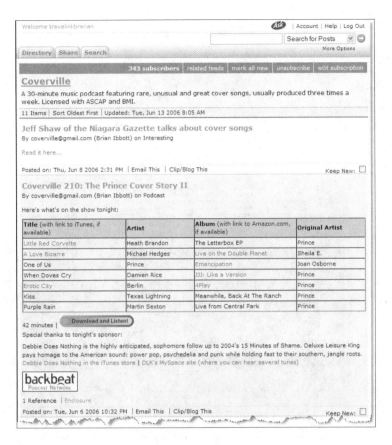

Figure 6.51   Looking at a podcast feed in Bloglines (top)
Figure 6.52   Three different podcast links on the Coverville Web site (bottom)

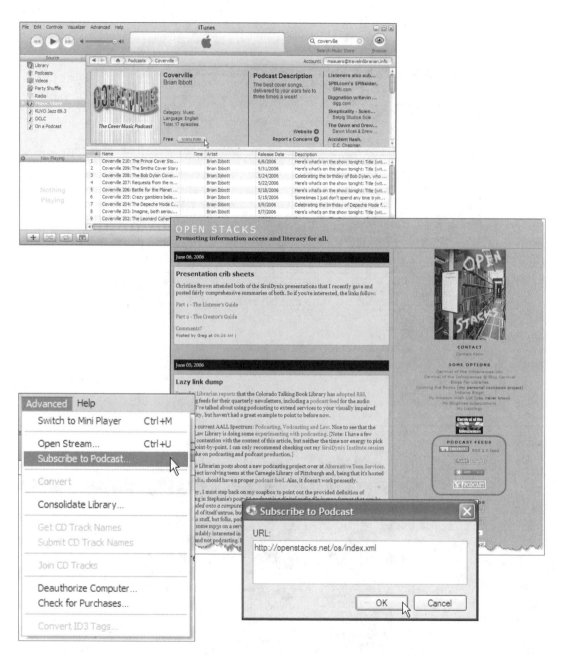

Figure 6.53   Subscribe via iTunes (top)

Figure 6.54   The "Podcast" icon on the Open Stacks blog (middle)

Figure 6.55   "Advanced/Subscribe to Podcast" in iTunes (bottom, left)

Figure 6.56   Subscribe to Podcast screen in iTunes (bottom, right)

Figure 6.57   iTunes' podcast area

you. To get additional episodes, click on the "Get" button to the right of the episode's title.

The small blue dot to the left of an episode title indicates that the episode has not been listened to yet. A dot to the right of a podcast's name indicates that it contains episodes that have not been listened to yet. To delete a particular episode or whole podcast, right click on the title and select "Clear."

iTunes offers several options for handling podcast subscriptions. These options can be found by clicking the "Settings ..." button in the bottom-right corner of iTunes. Here you can set how often iTunes should check for new episodes ("Every hour," "Every day," "Every week," or "Manually"), what to download when it finds new episodes ("Download all," "Download most recent one," or "Do nothing"), and which episodes to keep ("All episodes," "All unplayed episodes," "Most recent episodes," or the last two, three, four, five, or 10 episodes). The "iPod Preferences" button takes you to the general preferences for your iPod, providing it's connected.

Remember, you *do not* need an iPod or iTunes to listen to podcasts, they just make it much easier.

Now that you know how to use an aggregator, let's move on to Chapter 7 where we'll take a look at some feeds to which you may want to subscribe.

Endnotes

1. A more complete list of aggregators along with links to their Web sites can be found on the Weblogs Compendium site (www.lights.com/ weblogs/rss.html).

2. According to Bloglines' privacy policy (www.bloglines.com/about/ privacy): "Periodically, we may send e-mail to you if you have indicated a preference to receive news, updates, special offers, and other information relating to our service. You may unsubscribe from these e-mail subscriptions at the profile web page for your account on our website."

3. For more information, see "Targeting Windows" (wp.netscape.com/ eng/mozilla/2.0/relnotes/demo/target.html).

Chapter 7

Noteworthy Feeds

This chapter will introduce you to a number of potentially useful resources, including library, news, RSS (offering aggregated content), and miscellaneous feeds and services. Note that the library and librarian blogs covered in Chapters 2 and 3 have feeds available from their sites; these resources are not repeated in this chapter, so be sure to check them out in addition to those included here.

The URLs supplied here, in most cases, are for Web pages where the relevant feeds may be found. I provide these rather than the URLs of the feeds themselves both to minimize the chance of confusion (should the URL of a feed change) and because certain sites have multiple feeds available. In the few cases where I've listed the URL of the feed itself, it is so noted.

Library and Library-Related Feeds

Kansas City Public Library— Categories and Guides

www.kclibrary.org/guides

In 2004, the folks at the Kansas City Public Library (Figure 7.1) decided to take their online subject guides and make all of them available as feeds. Patrons can subscribe to more than 50 such guides, and receive notification when new items are added.

Hennepin County Library—Subject Guides and Search Results

www.hclib.org/pub/search/RSS.cfm

As with the Kansas City Public Library, Hennepin County Library (Minneapolis, MN) makes its subject guides available to patrons and anyone else interested in subscribing to them via RSS (Figure 7.2). As the librarians add new resources, subscribers are notified via the feeds. Subjects range from Library News to Genealogy to Jobs & Careers. There is also a single feed for those interested in being notified of all additions to every available subject.

In addition to the librarian-created subject feeds, the library now offers patrons the ability to create RSS feeds based on catalog searches. A patron performs an OPAC search and receives a link to an RSS feed of those results. Figure 7.3 shows the results of my author search for "koontz, dean." If I were to subscribe to the resulting feed, I would be notified automatically whenever a new Dean Koontz book was added to the library's collection.

Amazon.com Syndicated Content

www.amazon.com/exec/obidos/subst/xs/syndicate.html

Amazon.com currently offers feeds for new items in approximately 260 product categories (Figure 7.4). Feed categories range from horror novels to bridal magazines to headphones. These feeds are not customizable.

BCR Online

www.bcr.org/rss

BCR (Bibliographical Center for Research) was the first OCLC regional library network to offer feeds to its members (Figure 7.5), or to anyone else who wants to subscribe. At the time of this writing BCR is offering its newsletter, The Third Indicator, and its continuing education information as feeds, and has plans to make other feeds available in the future. In the case of the newsletter-based feed, BCR continues to offer the content as a monthly Web-based publication, but encourages readers to subscribe to the feed by making the articles available at an earlier time.

OCLC

www.oclc.org/rss

OCLC started offering feeds in early 2005. In May of the same year, the organization posted a single page of all its available feeds (Figure 7.6). With 20 feeds and counting, the topics range from the general (the 10 most recent OCLC news items) to specific products (WorldCat) and services (Dewey Journal: "all the latest Dewey Decimal Classification® news and announcements, DDC mappings, and tips").

Unshelved

www.overduemedia.com

Welcome to the Mallville Public Library and its wonderful cast of characters created by Bill Barnes and Gene Ambaum. If you're not already reading Unshelved (Figure 7.7), shame on you. Although you can read the daily strip (and access the archives) on the Web site, why not make it easier on yourself and receive the comic every morning in your aggregator?

Librarians' Internet Index

www.lii.org

When it comes to finding great sites online, the Librarians' Internet Index (LII) has long been a favorite of librarians. LII has a feed (Figure 7.8) available on its home page that syndicates all new listings as they're added to the site.

Encyclopædia Britannica Online—Daily Content

www.britannica.com/eb/dailycontent/rss

Encyclopædia Britannica Online offers a feed for the daily content as presented on its home page (Figure 7.9). The feed typically contains links to articles on current events, "this day in history," and highlighted biographies.

University of Saskatchewan Library— Electronic Journals

library.usask.ca/ejournals/rss_feeds.php

Darryl Friesen and Peter Scott at the University of Saskatchewan Library have made available an online directory of electronic journals that provide RSS feeds (Figure 7.10), usually of the tables of contents. The directory can be sorted alphabetically by title or by publisher/source and can be searched.

News Feeds

BBC

news.bbc.co.uk/2/hi/help/3223484.stm

At just 18 available feeds, the BBC (Figure 7.11) may not have

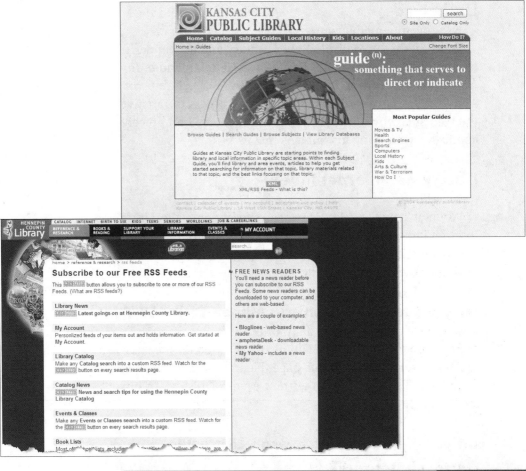

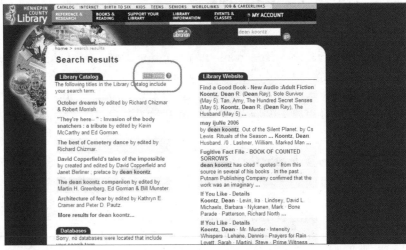

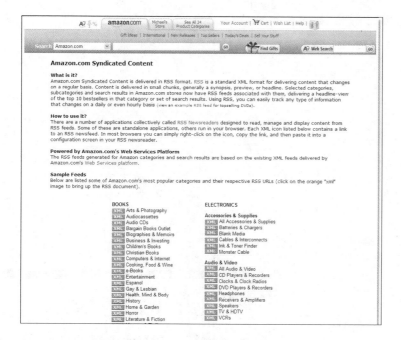

Figure 7.1   Kansas City Public Library feed link (left, top)

Figure 7.2   Hennepin County Library feed links (left, middle)

Figure 7.3   Hennepin County Library search results feed link (left, bottom)

Figure 7.4   Amazon.com feed directory (above, top)

Figure 7.5   RSS Feeds @ BCR (above, bottom)

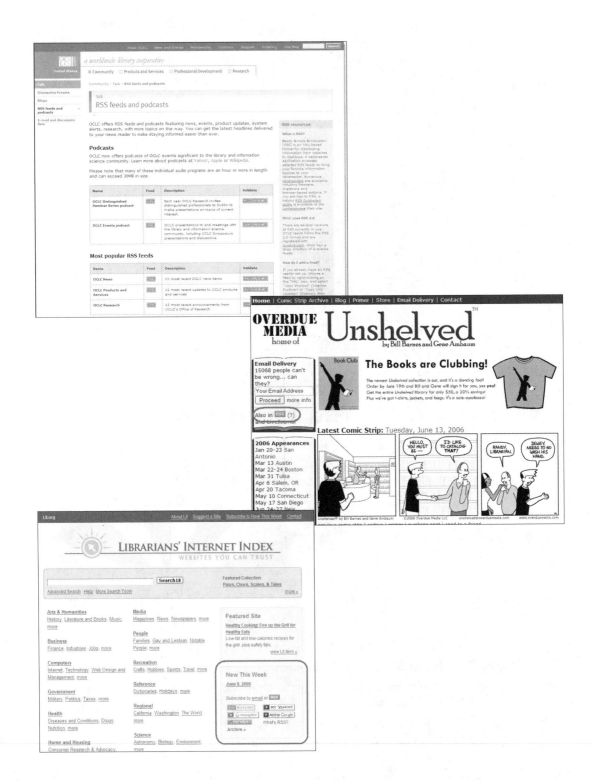

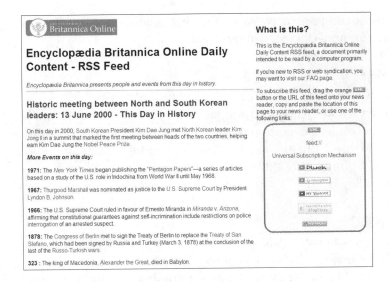

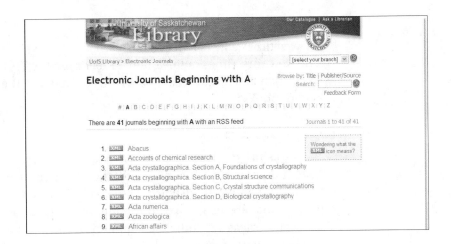

Figure 7.6   OCLC feed directory (left, top)

Figure 7.7   Unshelved feed link (left, middle)

Figure 7.8   Librarians' Internet Index feed link (left, bottom)

Figure 7.9   Encyclopædia Britannica Online—Daily Content feed link (above, top)

Figure 7.10   University of Saskatchewan Library—Electronic Journals feed directory (above, bottom)

the most comprehensive or specific list of feeds but it is a good source for non-U.S.-centric news.

C|Net

www.cnet.com/4520-6022-5115113.html

C|Net is a well-known authoritative site for news about technology. Each of its categories contains an average of a dozen specific feeds (Figure 7.12). Anyone in charge of keeping public computers up and running smoothly will want to check out the "Virus Threat Center Blog" feed.

MSNBC

msnbc.msn.com/id/5216556

Of the major online news sources that offer RSS feeds, MSNBC (Figure 7.13) comes in with the lowest number (19), but with NBC and Microsoft backing the site, the news coverage is excellent.

New York Times

www.nytimes.com/services/xml/rss

The New York Times online offers 31 feeds (Figure 7.14). As with MSNBC, only major news categories are covered, but there is also a feed for books.

Washington Post

www.washingtonpost.com/wp-dyn/rss

With more than 130 different feeds, the Washington Post online (Figure 7.15) comes in well ahead of the pack. Its feeds cover broad categories that are also broken down into narrower topics, such as discrete sports leagues, individual opinion writers, business policy, and specific world regions.

GovTrack.us

www.govtrack.us

The GovTrack.us Web site (Figure 7.16) collects legislative information from Thomas (Library of Congress) and the U.S. House and Senate Web sites and offers it in one convenient location. You can sign up for an account and track particular subjects or use the site without an account to track all legislation. Whichever method you use, you can elect to receive a feed of current legislation showing which votes have taken place. Selecting an item within a feed sends you back to the GovTrack.us site for more detailed voting information.

FARK

www.fark.com

Drew Curtis's FARK.com (Figure 7.17) is the single largest site for news of the weird and obscure. If it's an odd news story, you'll hear about it here first. In many cases, the headlines are even funnier than the stories themselves. Note, however, that some of the stories are not appropriate for all viewers (these are marked "NSFW" for "Not Safe For Work").

U.S. Government RSS Library

www.firstgov.gov/Topics/Reference_Shelf/Libraries/RSS_Library. shtml

FirstGov.gov is the official portal for all information relating to the U.S. Federal Government. This page is a directory of official government RSS feeds broken down into subject categories ranging from agriculture to "cyber security" to the military (Figure 7.18).

RSS Services

The feeds we've looked at thus far are known as static feeds—their content is written by a single individual (or organization) and then subscribed to by the reader. There are, however, a number of RSS-based services available, many of which allow the user to perform searches in various databases with results delivered via an aggregator as an RSS feed. Although some of the listed resources may not be seen as having direct library relevance, all illustrate the value of this type of service.

GoogleNews RSS

news.google.com

While the *New York Times* and *Washington Post* are considered the authority in news, people are often looking for multiple viewpoints on a particular topic. This is where the GoogleNews service can be of benefit. According to Google, "GoogleNews gathers stories

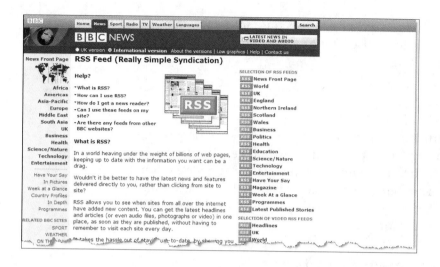

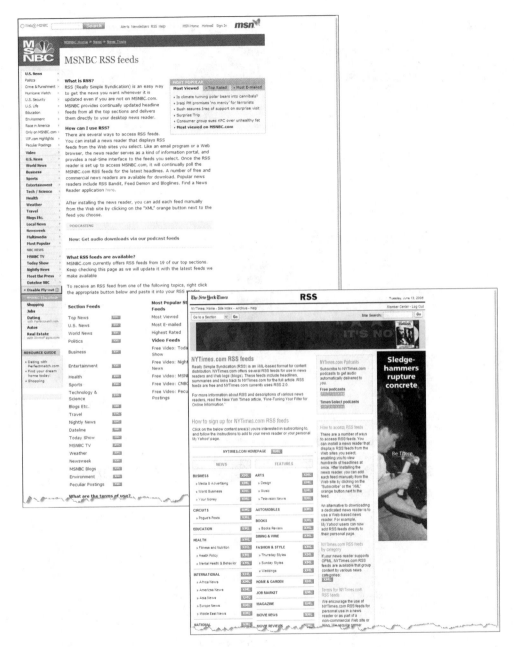

Figure 7.11   The BBC feed directory and Help page (left, top)

Figure 7.12   CINet feed directory (left, bottom)

Figure 7.13   MSNBC feed directory (above, top)

Figure 7.14   New York Times online feed directory (above, bottom)

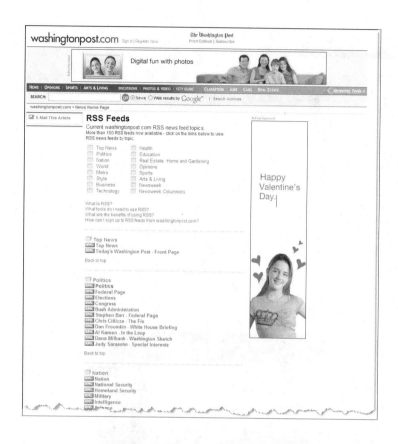

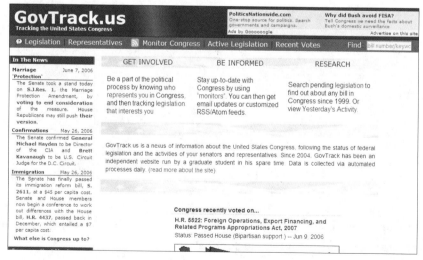

Figure 7.15   Washington Post online feed directory (left, top)

Figure 7.16   GovTrack.us home page (left, bottom)

Figure 7.17   FARK feed links (above, top)

Figure 7.18   U.S. Government RSS Library (above, bottom)

from more than 4,500 news sources in English worldwide" and is "updated every 15 minutes." In July 2005, Google announced the addition of RSS feeds to GoogleNews. To take advantage of this resource, perform a search (Figure 7.19) and then subscribe to the feed via the link on the results page. One word of warning: I sometimes receive many duplicate results from the feed. If you're willing to overlook this flaw—which I hope will be corrected soon—this is an amazing news-based resource.

Gmail

gmail.google.com/gmail/feed/atom (feed)

If you have a Gmail (Google's e-mail provider) account, you can read your messages in your aggregator. (You cannot, however, perform any other function such as replying or forwarding.) Any message in your Gmail inbox that is marked as unread will appear as part of the feed. Once you've logged into your Gmail account and opened a message, thereby marking it as read, it will no longer appear in the feed. This is basically an aggregator-based new mail notification.

The URL listed above is the URL of the feed itself—that is, what you subscribe to. Since each Gmail account is secured with a username and password, this service will only work with aggregators that support SSL/HTTPS and HTTP authentication. Consequently, it will not work in Bloglines.

isbn.nu

isbn.nu/ISBN.xml (feed)

isbn.nu is a service run by freelance writer Glenn Fleishman that allows you to search for books by title, author, subject, or ISBN. The results provide the prices for a given book in many different online bookstores, including Amazon.com, Barnes & Noble, Books-A-Million, Alibris, and ABEbooks. Fleishman has embedded links to RSS feeds on each result page, allowing you to subscribe to those results and track pricing changes and title availability.

Figure 7.20 shows Fleishman's blog post explaining how the system works (blog.glennf.com/mtarchives/004668.html) while Figure 7.21 shows a sample result. To subscribe to a feed, either perform an isbn.nu search and subscribe from the results page or build your own URL. To build your own URL, copy the URL listed for this entry and replace "ISBN" with the actual ISBN of the book you want to track.

XHTML Validator to RSS

www.benhammersley.com/tools/xhtml_validator_to_rss.html

Ben Hammersley's service is indispensable to me in my role as Web page author. This service allows me to subscribe to a customized feed that checks for validation errors in the code of my Web pages. Rather than worrying about revalidating my code every time I make a change, I let the feed do the work and notify me if there's something wrong. If I did make a validation mistake on a page I'm tracking, I'll be automatically notified in my aggregator, typically within the hour. (Happily, I'm not notified all that often.)

Figure 7.22 shows Hammersley's blog post explaining how the system works, while Figure 7.23 shows a sample result.

Feedster

www.feedster.com

Feedster is a search engine that allows you to search more than 4 million feeds, as well as blogs, jobs, and media content such as MP3s, video, pictures, and BitTorrents. What makes Feedster worthy of inclusion here is that you can receive your results as an RSS feed, thereby having your search automatically updated and receiving new results in your aggregator (Figure 7.24).

PubSub

www.pubsub.com

PubSub[1] (Publish and Subscribe) is similar to Feedster in that it is a search engine that allows you to subscribe to a feed of your results. PubSub indexes "over 8 million weblogs, more than 50,000 internet newsgroups, and all SEC (EDGAR) filings" with the promise of adding more types of information in the future. PubSub allows you to limit your searches to the following categories: Earthquakes, Airport Delays, Press Releases, SEC/EDGAR Filings, Newsgroup Posts, and Weblog Entries.

A significant difference between PubSub and Feedster is that the former creates an account within which you can save your searches. For example, Figure 7.25 shows that I have three saved searches: "dean koontz," "alias," and "michael sauers." I've subscribed to each of these in my aggregator, but I can also view and

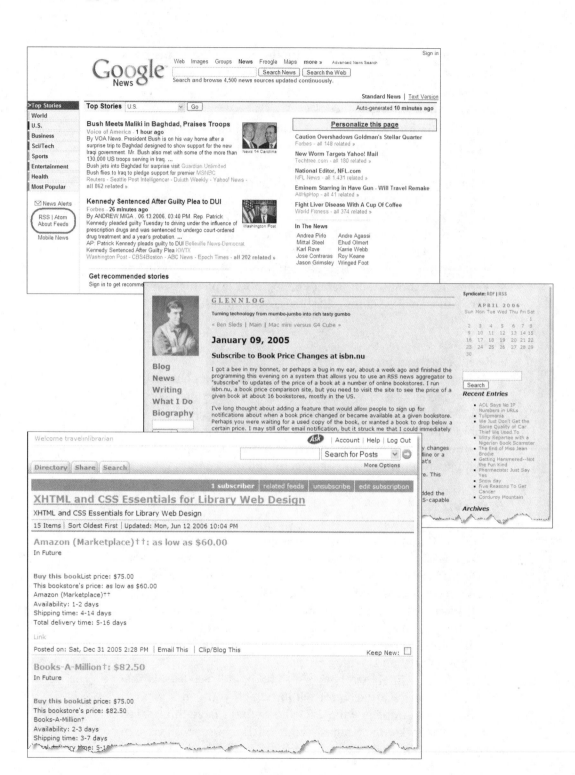

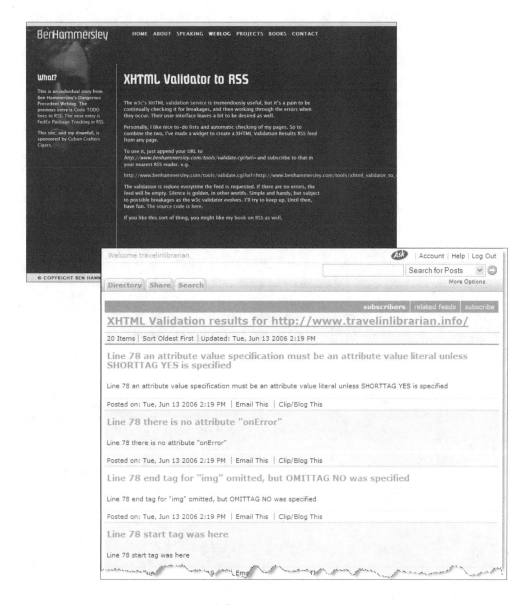

Figure 7.19   GoogleNews RSS (left, top)

Figure 7.20   Glenn Fleishman's blog post about isbn.nu feeds
(left, middle)

Figure 7.21   A sample isbn.nu feed (left, bottom)

Figure 7.22   Ben Hammersley's blog post about the XHTML Validator
to RSS service (above, top)

Figure 7.23   A sample XHTML Validator to RSS feed (above, bottom)

Figure 7.24   Feedster home page (top)

Figure 7.25   PubSub home page (middle)

Figure 7.26   The "dean koontz" search via PubSub (bottom)

delete them via the PubSub site. Figure 7.26 shows what the results of my "dean koontz" search look like in PubSub.

LibraryElf

www.libraryelf.com

LibraryElf may be the best current example of how RSS can and should be used in a library to the benefit of the patrons. My only disappointment is that neither a librarian nor a library vendor[2] developed it; JANDI Enterprises Inc.—"a privately held company based in Vancouver, British Columbia"—was the developer.

LibraryElf gives patrons access to notification of several events related to their library account. As a user, I'm automatically notified when a hold is ready to be picked up, when an item is due in three days, and when an item becomes overdue. What is truly amazing about this free service is that I can be notified via a feed in my aggregator *or* via e-mail *or* via an SMS text message on my cellphone. (Personally, I find the cellphone notification to be the most useful, but I also receive RSS notifications.)

Getting LibraryElf to work with your library account is, in most cases, a two-step process. First, you create an account with the system so that only you have access to your data. During this process, you set options including how you want to be notified (RSS, SMS, and/or e-mail), when you'd like to be notified of pending due items, and how often you'd like to be notified of overdue items (Figure 7.27).

The second step, which will be necessary for many users, is to add your particular library's system to the LibraryElf system. Because there are many different ILS systems containing many different options and customizations, LibraryElf needs to be set up to work with each one individually. In my experience, this setup generally takes only one or two days. (If your library is already listed in the system, there is no need to perform this step.) After that, just sit back and wait for the notifications to arrive.

Figures 7.28 and 7.29 show sample notifications in Bloglines and as an e-mail message, respectively.

Recently, library privacy advocates have expressed concerns about library patrons giving their login information to third parties (sunsite.berkeley.edu/Web4Lib/archive/0501/0221.html). LibraryElf does make clear the risks and that the decision to share

Figure 7.27   LibraryElf My Account screen (top)

Figure 7.28   LibraryElf feed results in Bloglines (middle)

Figure 7.29   LibraryElf results via e-mail (bottom)

such information should be that of the patron rather than the library.

Miscellaneous Feeds and Services

The feeds covered in this section aren't necessarily LIS-related or of particular use to most librarians, but they are interesting or creative enough to be of note.

Bloglines—News

www.bloglines.com/rss/about/news (feed)

If you're a user of Bloglines, you should definitely subscribe to its news feed. This is how you'll receive information about what's going on with the service. (The URL given above is for the feed.)

craigslist

www.craigslist.org

craigslist (Figure 7.30) was started in 1995 as a way for San Francisco Bay-area residents to sell and exchange items online. Since then it has grown to include more than 60 U.S. cities and more than 25 cities worldwide, and includes categories for personals, "free stuff," jobs, tickets, and housing, along with many discussion forums. Each category in each city has an associated RSS feed that can be found at the bottom right-hand corner of the page.

Tapestry

www.tapestrycomics.com

According to the Tapestry Web site (Figure 7.31), "Tapestry is a series of RSS feeds for online comics." This independent site offers feeds for such popular comic strips as *Dilbert, Get Fuzzy, Peanuts,* and *Wizard of Id*. Because this is an independent site, not all comics are available, while others are offered without the publisher's approval and are thus subject to cancellation without notice.

eBay Searches

www.rssauction.com

If you are a regular buyer and/or seller on eBay, you know that it's necessary to re-run your searches on a regular basis. Forgetting to run a search even one day can cause you to miss out on that perfect item you've been looking for at just the right price. With the help of a service from Lockergnome, you can create your perfect eBay search and then subscribe to the results as an RSS feed.

Complete all the information relevant to your search and then submit it (Figure 7.32). The service will return to you the URL for your new feed along with HTML and JavaScript code for including it within a Web page of your own. You can then subscribe to the URL in your aggregator.

iTunes Music Store RSS Feed Generator

phobos.apple.com/WebObjects/MZSearch.woa/wa/MRSS/rss Generator

Every Tuesday, Apple's iTunes service releases an electronic newsletter featuring music that is newly available through the service. Apple also provides this information via RSS. To take advantage of the feeds, you must first access the iTunes Music Store RSS Feed Generator (Figure 7.33). Select the types of music you're interested in, set a few additional options at the top, and then click the "Generate" button to receive the URL of the RSS feed.

Package Tracking

www.bloglines.com

If you've ever tracked a package online, you know that it can be inconvenient to return to a Web page every few hours and re-type a lengthy tracking number to see the status of your package. If you're a Bloglines user, there is an RSS-based solution available to you.

Log into your Bloglines account and select the "Add" link near the top of the left pane. Then in the right pane, click on the "Package Tracking" link (Figure 7.34). You will be presented with three boxes: one for UPS, one for FedEx, and one for the U.S. Postal Service. Enter your tracking number in the appropriate box and click on the corresponding "Track It!" button (Figure 7.35). As with any new feed, you have the option to place the feed into a folder (I'll discuss this option in Chapter 8).

Once you have successfully added the feed, it will appear in the left pane (Figure 7.36). Bloglines will check your package's status regularly and will notify you when the status is updated. Figure 7.37 shows you the output of a UPS package that has been successfully delivered.

Figure 7.30   A feed link in craiglist (top)

Figure 7.31   Tapestry's directory of comic strip feeds (middle)

Figure 7.32   Converting eBay searches to RSS (bottom)

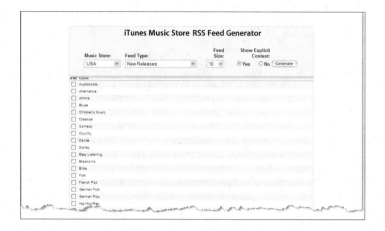

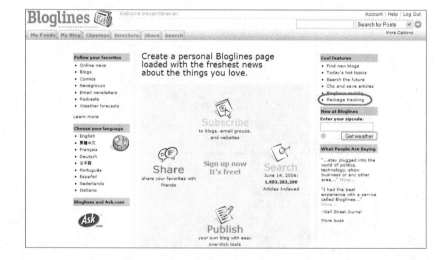

Figure 7.33   Creating iTunes new music feeds (left, top)

Figure 7.34   The Bloglines Package Tracking link (left, middle)

Figure 7.35   Entering a tracking number (left, bottom)

Figure 7.36   The Package Tracking feed as listed in My Feeds
(above, top)

Figure 7.37   A view of a Package Tracking feed (above, bottom)

del.icio.us

del.icio.us

del.icio.us (pronounced "delicious") is a "social bookmarks manager." It allows members to post their bookmarks and to add "tags"—metadata—to each posted link. Users of the site may then search through the combined collection based on the member or associated "tags" of the bookmarks. The social aspect is "its ability to let you see the links that others have collected, as well as showing you who else has bookmarked a specific site. You can also view the links collected by others, and subscribe to the links of people whose lists you find interesting." The "subscription" feature is why this site is listed here. Each "tag" and user has an associated RSS feed to which you can subscribe to receive automatic notification whenever a new bookmark relating to your topic of interest or a bookmark by a particular user is added to the system (Figure 7.38).

Topix.net

www.topix.net

Topix scours and indexes more than 10,000 news sources and organizes them into 150,000 topix.net pages. What makes Topix unique is that these pages cover more than "30,000 U.S. cities and towns [searchable by ZIP code], 5,500 public company and industry verticals, 48,000 celebrities and musicians, 1,500 sports teams and personalities, and many, many more." Each one of these pages, along with search results, can be syndicated via RSS (Figure 7.39).

Traffic Conditions Data—John Resig

ejohn.org/blog/traffic-conditions-data

John Resig, who created this feed service for anyone interested in traffic conditions, was "poking around the Dashboard Widget archive on the official Apple site and spotted a Yahoo! Traffic Conditions widget. This is interesting because they are somehow getting the data from their web site in an easy-to-parse format. So, I peeked under the hood and, sure enough, there's an RSS feed for traffic conditions!"

Resig's blog (Figure 7.40) explains how to construct a URL by hand for a feed appropriate for your area (to explain how it works to a more technical audience), and includes a form that helps you build the feed's URL automatically. Options for the feed results include setting a radius around your ZIP code area for which details are provided, and the level of severity of a given traffic condition (minor, moderate, major, or critical) (Figure 7.41).

Figure 7.38   My del.icio.us page for "rss" including the link to its feed
(top)

Figure 7.39   Topix.net search result for "rss libraries" (middle)

Figure 7.40   John Resig's blog for creating a Yahoo! traffic conditions
feed (bottom)

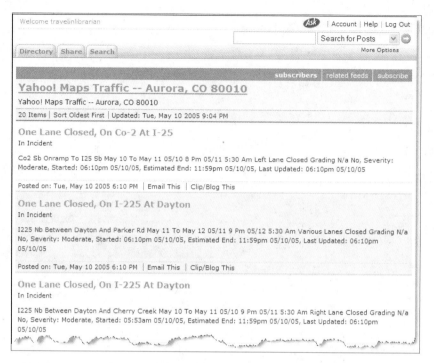

Figure 7.41   A Yahoo! traffic conditions feed as shown in Bloglines

Endnote

1. Shortly before publication, PubSub had become a virtually defunct company and should not be considered a reliable resource despite the Web site's availability. Details of PubSub's demise can be found at Forbes.com (www.forbes.com/entrepreneurs/2006/08/16/google-yahoo-entrepreneurs-cx_mr_0816friends.html) and co-owner Bob Wyman's Blog (www.wyman.us/main/2006/06/the_rumors_of_o.html).

2. By the summer of 2005, several ILS vendors including SirsiDynix (www.sirsi.com/Pdfs/Newsevents/sirsi_enterprise_portal_solution. pdf) and III (www.iii.com/pdf/it_2005_06.pdf) had announced implementation of RSS feeds in the latest versions of their products.

Chapter 8

Creating Feeds

Feeds can be created in three ways: Hand rolling, semi-automated, or fully automated. Which method you use depends largely on the source of your content: Is your feed based on a blog, in which case your content already exists, or are you creating a feed from scratch?

You may also want to consider the different feed versions available, as discussed under "Feed Types" in Chapter 5. However, before you flip back to review the features of the various versions, keep in mind that the specific software product or service you use to create your feed is unlikely to give you a choice. Each supports a given feed version that you cannot change. My suggestion is not to worry about the version—just create the feed. If at some point you feel that your feed would benefit from a particular feature that your current product or service does not support, you can consider other options.

Hand Rolling

"Hand rolling" is writing an RSS file completely by hand. Experienced coders generally hand roll feeds that are not associated with blogs. If your feed is providing syndication for a blog, there is no sense in writing the feed by hand, as you will end up writing your content twice—once for the blog and once for the feed. Still, I encourage you to try hand rolling at some point because it will give you a greater appreciation for the code, as well as some comfort with hand editing. If you decide to hand roll a feed, these guidelines will save you some time and aggravation:

- Use "copy and paste" to reproduce the content of your blog entries in the RSS file instead of retyping the content.

- Set up templates. Once you've decided which version of RSS to use, create a blank file containing all of the code but none of the content. Save this file and then use it to create future feeds. Additionally, within a feed, add a mini-template for a new item. Include items such as <item>, <title>, <link>, and <description> and place them within comment markers. Then when you want to add new items, simply make a copy of the code and add the relevant content.

Hand rolling is not a real-life solution for most of us since simple and time-efficient feed creation is our main goal.

Semi-Automated

If your RSS feed isn't blog-based, there are several programs designed to assist you in writing your code. I refer to these programs as "semi-automated" as they add the relevant code and, in some cases, even publish the feed to your server at the click of a button; however, you will still need to type the content yourself.

ListGarden

ListGarden is a free Perl program from Software Garden (www.softwaregarden.com/products/listgarden) that allows you to create RSS 2.0 feeds without writing any code. To use ListGarden, download either the Windows or Mac client or the UNIX/LINUX server version. Which version to use depends on your environment:

- If you have a Windows-based Web server, you must use the Windows client since there is no Windows server version.

- The client version is designed for use on a single machine. I was able, however, to successfully place the Windows client version on a LAN and run it from multiple computers in the building. Setting up the client version on a network location will allow for multiple users but will not allow for editing outside of the LAN.

- The server version, placed in the proper directory with permissions set accordingly and a password placed on the directory, lets users access the program and edit the feeds from any Internet-connected computer. Choose the server version if remote editing is a necessary feature for you.

Once the program is installed, it is a simple two-step process to access it. For the server version, enter the appropriate URL for your installation and submit the username and password as required. The client version requires that you run the program (which will place an icon in your system tray) and double-click the system tray icon (Figure 8.1) to open the program in your default browser.

Note that in the example shown in Figure 8.2, a feed already exists for a BCR Test RSS Feed. When you first install ListGarden, there will not be any feeds available—you'll need to create one. First, select a name for your feed that includes from one to 10 characters. (This is not the name your subscribers will see, but rather one that will be used by ListGarden to track your various feeds.) As a demonstration, we'll create a new feed for a library's public programs called "pubprogs," entering that title into the appropriate field and clicking the "Create" button (Figure 8.2).

Next we're presented with a screen requesting the channel's basic information to be entered into the following fields:

- *Title*. In this field, enter the name of the channel as you want your subscribers to see it. The title should be brief, yet sufficiently descriptive of the content of your channel.

- *Link*. This field should contain the URL of the Web page that corresponds to the channel of this field. If you're creating a channel based on a blog, enter the blog's URL. Otherwise, enter the URL of the corresponding Web page. For our demonstration, we'll use the URL of the page on the library's site that contains a public programs listing.

- *Description*. In this field, enter a narrative description of the content of the feed. Although you may write as much as you like, I recommend you limit the description to a few sentences. Do be creative, however, because potential subscribers may base a decision to subscribe to your feed solely on the description.

Figure 8.3 shows the basic channel information completed for our sample feed. Once you've completed the three fields, click the "Save" button to create your feed. You'll be sent back to the opening page of the program where you will see the new feed listed along with any others that you may have previously created. The feed you are currently working on ("pubprogs" in this example)

Figure 8.1 The ListGarden system tray icon

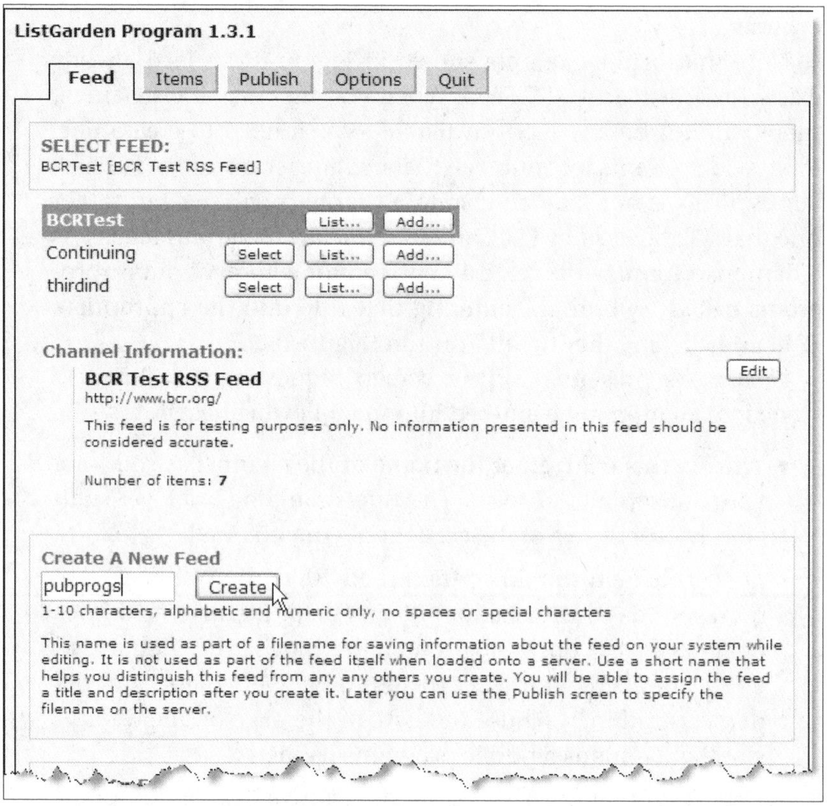

ListGarden Program 1.3.1

| Feed | Items | Publish | Options | Quit |

SELECT FEED:
BCRTest [BCR Test RSS Feed]

BCRTest		List...	Add...
Continuing	Select	List...	Add...
thirdind	Select	List...	Add...

Channel Information: Edit
  BCR Test RSS Feed
  http://www.bcr.org/

  This feed is for testing purposes only. No information presented in this feed should be
  considered accurate.

  Number of items: **7**

Create A New Feed

  pubprogs   Create
  1-10 characters, alphabetic and numeric only, no spaces or special characters

  This name is used as part of a filename for saving information about the feed on your system while
  editing. It is not used as part of the feed itself when loaded onto a server. Use a short name that
  helps you distinguish this feed from any any others you create. You will be able to assign the feed
  a title and description after you create it. Later you can use the Publish screen to specify the
  filename on the server.

Figure 8.2 Creating your first feed

will be highlighted in green. To work on a different feed, click on the "Select" button next to the name of the feed you want.

If at any time you want to change the title, link, or description of your feed, simply select that feed and click on the "Edit" button (Figure 8.4). This will take you back to the Channel Information screen.

You can also use the Channel Information screen to delete a feed. To do so, scroll down to "Delete An Existing Feed," select the appropriate feed, and click the "Delete" button (Figure 8.5).

Once you've created your feed, you'll need to put some items into it. The most straightforward method of doing this is to click the "Add…" button (Figure 8.6) for the feed on which you're working. You will then be taken to the Items screen (Figure 8.7), where you can add a new item to your feed. Complete the following fields:

- *Title.* Think of the title as the headline of the item. Make it concise, descriptive, and thought provoking. A great title will make the reader want to read the item.

- *Link.* Complete this field with the URL of the Web page that contains information about the item. This field is optional, as there may not be a Web page associated with a given item; for now, we'll work from the assumption that there is.

- *Description.* This field contains the narrative that will be associated with the feed. As discussed previously, some feeds provide the complete content of the item in the description while others offer only a summary. The "Includes HTML" option allows you to specify whether the Description field contains markup code. For the example feed, I'm leaving this option unchecked. If you do include HTML code and do not check this box, your readers will see your code in addition to your content.

- *Enclosure.* This field allows you to add a non-text file to your item. This is similar to attaching a file to an e-mail message. The main reason you may wish to do this is if you're creating a podcast. In that case, you would need to browse for and select the audio file appropriate for this post. The length of the file and MIME-type information also needs to be included. If you're not sure how to find that information on your own, click the "Get Info" button (after selecting your file) and the fields will be populated for you with the correct information.

- *PubDate.* Each item in your feed must contain a date and time stamp. This not only tells the reader when the item was posted but also allows aggregators to determine whether a particular item should be displayed to a subscriber. The option "Set to current time" (which is checked by default) directs the program to automatically set the date and time of the item to "now."

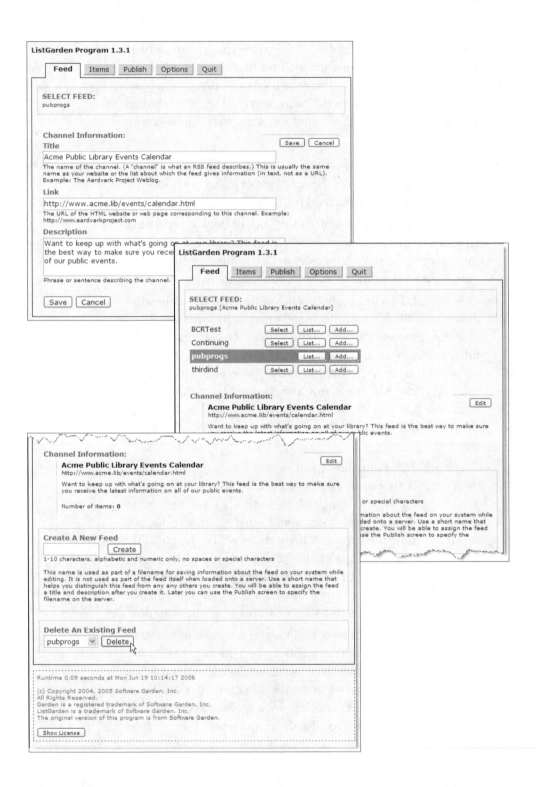

ListGarden Program 1.3.1

Feed   Items   Publish   Options   Quit

SELECT FEED:
pubprogs

Channel Information:
Title   Save   Cancel
Acme Public Library Events Calendar
The name of the channel. (A "channel" is what an RSS feed describes.) This is usually the same
name as your website or the list about which the feed gives information (in text, not as a URL).
Example: The Aardvark Project Weblog.

Link
http://www.acme.lib/events/calendar.html
The URL of the HTML website or web page corresponding to this channel. Example:
http://www.aardvarkproject.com

Description
Want to keep up with what's going on at your library? This feed is
the best way to make sure you rece
of our public events.

Phrase or sentence describing the channel.

Save   Cancel

ListGarden Program 1.3.1

Feed   Items   Publish   Options   Quit

SELECT FEED:
pubprogs [Acme Public Library Events Calendar]

BCRTest   Select   List...   Add...
Continuing   Select   List...   Add...
pubprogs   List...   Add...
thirdind   Select   List...   Add...

Channel Information: Edit
Acme Public Library Events Calendar
http://www.acme.lib/events/calendar.html

Want to keep up with what's going on at your library? This feed is the best way to make sure
you receive the latest information on all of our public events.

Channel Information: Edit
Acme Public Library Events Calendar
http://www.acme.lib/events/calendar.html

Want to keep up with what's going on at your library? This feed is the best way to make sure
you receive the latest information on all of our public events.

Number of items: 0

Create A New Feed
[   ]   Create
1-10 characters, alphabetic and numeric only, no spaces or special characters

This name is used as part of a filename for saving information about the feed on your system while
editing. It is not used as part of the feed itself when loaded onto a server. Use a short name that
helps you distinguish this feed from any any others you create. You will be able to assign the feed
a title and description after you create it. Later you can use the Publish screen to specify the
filename on the server.

Delete An Existing Feed
pubprogs   ▾   Delete

Runtime 0.09 seconds at Mon Jun 19 10:14:17 2006

Show License

- *GUID.* The Global Unique Identifier (GUID) field lets you specify a string that uniquely identifies the item from others in the feed. If you leave this optional field blank, you can choose to have ListGarden set the GUID based on the URL specified in the Link field or create a unique GUID on its own. Since unique identifiers aren't really necessary in this example, I'll leave this item set to the default. Figure 8.8 shows how I've filled in the fields for the first event.

After you've filled in the fields, you will have the following options:

- *Add Item.* This button adds the item you've just created to your feed but does not publish your feed to your server. Until your feed has been published, subscribers will not see any new items.

- *Add & Publish.* This button adds the new item to your feed and immediately publishes the feed to your server.

- *Cancel.* This button allows you to stop the process and does not add the new item to your feed.

Once the item has been added, you'll be taken back to the Items screen where you will see that the feed now has a single item in it (Figure 8.9 shows the "pubprogs" example added to the Items screen).

Now that there is an item in the feed, the Items screen has the following additional buttons:

- *Delete.* Clicking this button will present you with a list of your feed's items and give you the option to delete them. Clicking the "Delete" button next to a particular item will remove that item from your feed (see Figure 8.9).

- *Reorder.* Clicking this button will present you with a list of your feed's items along with "Up" and "Down" buttons next to each item (Figure 8.10). By clicking these buttons, you can modify the order in which your items are delivered within the feed. (Since we only have one item at this point, reordering won't make a difference.)

- *Add.* Clicking this button takes you to the Add Item screen, allowing you to add a new item to your feed.

- *Edit.* Clicking this button will take you to the same screen as the "Add" button, but instead of blank fields, the fields will be prepopulated with the information relating to the item, which you can edit as necessary.

It is important to note that added items and changes made using these buttons will only affect the version of your feed that's stored within the ListGarden program. You will need to publish the feed before anyone can subscribe to it or see changes you've made to a previously published feed.

To publish your first feed, click on the "Publish" tab at the top of ListGarden. You'll be presented with the Publish RSS Feed interface (Figure 8.11). Since you have not previously published this feed, you'll be informed that you must first provide the program with some information. To do so, click on the "Edit" button. This will take you to the Edit Publish Information screen (Figure 8.12), where you'll need to provide the following information:

- *FTP URL*. The domain name of your FTP server. Do not include "ftp://".

- *FTP Filename*. The filename of your RSS feed.

- *FTP Directory*. The path to the directory in which you want to place the RSS file. You will typically need to supply the full path from root.

- *FTP User*. Your username for the FTP server.

- *FTP Password*. Your password for the FTP server.

- *Local Filename*. If you want to save a copy of the RSS file on your local computer, enter the path and filename here. If you leave this blank, a local copy will not be created.

- *Maximum Items*. This is the maximum number of items you want to appear in your feed file. If you set this number at 25, only the most recent 25 items will be published in the RSS file, regardless of the number of items you've created in ListGarden.

- *Minimum Time To Publish Items*. This sets the minimum length of time that an item must appear in a feed, regardless of the maximum items setting. Your choices are None, 1 day, 2 days, 3 days, 1 week, and 2 weeks.

- *Item Sequence*. Choose between "As Listed" and "Reverse Chronological." Though the "Reverse Chronological" option is the most common choice, choosing "As Listed" gives you the

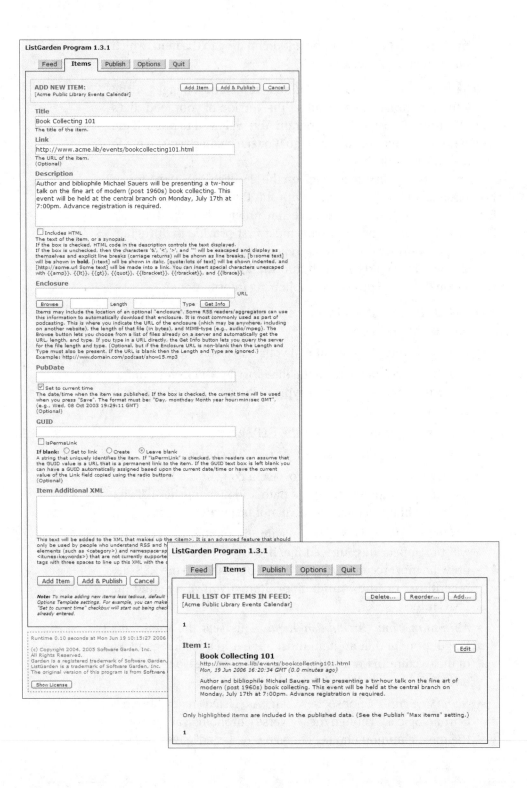

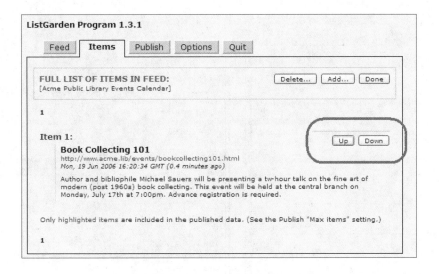

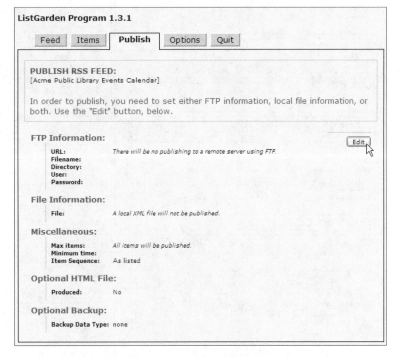

Figure 8.8   Fields completed on the Items screen (left, top)

Figure 8.9   The example feed with a single item (left, bottom)

Figure 8.10   Moving items up and down (above, top)

Figure 8.11   Publish RSS Feed interface (above, bottom)

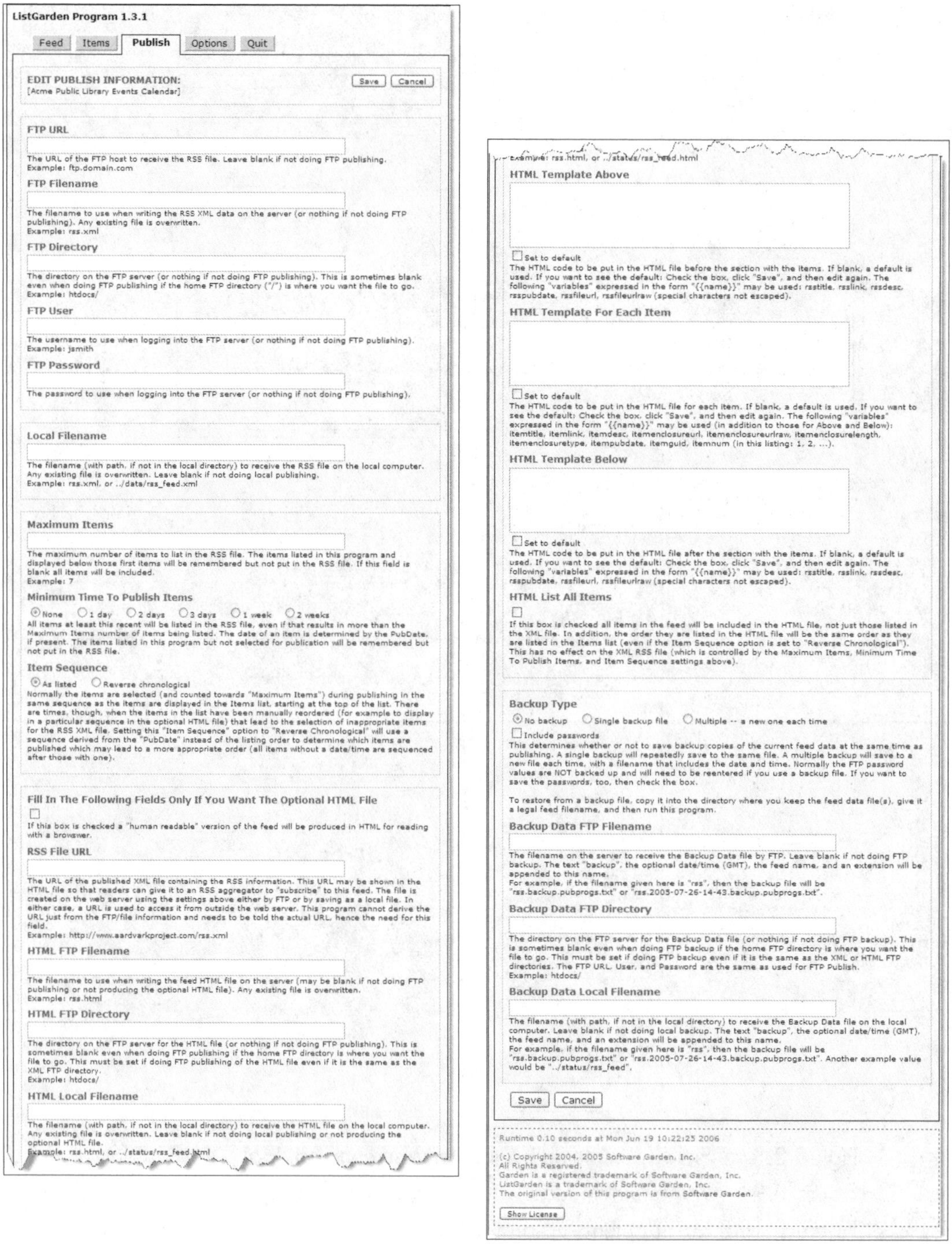

ListGarden Program 1.3.1

Feed   Items   **Publish**   Options   Quit

EDIT PUBLISH INFORMATION: [Save] [Cancel]
[Acme Public Library Events Calendar]

FTP URL

The URL of the FTP host to receive the RSS file. Leave blank if not doing FTP publishing.
Example: ftp.domain.com

FTP Filename

The filename to use when writing the RSS XML data on the server (or nothing if not doing FTP publishing). Any existing file is overwritten.
Example: rss.xml

FTP Directory

The directory on the FTP server (or nothing if not doing FTP publishing). This is sometimes blank even when doing FTP publishing if the home FTP directory ("/") is where you want the file to go.
Example: htdocs/

FTP User

The username to use when logging into the FTP server (or nothing if not doing FTP publishing).
Example: jsmith

FTP Password

The password to use when logging into the FTP server (or nothing if not doing FTP publishing).

Local Filename

The filename (with path, if not in the local directory) to receive the RSS file on the local computer. Any existing file is overwritten. Leave blank if not doing local publishing.
Example: rss.xml, or ../data/rss_feed.xml

Maximum Items

The maximum number of items to list in the RSS file. The items listed in this program and displayed below those first items will be remembered but not put in the RSS file. If this field is blank all items will be included.
Example: 7

Minimum Time To Publish Items

○ None ○ 1 day ○ 2 days ○ 3 days ○ 1 week ○ 2 weeks
All items at least this recent will be listed in the RSS file, even if that results in more than the Maximum Items number of items being listed. The date of an item is determined by the PubDate, if present. The items listed in this program but not selected for publication will be remembered but not put in the RSS file.

Item Sequence

⊙ As listed ○ Reverse chronological
Normally the items are selected (and counted towards "Maximum Items") during publishing in the same sequence as the items are displayed in the Items list, starting at the top of the list. There are times, though, when the items in the list have been manually reordered (for example to display in a particular sequence in the optional HTML file) that lead to the selection of inappropriate items for the RSS XML file. Setting this "Item Sequence" option to "Reverse Chronological" will use a sequence derived from the "PubDate" instead of the listing order to determine which items are published which may lead to a more appropriate order (all items without a date/time are sequenced after those with one).

Fill In The Following Fields Only If You Want The Optional HTML File
☐
If this box is checked a "human readable" version of the feed will be produced in HTML for reading with a browser.

RSS File URL

The URL of the published XML file containing the RSS information. This URL may be shown in the HTML file so that readers can add it to an RSS aggregator to "subscribe" to this feed. The file is created on the web server using the settings above either by FTP or by saving as a local file. In either case, a URL is used to access it from outside the web server. This program cannot derive the URL just from the FTP/file information and needs to be told the actual URL, hence the need for this field.
Example: http://www.aardvarkproject.com/rss.xml

HTML FTP Filename

The filename to use when writing the feed HTML file on the server (may be blank if not doing FTP publishing or not producing the optional HTML file). Any existing file is overwritten.
Example: rss.html

HTML FTP Directory

The directory on the FTP server for the HTML file (or nothing if not doing FTP publishing). This is sometimes blank even when doing FTP publishing if the home FTP directory is where you want the file to go. This must be set if doing FTP publishing of the HTML file even if it is the same as the XML FTP directory.
Example: htdocs/

HTML Local Filename

The filename (with path, if not in the local directory) to receive the HTML file on the local computer. Any existing file is overwritten. Leave blank if not doing local publishing or not producing the optional HTML file.
Example: rss.html, or ../status/rss_feed.html

Example: rss.html, or ../status/rss_feed.html

HTML Template Above

☐ Set to default
The HTML code to be put in the HTML file before the section with the items. If blank, a default is used. If you want to see the default: Check the box, click "Save", and then edit again. The following "variables" expressed in the form "{{name}}" may be used: rsstitle, rsslink, rssdesc, rsspubdate, rssfileurl, rssfileurlraw (special characters not escaped).

HTML Template For Each Item

☐ Set to default
The HTML code to be put in the HTML file for each item. If blank, a default is used. If you want to see the default: Check the box, click "Save", and then edit again. The following "variables" expressed in the form "{{name}}" may be used (in addition to those for Above and Below): itemtitle, itemlink, itemdesc, itemenclosureurl, itemenclosureurlraw, itemenclosurelength, itemenclosuretype, itempubdate, itemguid, itemnum (in this listing: 1, 2, ...).

HTML Template Below

☐ Set to default
The HTML code to be put in the HTML file after the section with the items. If blank, a default is used. If you want to see the default: Check the box, click "Save", and then edit again. The following "variables" expressed in the form "{{name}}" may be used: rsstitle, rsslink, rssdesc, rsspubdate, rssfileurl, rssfileurlraw (special characters not escaped).

HTML List All Items
☐
If this box is checked all items in the feed will be included in the HTML file, not just those listed in the XML file. In addition, the order they are listed in the HTML file will be the same order as they are listed in the Items list (even if the Item Sequence option is set to "Reverse Chronological"). This has no effect on the XML RSS file (which is controlled by the Maximum Items, Minimum Time To Publish Items, and Item Sequence settings above).

Backup Type

⊙ No backup ○ Single backup file ○ Multiple -- a new one each time
☐ Include passwords
This determines whether or not to save backup copies of the current feed data at the same time as publishing. A single backup will repeatedly save to the same file. A multiple backup will save to a new file each time, with a filename that includes the date and time. Normally the FTP password values are NOT backed up and will need to be reentered if you use a backup file. If you want to save the passwords, too, then check the box.

To restore from a backup file, copy it into the directory where you keep the feed data file(s), give it a legal feed filename, and then run this program.

Backup Data FTP Filename

The filename on the server to receive the Backup Data file by FTP. Leave blank if not doing FTP backup. The text "backup", the optional date/time (GMT), the feed name, and an extension will be appended to this name.
For example, if the filename given here is "rss", then the backup file will be "rss.backup.pubprogs.txt" or "rss.2005-07-26-14-43.backup.pubprogs.txt".

Backup Data FTP Directory

The directory on the FTP server for the Backup Data file (or nothing if not doing FTP backup). This is sometimes blank even when doing FTP backup if the home FTP directory is where you want the file to go. This must be set if doing FTP backup even if it is the same as the XML or HTML FTP directories. The FTP URL, User, and Password are the same as used for FTP Publish.
Example: htdocs/

Backup Data Local Filename

The filename (with path, if not in the local directory) to receive the Backup Data file on the local computer. Leave blank if not doing local backup. The text "backup", the optional date/time (GMT), the feed name, and an extension will be appended to this name.
For example, if the filename given here is "rss", then the backup file will be "rss.backup.pubprogs.txt" or "rss.2005-07-26-14-43.backup.pubprogs.txt". Another example value would be "../status/rss_feed".

[Save] [Cancel]

Runtime 0:10 seconds at Mon Jun 19 10:22:25 2006

Figure 8.12   Edit Publish Information screen

ability to control the order in which items are listed in your feed.

- *Create "human readable" version.* The remainder of the options relate to this section. If you check this box, choosing to create a "human readable" version, not only will the RSS file be created but an HTML version will also be created, allowing you to provide a link to a Web page of your feed content as well as to the RSS file for subscription purposes. If you do not check this box, all of the following settings will be ignored.

- *RSS File URL.* The full URL of the RSS file being generated.

- *HTML FTP Filename.* The filename of the HTML version to be created.

- *HTML FTP Directory.* The full path (typically from root) to the directory in which the HTML version should be placed.

- *HTML Local Filename.* Allows you to save a local copy of the HTML version. Enter the full path to the directory in which this copy should be placed.

- *HTML Template Above.* Any HTML code placed in this field will appear at the top of the HTML version ahead of any item content. This allows you to format the HTML version to fit your site's current style.

- *HTML Template For Each Item.* Allows you to format individual items in the HTML version using HTML code of your specification. For example, the following code will create a block quote for each item, with the title in bold.

```
<blockquote><b>{{itemtitle}}</b><br />
{{itemlink}}<br />
{{itemdesc}}<br />
{{itempubdate}}</blockquote>
```

- *HTML Template Below.* Any HTML code placed in this field will appear at the bottom of the HTML version after any item content. This allows you to format the HTML version to match your site's current style.

- *HTML List All Items.* If checked, this option causes all items to appear in the HTML version regardless of any settings limiting the items in the RSS version.

When you've filled in all the appropriate information, click on the "Save" button in the upper right to save your changes and return to the Publish screen. On that screen, click "Publish FTP," "Publish Local File," or 'Publish Both," as your situation requires. You should receive a message letting you know that publishing was successful (Figure 8.13). If any errors occurred during publishing you will be notified, and can then re-edit your publishing settings to correct the error.

To exit ListGarden, click on the "Quit" button at the top of any screen (Figure 8.14).

Fully Automated

To have a feed created for you automatically, your feed must be directly related to existing content, typically a blog of some sort. Let's take the Blogger.com example described in Chapter 4 and demonstrate how to make Blogger create a feed automatically. (Blogger uses the Atom feed format as opposed to RSS, but as all of today's aggregators handle both formats, this is not a concern.)

To set up a feed for your blog in Blogger, log into your blog and select the "Settings" tab. From there, select the "Site Feed" link. The Site Feed screen (Figure 8.15) gives you two options:

- *Publish Site Feed*. This is a "yes" or "no" choice. By default, it should already be set to "yes." Answering "yes" instructs Blogger to create the Atom feed and update it whenever you create a new posting. Switching this option to "no" turns off your feed.

- *Descriptions*. The "Full" option (the default) publishes the complete content of each post to the feed. The "Short" option publishes the first 255 characters of each post to the feed. Most users prefer to receive complete posts in their aggregators rather than having to link to the Web version to finish reading the article.

Also listed on this page is the URL of your generated feed. This is the address that you need to provide to readers along with a link to an RSS icon so they can subscribe to your feed.

If you've made any changes on this screen, be sure to click the "Save Settings" button before moving on or Blogger will abandon

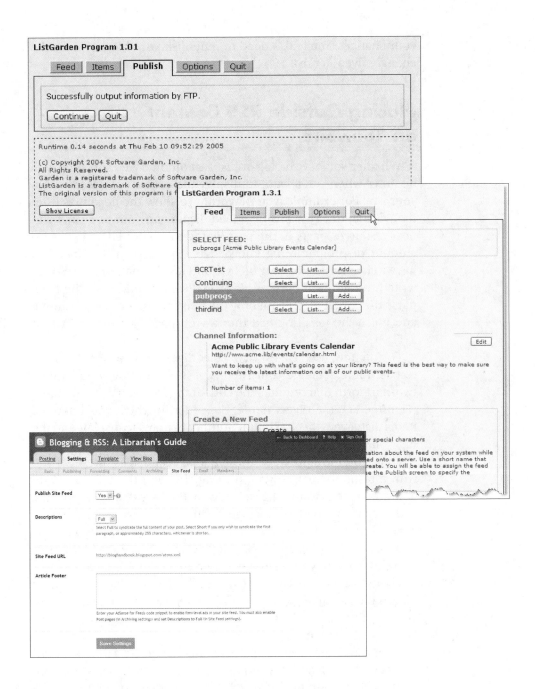

Figure 8.13 Publishing successful (top)

Figure 8.14 Quitting ListGarden (middle)

Figure 8.15 Site Feed screen in Blogger (bottom)

your changes. You'll also need to republish your blog to make the changes live (Figure 8.16).

Placing Outside RSS Content on Your Site

Whether you have a blog or just a traditional Web site, there will be times when you'll want to display the content of a feed within your site. For example, you may want to show the headlines from the Washington Post business feed display on your library's business resources page. In the past, doing this required an extensive amount of programming knowledge. An author would need to have a clear understanding of XML and RSS formats and be able to write a program in either ASP or PHP that would grab the feed, parse the contents, pull out only the information he or she wanted, and place the resulting text into a Web page as either HTML or XHTML.

Fortunately, Feed Digest (www.feeddigest.com) has come to our rescue. You can create your Feed Digest account by completing a two-part form that requires the URL of the feed you want to access (Figure 8.17), the digest name, the order in which you'd like the items displayed, the maximum number of items to display, and the digest layout (Figure 8.18).

Once you have provided these items, Feed Digest presents you with a results screen (Figure 8.19), giving you the option to add additional feeds to the digest, preview the digest, and receive the code necessary to place the digest within another site. The code is available in both PHP and JavaScript. Choose whichever you feel is appropriate for placement within your site. Additionally, you can also subscribe to your digest as either an RSS or Atom feed.

Figure 8.20 shows what the digest I've created looks like when placed on a sample page on my Web site, using the Javascript version of the code along with a "Washington Post Technology Headlines" citation.

With Feed Digest, you can also create a single feed from the content of multiple feeds. Beyond that, you can then create a feed with content that is limited by search terms that you specify. With the creation of a paid account, the number of digests you can create and the number of feeds that can be pulled into a digest are both increased.

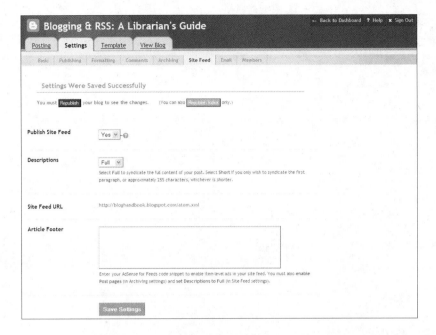

Figure 8.16   Republishing your blog (top)
Figure 8.17   Enter a URL to begin generating a digest (bottom)

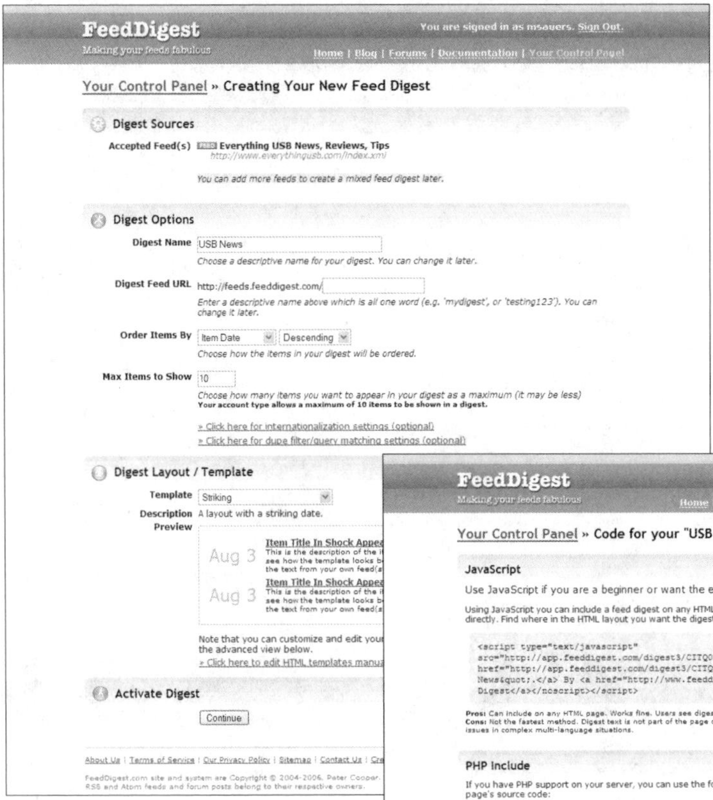

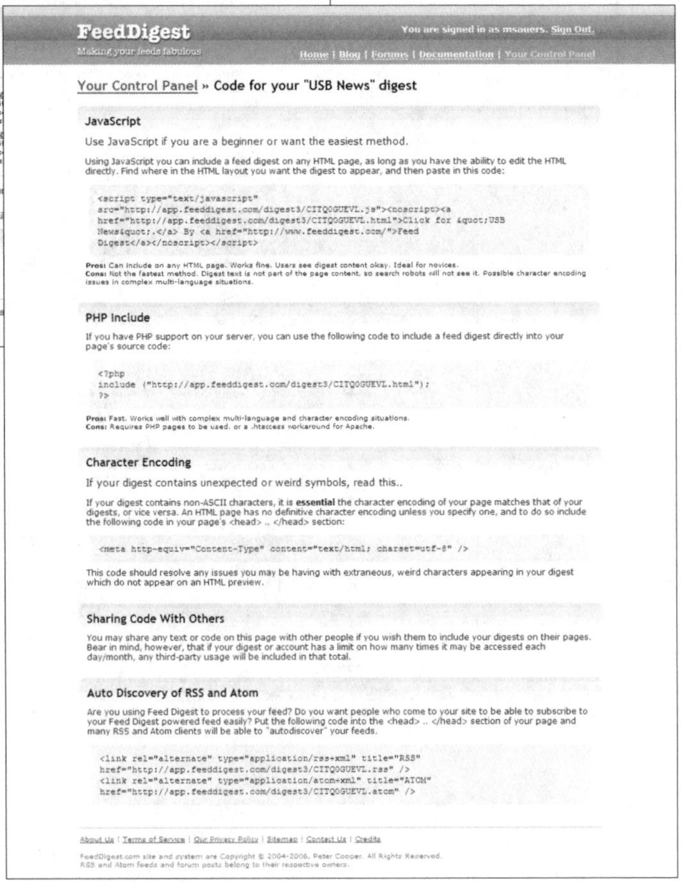

Figure 8.18   Feed Setup (top)
Figure 8.19   Feed Digest results screen (bottom)

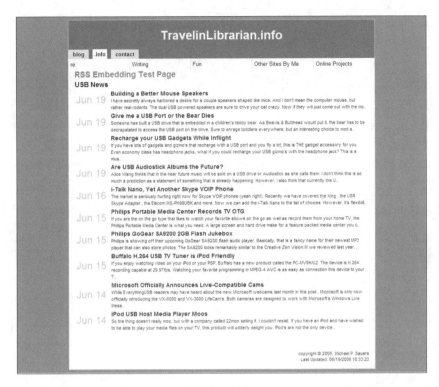

Figure 8.20   Feed Digest code in my blog

If you are planning to add outside feed content in this manner, keep in mind that there is a potential fair-use issue because you are placing someone else's content on your site. If you are going to include content from other sites, be sure to clarify to readers that your library is not the creator of the content. In other words, cite your sources.

Another issue is that when you rely on a third party to supply content, you run the risk of the content suddenly disappearing. Although this is unlikely with either Feed Digest or a major news source, it can happen.

Afterword

"What if the real attraction of the Internet is not its cutting-edge bells and whistles, its jazzy interface or any of the advanced technology that underlies its pipes and wires? What if, instead, the attraction is an atavistic throwback to the pre-historic human fascination with telling tales? Five thousand years ago, the marketplace was the hub of civilization, a place to which traders returned from remote lands with exotic spices, silks, monkeys, parrots, jewels—and fabulous stories."

—From *The Cluetrain Manifesto* by Rick Levine, Christopher Locke, Doc Searls, and David Weinberger (2000)

Will You Tell Me a Story?

In writing this book, I've focused mostly on the mechanics of creating blogs and RSS feeds, and my hope is that I've shown you how to use those mechanics easily. Now comes the hard part—putting those mechanics into action.

The next step is to take your blog or your library's and use it to its full advantage. The best way to go about that is to use it to tell a story—your story, the library's story, the conference's story. The story itself isn't as important as the fact that you tell it.

Libraries are notoriously bad at promotion. Every other time I've printed those words, the editor with whom I'm working has responded by telling me, "You can't say that. Be less direct. You'll upset people." The trouble is, every time I make that statement to a librarian, he or she instantly agrees with me. Sorry, folks, we librarians are *bad* at publicity.

Yes, we make fliers, post announcements on our Web sites, and use word of mouth to let people know what's going to happen at the library. Then we cross our fingers and hope that enough people show up at the event to make it worth the time and effort. We need a better way to promote both the library's events and the library itself.

One way is not only to promote the event before it happens, but also to promote the event *after* it happens. Tell the story of the planning, what happened at the event, and the results after the fact. Include pictures and comments from the participants. Tell a story and people will want to come back for more.

A blog can accomplish this. Blogs are inherently story-based. A blog tells the story of its author or authors. Let your blog be the place where your patrons come to hear that story.

Why does a blog work for storytelling? Because it takes the complexity out of Web publishing. No XHTML, CSS, or messing around with servers required. Blogs are conversational. If you let your blog have its own voice, people will respond as if they're talking to you—not reading a press release drafted by a PR department.

So, go forth and blog. Tell your story.

Recommended Reading

Following is a list of books and online resources that contain further information on blogs, blogging, bloggers, and RSS. This list is by no means complete and does not contain any of the blogs or feeds covered in previous chapters. Those interested in more items should look at BlogBib by Susan Herzog located at blog-bib. blogspot.com.

Books

Blood, Rebecca (ed.). *We've Got Blog: How Weblogs are Changing Our Culture.* Cambridge, MA: Perseus Publishing, 2002.

Clyde, Laurel A. *Weblogs and Libraries.* Oxford: Chandos House, 2004.

Gillmor, Dan. *We the Media: Grassroots Journalism by the People, For the People.* Cambridge, MA: O'Reilly, 2004.

Graham, Alan and Bonnie Burton (eds.). *Never Threaten to Eat Your Co-Workers: Best of Blogs.* Berkeley, CA: Apress, 2004.

Hewitt, Hugh. *Blog: Understanding the Information Reformation That's Changing Your World.* Nashville, TN: Nelson Books, 2005.

Scoble, Robert and Shel Israel. *Naked Conversations: How Blogs Are Changing the Way Businesses Talk with Customers.* Hoboken, NJ: John Wiley & Sons, 2006.

Stone, Biz. *Who Let the Blogs Out? A Hyperconnected Peek at the World of Weblogs.* New York: St. Martin's Griffin, 2004.

Trippi, Joe. *The Revolution Will Not Be Televised: Democracy, the Internet, and the Overthrow of Everything.* New York: Regan Books, 2004.

Wright, Jeremy. *Blog Marketing: The Revolutionary New Way to Increase Sales, Build Your Brand, and Get Exceptional Results.* New York: McGraw-Hill, 2005.

Online or Print Articles

Albanese, Andrew. UM Library Offers Free Blogs. *Library Journal* 129, no. 9 (May 15, 2004): 18.

Angeles, Michael. K-Logging: Supporting KM with Web Logs. *Library Journal* 128, no. 7 (April 15, 2003). Retrieved from www.libraryjournal.com/index.asp?layout=article&articleid=CA286642

Ayre, Lori Bowen. Want To Go Blogging? Infopeople Webcast. March 2004. Retrieved from infopeople.org/training/web casts/handouts/2004/03-09-04_handouts/want_to_go_blogging_ppt1.ppt#1

Balas, Janet L. Here a Blog, There a Blog, Even the Library Has a Web Log. *Computers in Libraries* 23, no. 10 (November–December 2003): 41–43.

Bannan, Karen J. RSS: Lo-fi Content Syndication. *EContent* 25, no. 1 (January 2002).

Barron, Daniel D. Blogs, Wikis, Alt Com, and the New Information Landscape: A Library Media Specialist's Guide. *School Library Media Activities Monthly* 20, no. 2 (October 2003): 48–51.

Bates, Mary Ellen. Would You Trust Joe Isuzu's Blog? *EContent* 27, no. 12 (December 2004).

Berger, Pam. Are You Blogging Yet? *Information Searcher* 14, no. 2:1–4. Retrieved from infosearcher.typepad.com/info searcher/articles/ISblogs2.pdf

Bradley, Phil. Weblogs: What, Why, Where & When. Retrieved from www.philb.com/weblogsppt/Weblogs_files/frame.htm

Broun, Kevin. New Dog, Old Trick: Alerts for RSS Feeds. *Library Journal*, Net Connect (Summer 2004).

Carver, Blake. Is It Time To Get Blogging? *Library Journal* 128, no. 1 (January 15, 2003). Retrieved from www.libraryjournal.com/article/CA266428

Cervone, Frank. Libraries, Blogs & RSS. Internet Librarian International 2004, London, October 12, 2004. Retrieved from www.internet-librarian.com/Presentations/Cervone_B201_B202.ppt

Clyde, L. Anne. Enterprise Blogging. Online Information 2004, London, December 2004. Retrieved from www.hi.is/~anne/entblogs. html

___. Library Weblogs. *Library Management* 25, no. 4/5 (2004): 183–189.

___. Shall We Blog? *Teacher Librarian* 30, no. 1 (October 1, 2002): 44–46.

___. Weblogs and Blogging, Part 1. *Free Pint* 111 (May 2, 2002). Retrieved from www.freepint.com/issues/020502.htm#feature

___. Weblogs and Blogging, Part 2. *Free Pint* 112 (May 16, 2002). Retrieved from www.freepint.com/issues/160502.htm

Cohen, Steven M. RSS for Non-Techie Librarians. LLRX, June 2002. Retrieved from www.llrx.com/features/rssforlibrarians.htm

Cohen, Steven M. and Jenny Levine. Weblogs/RSS 101. Internet Librarian 2004, November 13, 2004. Retrieved from www.librarystuff.net/presentations/11142004AM.ppt

___. Weblogs/RSS 201. Internet Librarian 2004, November 13, 2004. Retrieved from www.librarystuff.net/presentations/1114200 4PM.ppt

Cohen, Steven M. and Michael Stephens. Get 'Em Started—Teaching Weblogs to Staff. Internet Librarian 2004, November 16, 2004. Retrieved from www.tametheweb.com/presentation/getemstarted.ppt

Crawford, Walt. Starting a Bicycle Club: Weblogs Revisited. *American Libraries* 35, no. 1 (January 2004): 90–91. Retrieved from www.ala.org/al_onlineTemplate.cfm?Section=crawford2004&Template=/ContentManagement/ContentDisplay.cfm&ContentID=52691

___. 'You Must Read This': Library Weblogs. *American Libraries* 32, no. 9 (October 2001): 74–79.

Crego, Susannah. Breaking News: Law Librarians as Newscasters. *New Jersey Law Journal* 31 (August 2001). Retrieved from www.law.com/jsp/statearchive.jsp?type=Article&oldid=ZZZ4SS ME2RC

Curling, Cindy. A Closer Look at Weblogs. LLRX.com, October 15, 2001. Retrieved from www.llrx.com/columns/notes46.htm

Efimova, Lilia and Stephanie Hendrick. In Search for a Virtual Settlement: An Exploration of Weblog Community Boundaries. Retrieved from doc.telin.nl/dscgi/ds.py/Get/File-46041

Embrey, Theresa Ross. You Blog, We Blog: A Guide to How Teacher-Librarians Can Use Weblogs to Build Communication and Research Skills. *Teacher Librarian* 30, no. 2 (December, 2002): 7–9. Retrieved from www.teacherlibrarian.com/tlmag/v_30/v_30_2_feature.html

Estep, Erik S. and Julia Gelfand. Weblogs. *Library Hi Tech News* 20, no. 5:11–12.

Fichter, Darlene. Blogging Basics. Computers in Libraries 2004, March 11, 2004. Retrieved from library.usask.ca/~fichter/talks04/cil/2004.02.17.cyber.blogging.basics.ppt

___. The Blogging Explosion—Libraries and Weblogs. Computers in Libraries 2003, March 14, 2003. Retrieved from library.usask.ca/~fichter/talks03/cil/2003.03.10.blogging.pps

___. Blogging Software for Intranet Applications: You Can Put Your Own Creative Juices to Work Thinking Up Ways to Use Weblog Software. *ONLINE* 27, no. 1 (January–February, 2003): 61–64.

___. Blogging Tools. Internet Librarian 2003, November 5, 2003. Retrieved from library.usask.ca/~fichter/talks03/il/2003.11.04.cyber.blogging.tools.pps

___. Blogging Your Life Away. *ONLINE* 25, no. 3 (May 2001): 68–71.

___. Using RSS to Create New Services. *ONLINE* 28, no. 4 (July–August 2004).

___. Using Weblogs to Spread the Word About Libraries. Hawaii Library Association 2004 Annual Conference, October 23, 2004.

Retrieved from library.usask.ca/~fichter/talks03/cil/2003.03.10. blogging.pps

___. Weblogs—Opportunities for Special Libraries. Special Libraries Network, Saskatoon, SK, Canada, June 17, 2004. Retrieved from library.usask.ca/~fichter/talks04/saskatoon/ 2004.06.17.saskatoon.blogging.ppt (for Resources and Bibliography, go to library.usask.ca/~fichter/talks04/saskatoon/ 2004.06.17.saskatoon.blogging.bibl.doc).

___. Why and How to Use Blogs to Promote Your Library's Services. *Marketing Library Services* 17, no. 6 (November–December 2003): 1–4. Retrieved from www.infotoday.com/mls/nov03/ fichter.shtml

Garrod, Penny. Weblogs: Do They Belong In Libraries? *Ariadne* 40 (July 30, 2004). Retrieved from www.ariadne.ac.uk/issue40/ public-libraries

Goans, Doug and Teri M. Vogel. Building a Home for Library News with a Blog. *Computers in Libraries* 23, no. 10 (November– December 2003): 20–26. Retrieved from www.infotoday.com/ cilmag/nov03/goans_vogel.shtml

Grady, Jenifer. Who's Blogging? *Library Worklife* 1, no. 5. Retrieved from www.ala-apa.org/newsletter/vol1no5/worklife.html

Hammond, Tony, Timo Hannay, and Ben Lund. The Role of RSS in Science Publishing: Syndication and Annotation on the Web. *D-Lib Magazine* 10, no. 12 (December 2004).

Hane, Paula. Blogs Are a Natural for Librarians. *NewsLink*, no. 24 (October 2001). Retrieved from www.infotoday.com/newslink/ newslink0110.htm

Henning, Jeffrey. The Blogging Iceberg: Of 4.12 Million Hosted Weblogs, Most Little Seen, Quickly Abandoned. Retrieved from www.perseus.com/blogsurvey

Herring, Susan, Lois Ann Scheidt, Sabrina Bonus, and Elijah Wright. Bridging the Gap: A Genre Analysis of Weblogs. Proceedings of the 37th Annual Hawaii International Conference on System Sciences (HICSS'04)—Track 4 (January 5–8, 2004): 40101b. Retrieved from csdl.computer.org/comp/ proceedings/hicss/2004/2056/04/205640101b.pdf

Huwe, Terence K. Beyond Blogging 101: Applying Reference Skills to Weblogs. Computers in Libraries 2004, March 11, 2004. Retrieved from www.infotoday.com/cil2004/presentations/Huwe_Blogging101.pps

___. Born to Blog. *Computers in Libraries* 23, no. 10 (November–December 2003): 44–45.

International Association of School Librarianship (IASL). Weblogs and Blogging: Resources For School Libraries. School Libraries Online. Retrieved from www.iasl-slo.org/weblogs.html

Jacobs, James R. Blogosphere: Exploring the New Killer App for Librarians. *Documents to the People (DttP)* 31, no. 2 (Summer 2003): 6–7.

___. RSS: It's Only XML but I Like It. *Documents to the People (DttP)* 32, no. 2 (Summer 2004).

Johnson, Sarah L. and Rachel Singer Gordon. Library Job Gurus Create Career Blog Site. *Computers in Libraries* 24, no. 2 (February 2004): 48.

LaGuardia, Cheryl and Ed Tallent. Interviewing: Beware Blogging Blunders. *Library Journal* 127, no. 15 (September 15, 2002).

Lawley, Elizabeth Lane. Beyond Blogging. Internet Librarian 2003, November 4, 2003. Retrieved from www.it.rit.edu/~ell/il03-bb/

Levine, Jenny. Blogging and the Shifted Librarian. LISjobs.com. Retrieved from www.lisjobs.com/newsletter/archives/jul02 jlevine.htm

Levine, Jenny and Greg Schwartz. Making the Most of the Blogosphere. Internet Librarian 2004, November 16, 2004. Retrieved from www.infotoday.com/il2004/presentations/Levine_Schwartz.ppt

Mattison, David. So You Want to Start a Syndicated Revolution. *Searcher* 11, no. 2 (February 2003): 38–48.

Nardi, Bonnie, Diane Schiano, and Michelle Gumbrecht. Blogging as Social Activity, or, Would You Let 900 Million People Read Your Diary? *Proceedings of Computer Supported Cooperative Work 2004, November 6–10, 2004.* Chicago: ACM. Retrieved from home.comcast.net/~diane.schiano/CSCW04.Blog.pdf

Notess, Greg. The Blog Realm: News Sources, Searching with Daypop, and Content Management. *ONLINE* 26, no. 5 (September–October 2002). Retrieved from www.onlinemag. net/sep02/OnTheNet.htm

___. Harvesting Blogs for Emergent Information. Internet Librarian 2003, November 4, 2003. Retrieved from notess.com/speak/talks/il03harvestingblogs.pps

___. RSS, Aggregators, and Reading the Blog Fantastic. *ONLINE* 26, no. 6 (November–December 2002).

Quint, Barbara. Blogs and Currency. *Information Today* 21, no. 5 (May 2004): 7.

Rainie, Lee. The State of Blogging. Pew Internet & American Life Project, January 2005. Retrieved from www.pewinternet.org/ PPF/r/144/report_display.asp

Sauers, Michael. An Introduction to RSS. Business Information Alert, August 2003.

Schwartz, Greg. Blogs for Libraries. WebJunction, August 3, 2003. Retrieved from webjunction.org/do/DisplayContent?id=767

Skinner, Geoffrey. Filters and Rogue Librarians: Weblogs in the Library World. November 8, 2002. Retrieved from www. redgravenstein.com/people/gs/mlis/289/weblog

Stone, Steven A. The Library Blog: A New Communication Tool. *Kentucky Libraries* 67, no. 4 (Fall 2003).

Tennant, Roy. Feed Your Head: Keeping Up by Using RSS. *Library Journal* 128, no. 9 (May 15, 2003).

Thomsen, Elizabeth B. RSS: Really Simple Syndication. *Collection Building* 23, no. 4 (2004).

Viégas, Fernanda. Blog Survey: Expectations of Privacy and Accountability. 2004. Retrieved from web.media.mit.edu/~ fviegas/survey/blog/results.htm

Winship, Ian. Weblogs and RSS in Information Work. *Update* (August 11, 2004). Retrieved from www.cilip.org.uk/publications/ updatemagazine/archive/archive2004/may/update0405b.htm

Young, Jr., Terrence E. Blogs: Is the New Online Culture a Fad or the Future? *Net Worth* (May–June 2003). Retrieved from www.ala.org/ ala/aasl/aaslpubsandjournals/kqweb/kqreviews/networth/ v31n5.htm

Feed Code Examples

RSS 0.90

This version has been superseded by RSS 0.91 and is rarely used any more. The following sample was created for this book.

```
<?xml version 1.0"?>
<rdf:RDF xmlns:rdf=http://www.w3.org/1999/02/22-rdf-syntax-ns#
xmlns="http://my.netscape.com/rdf/simple/0.9">
  <channel>
    <title>Sample RSS 0.90 Feed</title>
    <link>http://www.foo.bar/</link>
    <description>A sample RSS feed for Blogs & RSS: A librarian's
    handbook</description>
  </channel>
  <image>
    <title>Michael rendered in Lego</title>
    <url>http://travelinlibrarian.info/blog/lego.jpg</url>
    <link>http://travelinlibrarian.info/</link>
  </image>
  <item>
    <title>The Misadventures of Hello Cthulhu</title>
    <link>http://www.hello-cthulhu.com</link>
  </item>
  <item>
    <title>Browse Happy</title>
    <link>http://browsehappy.com</link>
  </item>
</rdf:RDF>
```

RSS 0.91

This version has been superseded by RSS 0.92. The following sample is from Librarian's Rant, Louise Alcorn (lblog. jalcorn.net/rss.php?version=0.91).

```
<?xml version="1.0" encoding="utf-8" ?>
<rss version="0.91">
    <channel>
        <title>Librarian's Rant</title>
        <link>http://lblog.jalcorn.net/</link>
        <description>Planning the Revolution....</description>
        <language>en</language>
        <image>
        <url>http://lblog.jalcorn.net/templates/default/img/s9y_banner_small.png</url>
        <title>RSS: Librarian's Rant - Planning the Revolution....</title>
        <link>http://lblog.jalcorn.net/</link>
        <width>100</width>
        <height>21</height>
        </image>
        <item>
        <title>Our New Foreign Policy</title>
        <link>http://lblog.jalcorn.net/archives/615-Our-New-Foreign-Policy.html</link>
        <description>&lt;br /&gt;Talk tough, shoot first, ...&lt;a
        href=&quot;http://lblog.jalcorn.net/exit.php?url_id=1264&amp;amp;entry_id=615&quot;
        title=&quot;http://story.news.yahoo.com/news?tmpl=story&amp;u=/nm/20050128/pl_nm/
        holocaust_cheney_dress_dc&quot;
        onmouseover=&quot;window.status='http://story.news.yahoo.com/news?tmpl=story&amp;u=
        /nm/20050128/pl_nm/holocaust_cheney_dress_dc';return true;&quot;
        onmouseout=&quot;window.status='';return true;&quot;&gt;dress casual&lt;/a&gt;.
        &lt;blockquote&gt;&lt;b&gt;Cheney Criticized for Attire at Auschwitz
        Ceremony&lt;/b&gt;&lt;br /&gt; &lt;br /&gt; Vice President Dick Cheney raised
        eyebrows on Friday for wearing an olive-drab parka, hiking boots and knit ski cap
        to represent the United States at a solemn ceremony remembering the liberation of
        Auschwitz. &lt;br /&gt; &lt;br /&gt; ...&quot;The vice president...was dressed in
        the kind of attire one typically wears to operate a snow blower,&quot; Robin
        Givhan, The Washington Post's fashion writer, wrote in the newspaper's Friday
        editions. &lt;br /&gt; &lt;br /&gt; Between the somber, dark-coated leaders at the
        outdoor ceremony sat Cheney, resplendent in a green parka embroidered with his name
        and featuring a fur-trimmed hood, the laced brown boots and a knit ski cap reading
        &quot;Staff 2001.&quot; &lt;br /&gt; &lt;br /&gt; &quot;And, indeed, the vice
        president looked like an awkward boy amid the well-dressed adults,&quot; Givhan
        wrote. &lt;/blockquote&gt; &lt;i&gt; Thanks to Todd G.&lt;/i&gt;&lt;br /&gt; &lt;br
        /&gt;</description>
        </item>
        <item>
        <title>Education secretary condemns public show with gay characters</title>
        <link>http://lblog.jalcorn.net/archives/614-Education-secretary-condemns-public-
        show-with-gay-characters.html</link>
        <description>&lt;br /&gt;Cuz heaven forbid this administration shouldn't follow the
        oh-so-progressive viewpoint of James Dobson and Focus on the Family, a la &lt;a
        href=&quot;http://lblog.jalcorn.net/exit.php?url_id=1262&amp;amp;entry_id=614&quot;
        title=&quot;http://lblog.jalcorn.net/archives/609-UCC-Welcomes-
        Spongebob!.html&quot;
```

```
    onmouseover=&quot;window.status='http://lblog.jalcorn.net/archives/609-UCC-
    Welcomes-Spongebob!.html';return true;&quot;
    onmouseout=&quot;window.status='';return true;&quot;&gt;the Spongebob
    controversy&lt;/a&gt;.  Article about the Ed. Secy is at &lt;a
    href=&quot;http://lblog.jalcorn.net/exit.php?url_id=1263&amp;amp;entry_id=614&quot;
    title=&quot;http://www.cnn.com/2005/EDUCATION/01/26/education.secretary.pbs.ap/
    index.html&quot;
    onmouseover=&quot;window.status='http://www.cnn.com/2005/EDUCATION/01/26/education.
    secretary.pbs.ap/index.html';return true;&quot;
    onmouseout=&quot;window.status='';return true;&quot;&gt;CNN.com&lt;/a&gt;:
    &lt;blockquote&gt;The not-yet-aired episode of &quot;Postcards From Buster&quot;
    shows the title character, an animated bunny named Buster, on a trip to Vermont --
    a state known for recognizing same-sex civil unions. &lt;b&gt;The episode features
    two lesbian couples, although the focus is on farm life and maple
    sugaring&lt;/b&gt;.&lt;br /&gt; &lt;br /&gt; A PBS spokesman said late Tuesday that
    the nonprofit network has decided not to distribute the episode, called
    &quot;Sugartime!,&quot; to its 349 stations. She said the Education Department's
    objections were not a factor in that decision.&lt;/blockquote&gt;  I'm so
    disappointed with PBS...&lt;br /&gt; &lt;br /&gt; &lt;i&gt;Thanks to Amy M. on
    Library Underground.&lt;/i&gt;&lt;br /&gt; &lt;br /&gt;</description>
    </item>
  </channel>
</rss>
```

RSS 0.92

This version has been superseded by RSS 2.0. The following sample is from Thoughts From Eric, Eric Meyer (meyerweb. com/feed/rss).

```
<?xml version="1.0" encoding="UTF-8"?>
<rss version="0.92">
  <channel>
    <title>Thoughts From Eric</title>
    <link>http://meyerweb.com</link>
    <description>Things that Eric A. Meyer, CSS expert, writes
    about on his personal Web site; it's largely Web standards
    and Web technology, but also various bits of culture,
    politics, personal observations, and other miscellaneous
    stuff</description>
    <lastBuildDate>Thu, 03 Feb 2005 19:16:34
    +0000</lastBuildDate>
    <docs>http://backend.userland.com/rss092</docs>
    <language>en</language>
    <item>
      <title>S5 1.1b5</title>
      <description>The last beta before 1.1 final is released.
      The only change is the addition of Home and End handling,
```

```
        but we're still looking for a fix to alpha handling of
        background PNGs in IE/Win. (431 words | Tools S5 |
        comments and pings allowed)</description>
        <link>http://meyerweb.com/eric/thoughts/2005/02/03/
        s5-11b5/</link>
      </item>
      <item>
        <title>Be A Parent</title>
        <description>An old favorite returns, and in so doing
        inadvertantly touches off a rant about parenthood and baby
        blogs. (962 words | Personal | pings
        allowed)</description>
      </item>
    </channel>
</rss>
```

RSS 2.0

The following example is from Library Web Chic, Karen Coombs (www.librarywebchic.net/rss.xml).

```
<?xml version="1.0"?>
<!-- RSS generated by Radio UserLand v8.0.8 on Sun, 30 Jan 2005 20:55:47 GMT -- >
<rss version="2.0">
  <channel>
    <title>Library Web Chic</title>
    <link>http://www.librarywebchic.net/</link>
    <description></description>
    <language>en-us</language>
    <copyright>Copyright 2005 Karen Coombs</copyright>
    <lastBuildDate>Sun, 30 Jan 2005 20:55:47 GMT</lastBuildDate>
    <docs>http://backend.userland.com/rss</docs>
    <generator>Radio UserLand v8.0.8</generator>
    <managingEditor>kac@mailcity.com</managingEditor>
    <webMaster>kac@mailcity.com</webMaster>
    <skipHours>
      <hour>0</hour>
      <hour>2</hour>
      <hour>3</hour>
      <hour>4</hour>
      <hour>5</hour>
      <hour>1</hour>
      <hour>8</hour>
      <hour>23</hour>
      <hour>15</hour>
      <hour>16</hour>
```

```
    <hour>10</hour>
    <hour>6</hour>
    <hour>11</hour>
    <hour>7</hour>
    </skipHours>
<ttl>60</ttl>
<item>
    <title>Free E-books</title>
    <link>http://www.librarywebchic.net/2005/01/30.html#a196</link>
    <description>&lt;h4&gt;Free E-books&lt;/h4&gt; &lt;p&gt;This week I spent
    some time adding free e-books collections to our OpenURL resolver. The
    most important set I got added as the Escholarship editions from the
    University of California Press. Information about how to link to these
    titles and a list of them is available on the web at &lt;a
    href=&quot;http://texts.cdlib.org/escholarship/help.html&quot;&gt;&lt;a
    href=&quot;http://texts.cdlib.org/escholarship/help.html&quot;&gt;http:
    //texts.cdlib.org/escholarship/help.html&lt;/a&gt;&lt;/a&gt; This
    collection contains almost 500 publically available titles. The best
    part is if you have SFX (which we do) there is a target already set up
    for you. You don&apos;t have to create one on your own. This basically
    means all you have to do is turn things on. Since our monography budget
    has taken a serious hit this year, access to these e-books is very
    helpful. Does anyone have other collections of freely available e-books
    that they have added to their OPAC or OpenURL resolver? If so, drop me
    a note using the email link and let me know. I&apos;m very interested
    in trying to make as many free resources available to my users as
    possible.&lt;br&gt; &lt;/p&gt;&lt;br&gt;</description>
    <guid>http://www.librarywebchic.net/2005/01/30.html#a196</guid>
    <pubDate>Sun, 30 Jan 2005 20:55:47 GMT</pubDate>
    <category>Ongoing Projects</category>
    <category>OpenURL</category>
</item>
<item>
    <title>Integrateable Standards compliant WYSIWYG Editor</title>
    <link>http://www.librarywebchic.net/2005/01/27.html#a195</link>
    <description>&lt;h4&gt;Integrateable Standards compliant WYSIWYG
    Editor&lt;/h4&gt; &lt;p&gt;&lt;a
    href=&quot;http://www.themaninblue.com&quot;&gt;The Man in
    Blue&lt;/a&gt; has created a JavaScript-driven &lt;a
    href=&quot;http://www.themaninblue.com/experiment/widgEditor/&quot;&gt;
    web-based WYSIWYG editor&lt;/a&gt; that can be added to any web page.
    This is similar to tools such as &lt;a
    href=&quot;http://www.kevinroth.com/rte/demo.php&quot;&gt;RichText
    Editor&lt;/a&gt; and &lt;a
    href=&quot;http://www.dynarch.com/demos/htmlarea/examples/core.html&quo
    t;&gt;HTMLArea&lt;/a&gt;, but highly streamlined, standards-compliant,
    and much easier to integrate. It is very cool. If you have a home-grown
    content management system in which you have people contribute content
    by adding html into a textarea field, this tool will eliminate the need
    for content creators to know HTML. I&apos;m integrating it into our
    XML-base blogging tool (which was using RichTextEditor before) and a
```

```
            small content management system I&apos;ve built. Thanks Man in Blue for
            such a cool and very useful tool!&lt;br&gt;
            &lt;/p&gt; &lt;br&gt;</description>
            <guid>http://www.librarywebchic.net/2005/01/27.html#a195</guid>
            <pubDate>Fri, 28 Jan 2005 01:28:02 GMT</pubDate>
            <category>General Thoughts</category>
        </item>
    </channel>
</rss>
```

RSS 1.0

This version is not preceded or superseded by any other RSS version. The following sample is from Free Range Librarian, Karen G. Schneider (freerangelibrarian.com/index.rdf).

```
<?xml version="1.0" encoding="utf-8"?>
<rdf:RDF
 xmlns:rdf="http://www.w3.org/1999/02/22-rdf-syntax-ns#"
 xmlns:dc="http://purl.org/dc/elements/1.1/"
 xmlns:sy="http://purl.org/rss/1.0/modules/syndication/"
 xmlns:admin="http://webns.net/mvcb/"
 xmlns:cc="http://web.resource.org/cc/"
 xmlns="http://purl.org/rss/1.0/">
  <channel rdf:about="http://freerangelibrarian.com/">
     <title>Free Range Librarian</title>
     <link>http://freerangelibrarian.com/</link>
     <description></description>
     <dc:language>en-us</dc:language>
     <dc:creator></dc:creator>
     <dc:date>2005-02-01T08:11:58-08:00</dc:date>
     <admin:generatorAgent
     rdf:resource="http://www.movabletype.org/?v=3.14" />
     <items>
       <rdf:Seq>
         <rdf:li rdf:resource="http://freerangelibrarian.com/
         archives/020105/podcasting_test.php" />
         <rdf:li rdf:resource="http://freerangelibrarian.com/
         archives/013105/the_last_mile_a_cha.php" />
         <rdf:li rdf:resource="http://freerangelibrarian.com/
         archives/013105/mustread_blogs_lib.php" />
         <rdf:li rdf:resource="http://freerangelibrarian.com/
         archives/013005/frl_rss_1_or_rss_2.php" />
         <rdf:li rdf:resource="http://freerangelibrarian.com/
         archives/012905/lists_versus_blogs_.php" />
```

```
        <rdf:li rdf:resource="http://freerangelibrarian.com/
        archives/012905/newspaper_archives_.php" />
        <rdf:li rdf:resource="http://freerangelibrarian.com/
        archives/012805/frl_spotlight_review.php" />
        <rdf:li rdf:resource="http://freerangelibrarian.com/
        archives/012805/bookqueuetoo_previe.php" />
        <rdf:li rdf:resource="http://freerangelibrarian.com/
        archives/012805/proposals_and_dispos.php" />
        <rdf:li rdf:resource="http://freerangelibrarian.com/
        archives/012605/still_kicking_myself.php" />
        <rdf:li rdf:resource="http://freerangelibrarian.com/
        archives/012605/united_church_of_chr.php" />
        <rdf:li rdf:resource="http://freerangelibrarian.com/
        archives/012505/factcheck_asks_you_t.php" />
        <rdf:li rdf:resource="http://freerangelibrarian.com/
        archives/012405/pensees_du_webcred.php" />
        <rdf:li rdf:resource="http://freerangelibrarian.com/
        archives/012405/public_library_inter.php" />
        <rdf:li rdf:resource="http://freerangelibrarian.com/
        archives/012405/webcred_and_libraria.php" />
      </rdf:Seq>
    </items>
  </channel>
  <item rdf:about="http://freerangelibrarian.com/
  archives/020105/podcasting_test.php">
    <title>Podcasting Test</title>
    <link>http://freerangelibrarian.com/archives/020105/
    podcasting_test.php</link>
    <description>This is a test of podcasting (a special type
    of audio webcasting you can think of as &quot;radio on
    demand&quot;; the &apos;casters produce audio files which
    you can download to your MP3 player or--now you will
    understand the name--iPod). I...</description>
    <dc:subject>Podcasting</dc:subject>
    <dc:creator>kgs</dc:creator>
    <dc:date>2005-02-01T08:11:58-08:00</dc:date>
  </item>
  <item rdf:about="http://freerangelibrarian.com/
  archives/013105/the_last_mile_a_cha.php">
    <title>The Last Mile: A Chance to Get Started</title>
    <link>http://freerangelibrarian.com/archives/013105/
    the_last_mile_a_cha.php</link>
    <description>This Friday I&apos;m giving a talk at the
    Ontario Library Association Superconference , and months
    ago, I wrote a wide-open program description. I said I
    would &quot;describe the outer limits of digital
```

```
        libraries,&quot; share &quot;radical and contrarian
        views,&quot; and offer...</description>
        <dc:subject>The Last Mile (Digital Divide
        Issues)</dc:subject>
        <dc:creator>kgs</dc:creator>
        <dc:date>2005-01-31T10:31:41-08:00</dc:date>
    </item>
</rdf:RDF>
```

Atom

The following sample is from Travelin Librarian, Michael Sauers (www.travelinlibrarian.info/atom.xml).

```
<?xml version="1.0" encoding="UTF-8" standalone="yes"?>
<?xml-stylesheet href="http://www.blogger.com/styles/atom.css"
type="text/css"?>
<feed version="0.3" xml:lang="en-GB"
xmlns="http://purl.org/atom/ns#">
  <link href="http://www.blogger.com/atom/5543214"
  rel="service.post" title="Travelin' Librarian"
  type="application/atom+xml"/>
  <link href="http://www.blogger.com/atom/5543214"
  rel="service.feed" title="Travelin' Librarian"
  type="application/atom+xml"/>
  <title mode="escaped" type="text/html">Travelin' Librarian</title>
  <tagline mode="escaped" type="text/html"/>
  <link href="http://www.travelinlibrarian.info/" rel="alternate"
  title="Travelin' Librarian" type="text/html"/>
  <id>tag:blogger.com,1999:blog-5543214</id>
  <modified>2005-01-31T20:47:36Z</modified>
  <generator url="http://www.blogger.com/"
  version="5.15">Blogger</generator>
  <info mode="xml" type="text/html">
    <div xmlns="http://www.w3.org/1999/xhtml">This is an Atom
    formatted XML site feed. It is intended to be viewed in a
    Newsreader or syndicated to another site. Please visit the <a
    href="http://help.blogger.com/bin/answer.py?answer=697">Blogger
    Help</a> for more info.</div>
  </info>
  <entry xmlns="http://purl.org/atom/ns#">
    <link
    href="http://www.blogger.com/atom/5543214/110720445691459308"
    rel="service.edit" title="LC, ISBN &amp;amp; XML"
    type="application/atom+xml"/>
    <author>
```

```
      <name>Michael</name>
   </author>
   <issued>2005-01-31T13:45:36-07:00</issued>
   <modified>2005-01-31T20:47:36Z</modified>
   <created>2005-01-31T20:47:36Z</created>
   <link href="http://www.travelinlibrarian.info/2005/01/lc-isbn-
   xml.html" rel="alternate" title="LC, ISBN &amp;amp; XML"
   type="text/html"/>
   <id>tag:blogger.com,1999:blog-5543214.post-
   110720445691459308</id>
   <title mode="escaped" type="text/html">LC, ISBN &amp;amp;
   XML</title>
   <content type="application/xhtml+xml"
   xml:base="http://www.travelinlibrarian.info/"
   xml:space="preserve">
      <div xmlns="http://www.w3.org/1999/xhtml">This article, <i>
      <a href="http://www.xml.com/pub/a/2004/06/02/dijalog.html">
      Putting ISBNs to Work</a></i>, is going to take me a while to
      digest but it looks very interesting. What the author's done
      is "a command line tool that let me input an ISBN... which
      outputs a Library of Congress Call Number, which I could then
      affix to a book."</div>
   </content>
</entry>
<entry xmlns="http://purl.org/atom/ns#">
   <link
   href="http://www.blogger.com/atom/5543214/110720428926175088"
   rel="service.edit" title="Firefox 1.1 delayed"
   type="application/atom+xml"/>
   <author>
      <name>Michael</name>
   </author>
   <issued>2005-01-31T13:42:49-07:00</issued>
   <modified>2005-01-31T20:44:49Z</modified>
   <created>2005-01-31T20:44:49Z</created>
   <link href="http://www.travelinlibrarian.info/2005/01/firefox-
   11-delayed.html" rel="alternate" title="Firefox 1.1 delayed"
   type="text/html"/>
   <id>tag:blogger.com,1999:blog-5543214.post-
   110720428926175088</id>
   <title mode="escaped" type="text/html">Firefox 1.1
   delayed</title>
   <content type="application/xhtml+xml"
   xml:base="http://www.travelinlibrarian.info/"
   xml:space="preserve">
      <div xmlns="http://www.w3.org/1999/xhtml">According to <a
```

```
        href="http://weblogs.mozillazine.org/ben/archives/007434.html
        ">Ben Godger's blog</a>, Firefox 1.1 will not be making an
        appearance in March as originally scheduled. (He's the lead
        engineer on the project, he should know.) </div>
    </content>
  </entry>
</feed>
```

Glossary

Aggregator. A program or Web service that tracks and receives RSS feed content and presents that content to the user in a readable format.

Archive. To transfer old posts from a blog's homepage to pages that display posts only from a certain time period. Typically an archive page contains posts from a single month or week.

ASP. Active Server Pages. A Microsoft scripting language.

Atom. An XML-based structured language for syndicating content. Similar to RSS.

BitTorrent. A peer-to-peer Internet file-sharing system that uses a distributed model for sharing content.

Blog/blogging/blogger. A blog is a Web site in the form of an online journal that presents information in reverse chronological order. Blogging is the act of posting to a blog and a blogger is a person who is doing the posting.

Bloglines Notifier. A program available from Bloglines that monitors your account and notifies you when new information is available.

Blogosphere. A term denoting the totality of all blogs on the Web.

Blogroll. A list of blogs and/or feeds read by a user.

Client software. Software installed on a user's computer (typically a desktop or laptop) as opposed to software installed on a server.

Clipping. The act of saving a post for later access in Bloglines.

CSS. Cascading Style Sheets. A language for controlling the presentation of Web pages.

Enclosures. Non-text files that are attached to feed items. Similar to e-mail attachments.

Encoding scheme. The method used to control and identify which character set is being used in a file. For example, English and Russian use different encoding schemes.

Feed. Short for RSS feed or Atom feed. A file used to syndicate content.

FTP. File Transfer Protocol. An Internet protocol for transferring files from one computer to another.

FTP server. The computer that the user is either receiving from or sending to.

Google bomb. The act of millions of Web pages creating links of the same type in an attempt to influence the ranking of Google search results.

GUID. Globally Unique Identifier. A string of characters that identifies a feed item.

Hand rolling. Creating a feed without using any software. Through this method all feed code and content is entered by hand.

HTML. Hypertext Markup Language. A markup language used for creating Web pages.

HTTP authentication. A method of verifying the identity of a user attempting to access a Web page using a username/password combination.

LAN. Local Area Network.

Metadata. Information associated with an item (typically a document) that describes the content of that item.

Moblogging. Moblie blogging. Typically refers to the creation of a photo-based blog using a camera phone.

MP3. MPEG Level 3. An open-source standard for the creation of digital audio files.

PHP. An open-source scripting language. Typically used to automate the content of Web pages.

Podcast. Syndicated audio content using RSS.

Posts. Individual entries in a blog.

RDF. Resource Description Framework. An XML-based metadata format.

RFID. Radio Frequency Identification. A small chip containing data that can be read via radio frequency from a short distance.

RSS. Really Simple Syndication, Rich Site Summary, or RDF Site Summary. An XML-based language for syndicating content online.

Semi-Automated. A method for creating a feed in which a user types the content but software creates the required code.

Server root. The directory on the Web server that contains the homepage of the Web site.

Server software. Software installed on a server as opposed to software installed on a user's computer.

Server-based aggregators. An aggregator installed on a server.

SFTP. Secure File Transfer Protocol. A method of FTP that encrypts the content of the files being transferred.

SGML. Standard Generalized Markup Language. A set of rules for creating markup languages. Predates XML.

SMS. Short Messaging Service. The protocol used for sending text messages of up to 160 characters between cellphones.

SSL/HTTPS. Secure Sockets Layer/Hypertext Transport Protocol. Methods for encrypting and securing connections between a Web server and client computer.

Stand-alone clients. Software installed on a client computer that does not integrate into any other software on that computer.

Style sheet. File containing the code controlling the style of a document. Typically refers to files containing CSS code.

Sync. Synchronize. Comparing the data in two systems to make sure that both systems contain the same data.

Web server. Computer that houses Web site files.

Web-based aggregators. An aggregator housed on a Web server that can be accessed from any Web-accessible device.

Web-based service. Any program installed on a Web server and accessible from any Web-accessible device.

Weblog. Pronounced "We blog." The longer version of the more commonly used "blog."

WYSIWYG. What You See Is What You Get. Any interface that displays what you are typing exactly as you will see it once the information has been processed.

XHTML. eXtensible Hypertext Markup Language. A markup language used for creating Web pages. Similar to HTML but follows the rules of XML.

XML. A set of rules for creating markup languages. A follow-up to SGML.

About the Author

Michael Sauers is the Internet trainer for BCR's Member Services Division, which keeps him traveling throughout the country, and a part-time reference librarian for the Arapahoe County Library District. Michael, who currently lives in Aurora, CO, is on the Board of Trustees for the Aurora Public Library and the board of the Friends of the Aurora Public Library as the bookstore manager. Prior to moving to Colorado in 1997, he was an independent consultant and trainer in Las Vegas. He has also worked for both the New York State Library and the New York State Assembly. He earned his MLS from the University of Albany's School of Information Science and Policy in 1995 and a BS in American Studies from SUNY Brockport. Michael is the author of seven books on technology for librarians and has written dozens of articles for various journals and magazines. In his spare time, he reads about 130 books per year.

Index

More Great Books from Information Today, Inc.

The NextGen Librarian's Survival Guide

By Rachel Singer Gordon

Here is a unique resource for next generation librarians, addressing the specific needs of GenXers and Millenials as they work to define themselves as information professionals. The book focuses on how NextGens can move their careers forward and positively impact the profession. Library career guru Rachel Singer Gordon—herself a NextGen librarian—provides timely advice along with tips and insights from dozens of librarians on issues ranging from image to stereotypes, to surviving library school and entry-level positions, to working with older colleagues.

2006/224 pp/softbound/ISBN 1-57387-256-3 $29.50

The Accidental Webmaster

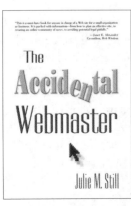

By Julie M. Still

Here is a lifeline for the individual who has not been trained as a Webmaster, but who—whether by choice or under duress—has become one nonetheless. While most Webmastering books focus on programming and related technical issues, *The Accidental Webmaster* helps readers deal with the full range of challenges they face on the job. Author, librarian, and accidental Webmaster Julie Still offers advice on getting started, setting policies, working with ISPs, designing home pages, selecting content, drawing site traffic, gaining user feedback, fundraising, avoiding copyright problems, and much more.

208 pp/softbound/ISBN 1-57387-164-8 $29.50

The Librarian's Internet Survival Guide, 2nd Edition
Strategies for the High-Tech Reference Desk

By Irene E. McDermott

In this updated and expanded second edition of her popular guidebook, *Searcher* columnist Irene McDermott once again exhorts her fellow reference librarians to don their pith helmets and follow her fearlessly into the Web jungle. She presents new and improved troubleshooting tips and advice, Web resources for answering reference questions, and strategies for managing information and keeping current. In addition to helping librarians make the most of Web tools and resources, the book offers practical advice on privacy and child safety, assisting patrons with special needs, Internet training, building library Web pages, and much more.

2006/328 pp/softbound/ISBN 1-57387-235-0 $29.50

Teaching Web Search Skills
Techniques and Strategies of Top Trainers

By Greg R. Notess

Educators and information professionals who teach Web searching will welcome this instructor's guide from trainer and search guru Greg Notess. Greg shares his own training techniques along with tips and strategies from savvy search trainers Joe Barker, Paul Barron, Phil Bradley, John Ferguson, Alice Fulbright, Ran Hock, Jeff Humphrey, Diane Kovacs, Gary Price, Danny Sullivan, Rita Vine, and Sheila Webber. In addition to presenting expert training strategies, *Teaching Web Search Skills* demonstrates a variety of approaches to instructional design and methodology, recommends a range of essential resources, and features dozens of helpful figures, search screens, worksheets, handouts, and sample training materials.

2006/368 pp/softbound/ISBN 1-57387-267-9 $29.50